Joseph Dennie
and His Circle

AMS PRESS
NEW YORK

Reprinted from the edition of 1915, Austin
First AMS EDITION published 1971
Manufactured in the United States of America

International Standard Book Number: 0-404-02308-8

Library of Congress Number: 73-131489

AMS PRESS INC.
NEW YORK, N.Y. 10003

BULLETIN

OF THE

UNIVERSITY OF TEXAS

1915: No. 40

JULY 15 1915

Joseph Dennie and His Circle

A Study in American Literature From 1792 to 1812

BY

Harold Milton Ellis, Ph. D.

Instructor in English in the
University of Texas

STUDIES IN ENGLISH NO. 3

Published by the University six times a month and entered as second-class matter at the postoffice at
AUSTIN, TEXAS

The benefits of education and of useful knowledge, generally diffused through a community, are essential to the preservation of a free government.

Sam Houston.

Cultivated mind is the guardian genius of democracy. . . . It is the only dictator that freemen acknowledge and the only security that freemen desire.

Mirabeau B. Lamar.

PREFACE

At the beginning of the nineteenth century one John Davis, an English traveler, asserted in his *Travels in the United States of America,* published in 1803, that "the most popular work on the American continent" was in his opinion, "the essays of the *Lay Preacher.*" In 1824 a New Hampshire poet, Jeremiah Fellowes by name, in the preface to a little volume of *Reminiscences, Moral Poems and Translations,* published at Exeter, proudly exclaimed, "The English may boast as much as they please, and they have certainly great reason to be proud of their men of science; but where, particularly in the belles-lettre department, have they produced the superior of Oliver Oldschool? *Etiam mortuus loquitur.*" Fourteen years later a better-known man of letters, Nathaniel Hawthorne, in his biographical sketch of Thomas Green Fessenden, printed in the *American Monthly Magazine,* January, 1838, said that the fame of none of Fessenden's early literary associates had survived, "save that of Joseph Dennie, once esteemed the finest writer in America."

Who was this Joseph Dennie, this Oliver Oldschool, this Lay Preacher, who loomed so large in American letters in the first decades of the last century, and who has been so completely forgotten since? To answer this question, as fully as may appear profitable, by giving an account of his life and work, his friends and enemies, his hopes and follies, his successes and failures; and incidentally to present a picture of literary conditions in the United States during the twenty years or so of his activity, is the purpose of this treatise.

Nothing needs to be said, I think, about the plan and order I have followed, which in general is chronological, after the custom of biographers; except in justification of one entire chapter and portions of others, devoted to brief biographical sketches of Dennie's literary contemporaries and associates. The history of American letters during the decades in question has been so imperfectly written that it has seemed advisable to incorporate a large amount of such material, from many and scattered sources, into our picture, even at the risk of decreasing its interest and injuring its symmetry.

The idea of this treatise, which was produced as a doctoral dissertation at Harvard University, in 1913, was first suggested to me, I believe, by a few paragraphs concerning Dennie in Professor W. P. Trent's *History of American Literature.* Since undertaking the work on the recommendation of Professors Kittredge, Greenough, and Neilson, I have incurred obligations on every hand. My thanks are especially due to Professor C. N. Greenough, not only for constant and helpful advice, but for frequent and valuable personal assistance as well. Miss Mary H. Dennie, of Boston, very kindly permitted me to make free use of the extensive correspondence and manuscripts of Joseph Dennie in her possession, and other members of the family have given me courteous assistance. Miss Kate V. Marcy, of Royalton, Vermont, through her attorney, R. G. DeForest, Esq., also placed the Vose-Dennie letters at my disposal. While it is impossible, within the limits of this preface, to make acknowledgment of all the favors I have received, it would be churlish not to mention the names of Professor Barrett Wendell, Miss E. D. Boardman, and Mr. Albert Matthews of Boston, Mr. Edward Biddle of Philadelphia, Doctor S. A. Green of the Massachusetts Historical Society, Professor Robert A. Law, of the University of Texas, and Mr. Clarence S. Brigham, Librarian of the American Antiquarian Society, at Worcester, to whom, among many others, I am deeply grateful.

TABLE OF CONTENTS.

CHAPTER I

TWO EIGHTEENTH CENTURY BOSTON FAMILIES

Joseph Dennie, once widely known in this country as the American Addison, was born in Boston, 30 August, 1768, the son of Joseph and Mary (Green) Dennie. Since the Dennies and Greens played a somewhat prominent part in the life and activities of Boston in the eighteenth century, some account of them is desirable for an understanding of the influences of environment, as well as heredity, upon their descendant.

The Dennies belonged to that merchant aristocracy which became dominant in the New England capital with the decline of the theocratic system soon after the beginning of the century. The family is of Scottish origin. The first member to appear in America was Albert Dennie, who was a resident of Fairfield, Connecticut, as early as 1684. In that year he appeared with two other Scotchmen in a transaction concerning a grant of land.[1] He married Elizabeth Wakeman, daughter of the Reverend Samuel Wakeman, minister at Fairfield, and his wife Hannah, daughter of Governor Stephen Goodyear. Since Albert Dennie's estate was in probate in 1708, he probably died in that year or in 1707. Little else is known of him.[2]

John (2) Dennie, probably the oldest child, baptized at Fairfield, 7 October, 1694, was the founder of the family in Boston. He was engaged in business in that town as early as 11 August, 1719, when a sale to him of "one dozen verses"—rhymes of the Mother Goose sort—was recorded by Thomas Fleet, printer.[3] Probably his home, however, was at Fairfield for some time, since most of his children were baptized there, though the absence of two names from the Fairfield church register may denote an occasional residence at Boston. By

---

1. Fairfield County, Connecticut, Registry of Deeds.
2. His children, all baptized at Fairfield, were the following:
   John Dennie, baptized 7 Oct., 1694.
   Grizzel Dennie, baptized 28 Feb., 1696.
   Margaret Dennie, baptized 30 Apr., 1696-7.
   Annabel Dennie, baptized 30 Nov., 1701.
   James Dennie, baptized 4 Mar., 1702-3.

Schenck, *History of Fairfield, Connecticut*, 1889.
Wakeman, R. P., *Wakeman Genealogy*, 1900.

3. *New England Historical and Genealogical Register*, 1873, p. 144.

the thirties, at any rate, he was established at the latter place, and from then until his death his name appears frequently in deeds and other records there. From 1743 to 1747 he had the direction of the town warehouse.[1] His will was presented for probation 19 January, 1747, and his estate was inventoried at £22,909, on 28 June, 1748. His widow, Sarah Dennie, died before 17 February, 1749, when guardians were appointed for her minor children, Thomas, Abigail, and Joseph.[2] She was his second wife; the first was Mary Edwards, daughter of John and Mary (Hanford) Edwards, of Stratfield, Connecticut. After her death he married, about 1724, Sarah Webb, daughter of the Reverend Joseph Webb, minister at Fairfield, and his wife Elizabeth, daughter of Isaac Nichols, of Stratford. She was a descendent from Robert the Bruce.[3]

The five sons of John (2) Dennie who lived all became merchants, dealing for the most part in West India commodities, such as molasses, sugar, rum and hemp. Albert (3) Dennie, the eldest, followed the example of his father and grandfather by marrying a minister's daughter, though under circumstances distasteful to her family. She was Abigail Colman, daughter of the Reverend Benjamin Colman, the liberal-minded pastor of the Brattle Square Church. Her local reputation as a poetess was little less than that of her sister Jane, wife of the Reverend Ebenezer Turell, of Medford.[4] She died 17 May, 1745, leaving a son John. Two other children had died in infancy.

---

1. *Selectmen's Minutes*, 1743-1753.
2. Probate Records of Suffolk County, Mass.
3. Five children were born to John and Mary (Edwards) Dennie, and six to John and Sarah (Webb), as follows:
   1. Albert Dennie, baptized ....
   2. John Dennie, baptized 4 Mar., 1716, at Fairfield, Conn.
   3. Mary Dennie, baptized 11 Dec., 1717, at Fairfield, Conn.
   4. Grissel Dennie, baptized 18 Feb., 1720, at Fairfield, Conn.
   5. Elizabeth Dennie, baptized ... ., ...
   6. Sarah Dennie, baptized 2 May, 1725, at Fairfield, Conn.
   7. William Dennie, baptized 23 Oct., 1726, at Fairfield, Conn.
   8. Thomas Dennie, baptized 5 May, 1728. Died young.
   9. Thomas Dennie, baptized 11 Oct., 1730, at Fairfield, Conn.
   10. Abigail Dennie, baptized — Apr., 1733, at Fairfield, Conn.
   11. Joseph Dennie, born c. 1743.
4. For an account of these people, see *The Life and Character of the Reverend Benjamin Colman*, by Ebenezer Turell, 1749. See also *N. E. Hist. & Gen. Register*, Vol. 3 (1849), page 232. According to Bond's *Charlestown Genealogies and Estates*, Albert Dennie married Abigail Turell, 21 Sept., 1737. Either the Turell is a mistake or, as is not impossible, she was married under an assumed name.

John (3) Dennie and his half brother William were among the most important Boston merchants of the fifties, sixties and seventies. Both were among the gentlemen occasionally invited to accompany the governor's train on a formal tour of the Boston schools; and their names appear frequently, in different capacities, in the records of the period. John married, 8 September, 1743, Sarah Wendell, cousin of the Sarah Wendell who became the wife of Abiel Holmes and mother of Oliver Wendell Holmes. From John and Sarah Dennie are descended all of the name now living in or around Boston. He lived in Brighton, then part of Cambridge, in a palatial residence described by Drake,[1] which was burned in 1770, despite the assistance of the Harvard students, but soon rebuilt with the ready assistance of his friends, most of whom were Tories. Like many men of wealth and rank, he was loyal to the King's cause, and may have escaped expatriation as a Loyalist by his death early in the war, 7 August, 1777. He had five children, of whom Capt. Thomas (4) Dennie, the youngest son (married Sarah Bryant, 5 February, 1778) was a prominent merchant and trader, making voyages to the West Indies.

Mary (3) Dennie married, 15 October, 1739, the Reverend William Hooper, a Scotchman, then pastor of the West Church. Later he became an Episcopalian and was pastor of Trinity for twenty years. His oldest son, William, studied law under James Otis, and was member of Congress from North Carolina in 1776, and a signer of the Declaration.

Grissel (3) Dennie married, first, in November, 1747, Nathaniel Martin; and second, 5 April, 1753, Dr. Simpson Jones, of Hopkinton, Mass. Elizabeth (3) Dennie married (Intention 10 May, 1743) William Fletcher, a respectable West India trader, and was living in Jamaica in 1783. Sarah (3) Dennie married, 24 December, 1747, William Merchant, and died before 1783.

William (3) Dennie was a wealthy bachelor. Like his half brothers, John and Albert, he was a town constable in his youth; and he succeeded his father, John Dennie, as director of the town's warehouse, "opposite the Golden Ball," at the decreased charge of £24 per annum. He was active in the interest of the

---

1. *History of Middlesex County.* Vol. 1, page 294.

colonists from 1770 to 1775, serving on several important committees with Hancock, Otis, Warren and the Adamses; but after Concord and Lexington he declined to go further. Though elected to the Committee of Safety, he refused to serve, and a substitute was elected, 29 August, 1776. His will was probated in 1783, generous legacies being left to numerous relatives. A large part of his property was left to Mrs. Elizabeth Swan, wife of Major James Swan, merchant, of Dorchester.[1]

Thomas (3) Dennie engaged in the West India trade, and removed to Kingston, Jamaica, where he left descendants. Of his sister Abigail I have no note after 1749, when she was placed under the guardianship of her brother William, she being then seventeen.

Joseph (3) Dennie, the youngest child, and father of the subject of this book, was about five years old when made a ward of his elder brother, 17 February, 1749. I have found no record of his birth or of his marriage to Mary, daughter of Bartholomew Green, Jr., which occurred sometime before 1768. Like his brothers, he became a merchant, and might have shared their wealth and prominence, had his business career not been arrested by mental disease. Soon after 24 April, 1775, he left the beleaguered town of Boston for Lexington, where he remained, subject to periods of insanity, of increasing duration and severity, until his death, 11 September, 1811. During lucid intervals he attended for a time to his business in Boston, and took an active and scrupulous interest in his only son. He was tenderly cared for during his illness by his wife and a kinsman of hers, Harriet Green, who after the death of his son in 1812, and his widow, 6 September, 1819, inherited most of his property. His obituary, in the *New England Palladium*, 4 October, 1811, says of him:

"Died: In Lexington, where his remains were respectfully entombed on Monday last,[2] Mr. Joseph Dennie, aet. 68, formerly a merchant in this town. For nearly 40 years preceding his death he was subject to great sufferings arising from bodily indisposition and mental derangement. The last 20 years he was

1. See page 25.
2. Some months later on 19 October, 1811, he was reinterred in the family tomb at King's Chapel. Recently, I understand, all the family remains have been transferred to Mount Auburn.

- Joseph Dennie 1768-1812
  - Joseph Dennie 1743-1811
    - John Dennie 1694-1747
      - Albert Dennie -1708
      - Elizabeth Wakeman -1721
    - Sarah Webb 1704-1749
      - Rev. Joseph Webb -1718
      - Elizabeth Nichols 1618-
  - Mary Green 1742-1819
    - Bartholomew Green 1701-1757
      - Bartholomew Green 1667-1732
      - Mary ——— -1709
    - Hannah Hammond 1704-
      - Eleazer Hammond 1677-1760
      - Hannah Harrington 1678-1775

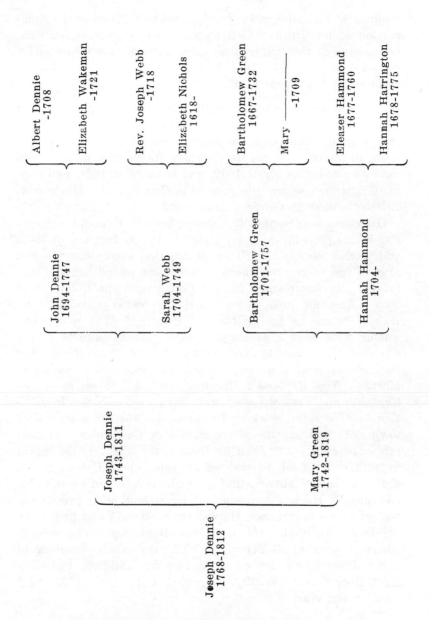

ANCESTRY OF JOSEPH DENNIE (1768-1812).

confined to his house, principally to his bed. During the small portion of his life in which he was able to transact business, he maintained the character of strict integrity, and was justly regarded by those who knew him, as possessing an enlightened mind and a benevolent heart."

The Greens of Cambridge and Boston, descendants of Samuel Green (c. 1614-1702), have been probably the most remarkable family in the annals of American printing. The earliest ancestor in this country was Bartholomew Green, who, Savage says, came to Cambridge about 1632, was freeman in 1634, and died in 1635, while preparing to proceed to Connecticut. His widow, Elizabeth, died 28 October, 1677, aged 88.

His eldest son, Samuel (2) Green, born in England, came to Cambridge probably with his father. He was freeman in 1635, and became the second printer in America, succeeding Stephen Daye a few years after the first press was established at Cambridge. He was printer for the College and the Colony, and issued from his press some ninety-five books enumerated by Isaiah Thomas in his *History of Printing*.[2] The most noteworthy were Eliot's *Algonquin Bible*, various editions of the Laws of Massachusetts Bay, Plymouth, and Connecticut, *The Bay Psalm Book* (second, revised edition, 1650), Nathaniel Morton's *New England's Memorial*, and the *Narrative of the Captivity and Restoration of Mrs. Mary Rowlandson*. In addition to fifty years' work at the press, he was for a long time town clerk and captain of the militia of Cambridge. Thomas relates of him that, "when he became, through age, too infirm to walk to the field, he insisted on being carried there in his chair, on days of muster, that he might review and exercise his company." He was a pious and benevolent man, greatly esteemed by his neighbors. He was twice married and had many children. His first wife was Jane Banbridge. The second, whom he married 23 February, 1662, was Sarah, daughter of Elder Jonas Clark, by whom he had five children, including Bartholomew and Timothy. He died 1 January, 1702, aged eighty-seven years.

---

1. James Savage: *Genealogical Dicitonary of the First Settlers of New England.*
2. Vol. I, pages 252 to 263. Thomas' account, though erroneous in some particulars, is the best source of information about Samuel Green and his descendants.

Three of his sons, Samuel, Bartholomew, and Timothy, became printers, and no fewer than fifteen of his descendants in the male line in three generations, besides numerous others in various female lines, followed the same trade. Samuel (3) Green, who married Elizabeth Sill and died in 1690, was a printer in Boston. Deacon Timothy (3) Green (c. 1679-1757) moved to New London, Connecticut, and founded a prolific race of printers, who conducted presses not only in Connecticut but also elsewhere in New England, and as far south as Annapolis, and Fredericksburg, Virginia. Two of his sons, Timothy (4) (1703-1763) and Samuel (4) (1712-1752), accompanied him to New London and carried on the business there. They, and Samuel's sons, Thomas (5), Timothy (5), and Samuel (5) Green, also conducted several newspapers, including the *New London Gazette* and the *Connecticut Journal and New Haven Post Boy*. Timothy (5) Green (1737-1796), after carrying on a printing business in Norwich during the war, struck out northward, and established at Westminster, in 1781, the first press and the first newspaper in the present state of Vermont. Timothy's son, Samuel (6) Green, and Thomas (6), son of Thomas (5), continued their father's businesses, while Thomas (6) and John (6), sons of Timothy, were booksellers and binders. Jonas (5) Green (1711-1767), brother of Timothy and Samuel, moved to Philadelphia, and later to Annapolis, where he was succeeded by his sons, Samuel (6), William (6), and Frederick (6).

Bartholomew (3) Green was the son of Samuel (2) and his second wife, Sarah (Clark); and brother to Samuel (3) and Timothy (3) Green. He was born in Cambridge, 26 October, 1667, and baptized 3 November, the same year. He set up a press in Boston in 1690, but was burned out in that year and returned to work with his father. In 1692 he resumed business in Boston, on Newbury Street. He was the printer of the first newspaper in America, the *Boston News-Letter*, from its beginning, 3 April, 1704, to 4 November, 1707, and again from October, 1711, to his death, 28 December, 1732. After December, 1722, he was editor as well as publisher, and the paper was considerably improved under his management. He was a pious man, a deacon of the Old South Church, and liked to attach moral lessons to the news articles he printed. He was printer for the College thirty years, and nearly forty years for the Governor and Council of Massachusetts Bay, and he is said to have been the most distinguished and busiest member of his profession in the country. His first wife, Mary, died 26 March, 1709. The following year he married Jane Tappan, niece of Judge Sewall, the diarist.

Three daughters of Bartholemew (3) Green, Mary, Deborah, and Elizabeth, married respectively three of his apprentices, Bozoan Allen, John Draper, and Samuel Kneeland, all of whom became prominent printers and had sons devoted to the same trade. Samuel (4) Green was a fourth apprentice of his father's, but I have no further note of him.

Another son, John, had a daughter, Margaret, who married Richard, son of John Draper, above. After her husband's death she conducted, from 1774 to 1776, the *Massachusetts Gazette and Weekly News-Letter* (previously the *Boston News-Letter*), the only paper published in Boston during the siege. She was an ardent Tory and at the Evacuation of Boston went with the Royal army to Halifax, and thence to England, where she is said to have enjoyed a royal pension.[1]

Bartholomew Green, Jr., born in Boston 22 October, 1701, the son of his father's first wife, Mary,[2] was likewise a printer. He worked first with his father on the *News-Letter;* later in partnership with his brother-in-law, John Draper; and still later with another brother-in-law, Bozoan Allen, and John Bushell. He also printed the *Boston Gazette* for Henry Boydell, postmaster, from 1727 until 1732, when Boydell died. Green took part in the expedition against Louisburg as a Lieutenant of Artillery, and on his return found his business much impaired by his absence. There is on file in the Massachusetts Military Archives a petition bearing the signature of Bartholomew Green, Jr., stating his losses, and asking to be appointed doorkeeper of the General Court, *vice* Richard Hubbart, deceased.[3] In August or September, 1751, he went to

1. Her will was dated at Pimlico, Middlesex, England, 1 Dec., 1802, and probated in Boston 12 Feb., 1807.
2. The confusion of the compiler of the *Historical Catalogue of the Old South Church* concerning Maria Mather is due to the existence of another family of Greens, in Charlestown, using the Christian name Bartholomew. See Wyman's *Charlestown Genealogies and Estates.*
3. Winsor's *Memorial History of Boston*, Vol. II, page 400, footnote.

Halifax, Nova Scotia, intending to start a press in that town, but he fell ill and died there in October.[1] His wife, whom he married 19 November, 1724, was Hannah Hammond,[2] daughter of Eleazer Hammond, a selectman of Newton, and his wife, Hannah Harrington. Mrs. Green survived her husband more than thirty years.[3]

Bartholomew (5) and John (5) Green carried on the traditions of the family at the press. The elder brother was the less successful, and never owned a press himself. He is best known for an accomplishment thus described by Thomas.[4] "He made himself so well acquainted with every vessel which sailed out of the port of Boston, as to know each at sight. Perpetually on the watch, as soon as a vessel could be discovered with a spyglass in the harbor, he knew it, and gave immediate information to the owner; and by the small fees for this kind of information, he principally maintained himself for several years." He married Hannah Foster, 7 March, 1771. His will, made 18 March, 1778, was probated 17 April, 1778, his estate being inventoried at £62, including "five very old sheets, s. 10" and "sundry old trumpery in the garrett, s. 6." The account of Hannah Green, executrix, 21 November, 1781, presents a charge "For

---

1. Buried 29 Oct., 1751. (Burial Record of St. Paul Parish, Halifax.) See Matthews, *Bibliographical Notes on Boston Newspapers, 1700-1780;* also, *Boston News Letter*, 14 Nov., 1751.

2. *Newton Vital Records*, p. 300. *Hammond Genealogies*, F. S. Hammond, Vol. II, pp. 12 and 13. Also Probate Records of Middlesex Co. In the intention of marriage, recorded at Boston, 7 Oct., 1724, her name is incorrectly given as Henson.

3. They had nine children baptized at the Old South Church between 1726 and 1742, as follows:

Mary, baptized 2 Jan., 1726. [Born 24 Dec., 1725.]
Bartholomew, baptized 24 Sept., 1727.
Hannah, baptized 31 Aug., 1729.
John, baptized 15 Aug., 1731.
Samuel, baptized 24 Feb., 1733.
Nathaniel, baptized 25 Apr., 1735.
Elizabeth, baptized 14 May, 1738.
Peter, baptized 26 Oct., 1740.
Mary, baptized 27 Feb., 1742.

The first Mary probably did not live. Hannah married James Withington, 18 July, 1784, and was living in 1813. Samuel married Ann Geoghean, 30 Dec., 1769, and was perhaps father of Harriet Green, who lived with the Dennies. Elizabeth married Thomas Hichborn 30 Aug., 1759, and lived in Charleston, South Carolina. Of Nathaniel and Peter I know nothing—marriages of men with both names are found in the Boston records. The second Mary married Joseph Dennie, Sr.

4. *History of Printing*, Vol. I, page 322.

pipes and Tobacco, Rum, Lemmons, etc. at the funeral, s. 6,'' and names daughters, Elizabeth, Hannah, Polly and Lydia.

John (5) Green (1721-1794), brother of Mary (Green) Dennie, was a prominent printer during the last third of the century. He and his partner, Joseph Russell (1734-1795), at their office in Queen, now Court Street, printed the laws of the Colony, and, from 1758 to 1773, the *Boston Weekly Advertiser*. After the war he had a share in the office of Adams and Nourse, publishers of the *Independent Chronicle*. He acquired a considerable fortune and owned a ''mansion'' in Newbury Street. He married first, 24 July, 1755, his cousin, Lydia Draper, daughter of John and Deborah (Green) Draper, above; and second, 15 March, 1759, Rebecca, daughter of Knight Leverett. There were no children who survived.

The Greens of Boston were people of property and good standing, who enjoyed an excellent reputation for uprightness and for honesty in business. They were good Calvinists, members of the Old South and Brattle Square Churches, and like the Drapers, with whom they intermarried, were for the most part Loyalists. Their family connections were eminently respectable, and they have many descendants in Boston and elsewhere.

CHAPTER II

BOSTON AND LEXINGTON, 1768-1787—BOYHOOD

Joseph, the only child of Joseph and Mary Dennie, was baptized 4 September, 1768, at the Church in Brattle Square,[1] of which his parents were probably members. His father was then a prosperous young merchant, about twenty-five years old, probably engaged, like his brothers, in the importation and sale of such West India staples as molasses, rum, hemp, and sugar. He is said to have enjoyed, during his brief mercantile career, a high reputation for integrity in business transactions.

The years during which the younger Dennie grew from infancy to boyhood in Boston were crowded with the exciting events which led up to the Revolution. In 1768, the year of his birth, the sloop *Liberty*, owned by John Hancock, was seized in the Harbor by the frigate *Romney* for evading the provisions of the Townshend Acts. A riot ensued, and the Commissioners of Customs fled for refuge to the fort on Castle Island. As a result of this disturbance, two British regiments were henceforth quartered in the town, whose presence provoked constant and increasing friction. This culminated, on 5 March, 1770, in the memorable Boston Massacre, in King Street. Though John Adams and Josiah Quincy, two of the most influential citizens of Boston, defended the soldiers in their trial for murder, the bitterest feelings were maintained toward the troops, and on the third anniversary of the Massacre, in March, 1773, William Dennie, brother of Joseph, Senior, was a member of a committee to arrange for fitting commemorative exercises.[2] One night in December of the same year, when young Joseph was five years old, occurred the Boston Tea Party. After waiting all day for Governor Hutchinson to promise to send back the tea-ships, a band of citizens in the garb of Indians took possession of the ships and poured 342 chests of tea into the bay. From this time on, the hostility between the majority of the colonists on one hand and the adherents of the Crown on the other was at

---

1. *Records of the Church in Brattle Square, Boston*, page 185.
2. *Boston Town Records, 1770-1777.*

fever pitch. The Tea Party was soon followed by the Boston Port Bill, and in June, 1774, Massachusetts issued the first call for a Continental Congress. Meanwhile writers like "Mucius Scaevola" in the *Massachusetts Spy* and "Lucius" and "Novanglus" in the *Boston Gazette* were arousing the public with their able pens, to be answered by equally heated Tory arguments in Richard and Margaret Draper's *Boston News Letter.* John Trumbull, a young lawyer in the office of John Adams, was issuing his *Elegy of the Times*[1] and the first cantos of *M'Fingal.*[2] Committees of Correspondence and Safety were forming to unite the towns and present solid front to royal oppression, and in all the eastern counties the Minute Men were preparing for a grapple with the troops in Boston.

That the conflict to follow was a civil rather than a national one, is shown by the divisions of families it brought about. Thus John Dennie of Cambridge, a brother of Joseph, Senior, and a firm Loyalist, undoubtedly viewed with disapproval the violence of a lawless mob pillaging ships sent to the colonies by His Majesty's orders. William Dennie, however, was one of the committee which had that day demanded the return of the tea-ships,[3] and remained prominent in the colonists' cause until the actual outbreak of hostilities. Margaret (Green) Draper, after the siege of Boston ended, left her native country with the King's forces, never to return. On the other side was William Hooper the younger, son of the Reverend William and Mary (Dennie) Hooper, a signer of the Declaration of Independence from his adopted state, North Carolina. And when the first armed clash came, on 19 April, 1775, there had fallen on Lexington Green, on the colonists' side, a cousin of Mary Dennie—that Jonathan Harrington who, as the record says, wounded to death, dragged himself to the threshhold of his house and died at his wife's feet. The boy Joseph Dennie was six years old then, and may have seen some of the wounded grenadiers brought across from Charlestown on the evening of the nineteenth. Scenes and events like these, at any rate, must have made a deep impression upon his mind and sensibilities.

---

1. Published at Boston in September, 1774.
2. Written in 1774. See Marble. *Heralds of American Literature,* pp. 126 ff.
3. *Boston Town Records, 1770-1777.*

The pursuing colonists, after the British retreat from Concord, instead of dispersing, remained encamped at Cambridge, and the siege of Boston had begun. Immediately the town was thrown into a state of alarm and confusion. Many families, in the expectation of immediate hostilities, desired to depart for the country. A town meeting was accordingly held on Sunday, 23 April, with General Gage present, at which it was agreed "That upon the inhabitants in general lodging their arms in Faneuil Hall, or any other convenient place, under the care of the selectmen, marked with the names of their respective owners, that all such inhabitants as are inclined might depart from the town, with their families and effects, and those who remain might depend upon his [Gage's] protection; and that the arms aforesaid, at a suitable time, would be returned to the owners."[1] The only mention of Joseph Dennie, Sr., to be found in the published records of the city of Boston is a memorandum stating that on 24 April, 1775, he gave over to the selectmen one pair of pocket pistols.[2] Immediately after the fulfillment of this condition by the inhabitants hundreds of people left the town with such furniture as they could carry. Among them was Joseph Dennie, Sr., who took his small family to the neighboring village of Lexington, where he was to spend most of the remainder of his life.

Lexington, in the decade between 1775 and 1785, was a small and very rustic hamlet, with an almost wholly agricultural population of between 800 and 900 people.[3] Boston, itself not alarmingly large and busy, was a long forenoon's ride away. Altogether, a quieter, more orthodox village in which to bring up a boy, would have been hard to find. A spirit of intense democracy prevailed, as was natural in the home of the Hancocks, the scene of the first armed resistance to British authority, and the parish of the militant pastor, Jonas Clarke. This gentleman, who succeeded in 1755 the Reverend John Hancock, grandfather of the patriot, was pastor at Lexington for fifty years. He was a survivor of the old theocracy, dominating his parish not by reason of his profession but by his native

---

1. Frothingham's *History of the Siege of Boston*, page 94.
2. *Miscellaneous Papers*. City Papers. Boston.
3. Hudson. *History of Lexington*, page 487.

ability as a leader. Samuel Adams and Hancock were his guests on the memorable night of 18 April, 1775. In 1795, as chairman of a committee of the town, he drew up a protest against Jay's treaty with England.[1] His patriotic and democratic sentiments were doubtless distasteful to the Dennies, who like very many, perhaps most, people of property in Massachusetts, were Loyalists during the Revolution and staunch Federalists after it. They appear to have held aloof from their rustic fellow-townspeople, except Doctor Fiske and their neighbors, the Parkhursts. The ill health to which the elder Dennie was subject soon set in, and was an additional reason for the seclusion in which the family lived. The siege of Boston ended with the evacuation by the British troops, 17 March, 1776, but Mr. Dennie never permanently resumed his business there.

At that time there was a grammar school in Lexington, situated centrally, but elementary instruction was provided by several schools in different parts of the town, "generally taught by females."[2] These were the time-honored dame-schools of New England. In one of them, taught by a certain Dame Rogers, as Dennie himself informs us,[3] the future essayist received the rudiments of an education, consisting of the "three R's." He may have supplemented this by attendance at the grammar school, which is described by Hudson in his *History of Lexington*. It had been built in 1761 at a cost of £42. It was twenty feet square, and as there was a space of only six and a half feet between floors it must have been dingy enough. This school was usually conducted by a man, often a Harvard student seeking to defray college expenses.

The more important part of his education, however, Dennie probably secured at home, from his parents and in his father's library. A few lines from one of the Lay Preacher's sermons, written in 1797,[4] give us a glimpse of this early period. "In my boyhood, I remember that a parent would sometimes repeat lessons of economy as I sat on his knee, and then lift me in his

1. This drew upon him an attack in Dennie's *Farmer's Weekly Museum*, 5 December, 1795, in which Mr. Clarke was called "the clerical Democrat who snores over sermons at Lexington with immeasurable periods and grievous tautology."
2. Hudson. *History of Lexington*, page 367.
3. In a letter to his parents, January, 1794.
4. Sermon 62. *On Reckless Haste.* May 23, 1797.

arms, that I might look on Hogarth's plates of Industry and Idleness. On youthful fancy the picture was more impressed than the precept." The elder Dennie was a man of intelligence, wit and taste, combined with shrewd Scotch thrift. In later years he was a frequent and appreciative correspondent of his son, whom he resembled in occasional and deep depression of spirits. His wife was of a more sentimental and pious nature, but possessed considerable independence of mind. Many years after, Dennie wrote of her:[1]

"For I have a mother. A sickly infancy, nurtured into health, a giddy and dangerous season of childhood and youth, carefully devoted to letters, attest the salutory cares and preserving affection of a wise and amiable woman. . . . By a mother he [the author] was presented with the keys of knowledge, and her liberal spirit sanctioned that scheme of life which it has been his delight to pursue; a scheme elevated above 'low-thoughted care,' and 'creeping gain.' By her he was exhorted, even though poverty should obstruct his path, to 'walk honestly as in the day.' "

Both his parents were deeply interested in the education of their son, and provided him with all the advantages which a liberal purse and a well-selected library could afford. Some idea of the books likely to be found in an enlightened New England household in 1775 may be gathered from a perusal of the titles in the library of the boy's uncle, John Dennie, of Cambridge. The list follows:[2]

21 vols.	Universal History	4to	£12	s.—
2 vols.	Temple's Works	Fo.	3	—
	Luther on Gall's.		1	—
	Addison's Works	4to	3	12
	Religion of Nature		—	12
4 vols.	Burns' Justice		3	—
	Nature Display'd		3	—
	Travels of Cyrus		—	8
	Jewish Spy		1	12
	Terence's Comedy		—	4
	Sherlock on Judgment		—	8
	Gulliver's Travels		—	6
	Treatise on Minut. Philos.		1	4
	Stanhope's Epictetus		—	10
	Lard's Gospel History		1	1
	Foster's Sermons		1	—

1. *Lay Preacher of Pennsylvania; Gazette of the U. S.*, 30 Dec., 1799.
2. This list is copied from an inventory made 3 Dec., 1777. Probate Records of Middlesex County, Mass.

3 vols.	Tillotson's Sermons Fo.	2	—
	Burkett's New Testament	1	5
	Henry on 4 Books Moses	1	15
5 vols.	Spectator	—	6
4 vols.	Cato's Letters	1	10
4 vols.	Spy at Paris	1	4
2 vols.	Zoroaster's Travels	—	12
	Boyle's Style of Scriptures	—	3
	Pope's Letters	—	4
	Free Thoughts on Religion	—	5
	Paradise Regain'd	—	6
	On the State of the Dead	—	6
	Marcus Antoninus	—	5
	Fiddes on Morality	—	6
	Gally's Characters on Thess.	—	4

The predominance of essays and works of a religious nature is significant in connection with the study of Dennie's literary output. The library of the younger brother was probably of greater variety and more general interest. His son's letters and other writings mention the works of Churchill, Atterbury, Bolingbroke, Seneca, and Pindar as belonging to it. Here he began to acquire that familiarity with the classics of English and other literatures which later aroused the surprise and admiration of his friends.

One unfortunate result of the lack of sympathy between the Dennies and their neighbors at Lexington was the fostering in the son of an aristocratic and cavalier attitude toward his fellow-townsmen, which was soon to be extended to the majority of his countrymen as well. The former he characterized in after years[1] as "the wretched and ignorant cottagers who surround that 'glorious' green where the first American blood was shed." Being the proverbial only child, moreover, and of a feeble physique, he was doubtless shielded and indulged, especially by his mother, who seems to have been somewhat awed by her son's precocity. Of his earliest literary achievements she once said,[2] "He wrote poetry in early life after the manner of Horace and various other modes, but never pleased himself. Some of these pieces were so pathetic that he could not read them without the tears running down his cheeks."

His less sentimental father "persuaded him to quit a pursuit where he would kill himself with his own sword."[3] He had other

1. *Farmer's Weekly Museum*. 13 Oct., 1795.
2. In a letter to J. E. Hall, quoted in his *Philadelphia Souvenir*, 1827.
3. Ibid.

ends in view for his son, in accordance with which the youth was sent, in 1783, to a commercial school in Boston to learn bookkeeping. After remaining here a year he was taken as a clerk into the counting house of Major James Swan. This gentleman had a remarkable and checkered career as merchant, author, soldier, and diplomat. An affluent man in 1796, when he built a palatial residence in Roxbury, he spent his last twenty-two years in a French debtors' prison, as a matter of principle.[1] A passage from one of Dennie's writings already quoted[2] may be autobiographical with reference to his work at this period. "He swept and garnished a counting-house. . . . opened it at five and did not bar it until nine; sold ropes and boxes for himself as well as bales for his master."

Two letters to his parents, dating from this period, have been preserved, the first of which, as his earliest extant writing, I will quote entire:

"Boston, 16th Oct'r., 1784.

"Dear Mama

"I hope to have the pleasure of hearing by Amos that you are in good health. Sir is gone to the southward this forenoon and expects to go to Dorchester. He is well and will write to you next week. Yesterday arrived in town from Philadelphia the Marquis de la Fayette. He was met at Dorchester by the Militia of that Town and accompanied as far as Boston Neck there was met by the Train of Artillery led by Major Davis and escorted into Town through the principal Streets, amidst the Acclamation of the People. The greatest Attention and every possible respect is paid to him. Next Sunday being the Nineteenth of this Month and the Anniversary of Cornwallis' Capture a most superb Entertainment is to be given to him at Faniuel[*sic*] Hall. Mr. Swan has given him an Invitation to pass a week at his Country Seat.

I am Dear Ma'am yours,

Joseph Dennie."

A year's employment was enough to convince all concerned that Dennie's talents were not of the mercantile variety. It was therefore decided that he should be sent to college, and in

1. Drake's *Town of Roxbury*, pp. 135-138, gives an account of his life.
2. Sermon *On Reckless Haste*, 23 May, 1797.

1785 he was placed in the charge of the Reverend Samuel West of Needham, to be prepared for Harvard. The influence of this excellent man upon young Dennie was far-reaching and for the most part salutary.[1] He was a son of the Reverend Thomas West, of Rochester, Mass., and was born in Martha's Vineyard in 1738. The early years of his life, during which he was educated by his father, were years of hard labor on the farm. He worked his way through Harvard, graduating in 1761. For a year he was chaplain of the garrison of Fort Pownal, in Maine. In 1763 he was ordained pastor of the church at Needham. Here he was insufficiently and irregularly paid, and his Loyalist sympathies during the Revolution caused some friction in his parish. In 1789 he accepted a call from the Hollis Street Church in Boston, where he preached until his death in 1808. He was an able, eloquent preacher of liberal views, a friend of Jonathan Mayhew, and is usually grouped with the early Unitarians. In his later years he wrote an autobiography and an interesting series of essays entitled *The Old Man*, in the *Boston Centinel.* During his pastorate at Needham he was obliged, in order to support his family, to tutor boys for entrance to Harvard. In this service he was very successful and endeared himself to all who came under his instruction.

The two years that Dennie spent with West were employed in diligent application to study, and pleasant association with his preceptor. The boy's fondness for literature was encouraged, and his sympathies with British rather than American ideas were not discouraged. By the summer of 1787 Joseph Dennie, a slightly built but spirited youth of nearly nineteen, imbued with a passionate love of letters, an exuberant wit, some strongly marked likes and dislikes, and a vigorous self-esteem, was ready to enter the sophomore class at Harvard.

---

1. His life is outlined in Sprague's *Annals of the American Pulpit*, vol. VIII, pp. 50-55.

CHAPTER III

AT HARVARD AND GROTON, 1787-1790

The Records of the Faculty of Harvard College, under the date of 20 August, 1787, contain the following entry:

"Joseph Dennie of Lexington, born August 30, 1768, now applied for admission into the Class of Sophimores; and after examination had,

"Voted, that upon his paying into the College Treasury the sum of twenty pounds and complying with the laws respecting admission, he be admitted into the Class of Sophimores in the University."

Some idea of what the Harvard College of 1787-90 was like may be gathered from various contemporary sources, including the journals and biographies of men who studied there about that time.[1] The students numbered about 140 and the faculty nine,[2] comprising the President, three professors and four or five tutors. Of the present buildings only Massachusetts, Harvard, and Hollis Halls and Holden Chapel were then in existence.[3] Massachusetts and Hollis were dormitories, each containing thirty-two chambers for students. Harvard Hall must be regarded as sufficiently versatile, with the following rooms and departments. "On the lower floor at the East end is the *Hall*, which serves as a dining room and is paved with stone. The west end is a *Chapel*, for devotions, lectures and exhibitions. . . . Over the Chapel, on the second floor, is the *Library*, containing 13,000 books, disposed in the alcoves, in each of which is a window. . . . At the east end, over the Hall, is the *Philosophy Room*. In this chamber are held the meetings of the corporation and overseers, and of the American Academy of Arts and Sciences, and here the professor of natural philosophy delivers his experimental lectures. . . . In a lesser

1. John Quincy Adams, Joseph Story, Horace Binney, and others. See also Quincy's *History of Harvard University*.
2. Exclusive of three professors in the Medical School.
3. A careful detailed description of these buildings and their equipment, with a view of the old Yard, appeared in the *Massachusetts Magazine*, June, 1790.

apartment adjoining this is kept the *Apparatus* for experimental philosophy. . . . In another apartment is the *Museum.*"[2] Holden Chapel was used for recitations. President Willard lived in Wadsworth House and took some of the students as lodgers there.

The regular undergraduate course, meagre and inadequate, included the following studies:

Latin: Livy, Sallust, Horace, Cicero *De Oratore.*
Greek: Xenophon, the *Iliad*, and the *New Testament.*
Mathematics: Arithmetic, required of freshmen; Algebra (Sanderson's) and Euclid, required of sophomores.
Natural Philosophy: Guthrie's *Geography*, Burlamaqui's *Natural Philosophy*, and Ferguson's *Astronomy.*
Rhetoric: Blair's *Lectures on Rhetoric* and Lowth's *Grammar.*
Metaphysics: Watts' *Logic*, and Locke *On the Human Understanding.*
History: Millott's *Elements* (all classes).
Theology: Doddridge's *Lectures*, and public lectures, required of juniors.

Declamations were required of all classes. The only modern language offered was French, which was prescribed for all students not electing Hebrew. It was not taught, however, by the regular faculty, but by occasional instructors from Boston, one day in the week.[2]

The diary of John Quincy Adams, H. C. 1787, describes the routine of a college day. The following entry is for 3 May, 1786, the year before Dennie entered:[3]

"This morning (Wednesday) at 6 we went in to prayers, after which we immediately recited (Homer). This took us till 7-¼. At 7-½ we breakfasted. At ten we had a lecture on

1. *Massachusetts Magazine*, June, 1790.
2. Albert Gallatin, a Swiss, later the financier of the Jeffersonian administration, gave instruction in French at Harvard in 1782 and 1783.
3. Henry Adams. "Harvard College in 1786-87," in *Historical Essays*, pp. 80-121.

Divinity from Mr. Wigglesworth; it was upon the wisdom of all God's action, and justifying those parts of Scripture which some have reproached as contrary to justice. At 11 we had a philosophical lecture from Mr. Williams upon the mechanical powers, and particularly the lever and the pulley. At 12-½, dinner. At 3, an astronomical public lecture upon the planet Mercury, a very circumstantial account of all its transits over the sun's disk. At 4 again we recited (Greek Testament), and at 5 attended prayers again, after which there are no more exercises for this day, but we are obliged in the evening to prepare our recitation for tomorrow morning. This I think is quite sufficient employment for one day, but the three last days in the week we have very little to do. Thursdays and Saturdays reciting only in the morning, and Friday a philosophical lecture."

Of the life and character of the students, Joseph Story, who entered Harvard in 1794, wrote,[1] "The students were generally moral, devoted to their studies, and ambitious of distinction. There would be, then as now, an occasional outbreak; but I am not aware that immorality or dissipation or habitual indolence was more in fashion then than in succeeding times. . . . There is universally far more temperance now in the use of wine and spirituous liquors.

"The college library was at that time far less comprehensive and suited to the wants of the students than it now is. It was not as easily accessible, and was not frequented by them. . . . Even in respect to English literature and science we had little more than a semi-annual importation of the most common works. . . . The English periodicals were then few in number; and I do not remember any one that was read by the students except the *Monthly Magazine* (the old *Monthly*), and that was read but by a few. I have spoken of our semi-annual importations; and it is literally true, that two ships only plied as regular packets between Boston and London—one in the spring, and the other in the autumn, and their arrival was an era in our college life.

"In respect to academical intercourse, the students had lit-

1. *Life and Letters of Joseph Story*, Vol. I, pp. 47-55. Two letters to W. F. Channing, 23 Sept. and 12 Oct., 1843.

erally none, that was not purely official, except with each other. The different classes were almost strangers to each other, and cold reserve generally prevailed between them. The system of 'fagging' (as it was called) was just then dying out, and I believe my own class was the first that was not compelled, at the command of the senior class, to perform the drudgery of the most humble services. . . . The intercourse between the students and Boston . . . was infrequent and casual[1] . . . and the inducement to visit in private circles was far less attractive than at present. The literature and science, the taste, talent, and learning now so abundantly found in that interesting city, have been in great measure the growth of later time and the result of the gradual progress of wealth and refinement and a more comprehensive education."

The relations between students and faculty were far from being close and cordial. Story says,[2] "The President and Professors were never approached, except in the most formal way, and upon official occasions; and in the college yard (if I remember rightly) no student was permitted to keep his hat on if one of the Professors was there. President Willard was a sound scholar, of great dignity of manners, but cold and somewhat forbidding in his demeanor. . . . Professor Webber[3] was modest, mild and quiet, but unconquerably reserved and staid. Professor Pearson[4] was an excellent critic, but somewhat severe and exact in his requirements." He was pretty cordially disliked by the students on this account. Professor Wigglesworth, Hollis Professor of Divinity, who deserves to be remembered for his remarkably accurate calculations of the probable increase in population in America, was so aged and feeble that his duties were often neglected and his lectures ill attended. The relations were still less pleasant with the tutors. Most of them were disliked by the general body of the students and constant friction was the result. This was due chiefly to the practice of regard-

1. The West Boston Bridge was not yet constructed, and the only means of communication was by means of the Charlestown ferry or by the roundabout route through Brighton and along Boston Neck.
2. Op. cit. Page 48.
3. Hollis Professor of Mathematics and Natural Philosophy.
4. Hancock Professor of Hebrew and Oriental Languages. He also gave instruction in English.

ing the students, most of whom were young, as inferiors, an attitude especially galling if coupled with a churlish disposition in the instructor. To seek the counsel or confidence of the faculty was regarded as intrusion on one hand, and exposed one to distrust as a "fisherman"—as the term was—on the other.

The class of 1790, to which Dennie belonged, was neither exceptionally brilliant nor unusually dull. Nearly all of its forty-two graduates attained some distinction in after life. Eleven became ministers, three physicians, and twelve lawyers, of whom five were at different times members of Congress.[1] Thomas Boylston Adams (1772-1832), son of Vice-President, later President, Adams, became Chief Justice of the Massachusetts Court of Common Pleas. Samuel C. Crafts (1768-1853) was Representative from Vermont, 1817 to 1825, and Governor of that state, 1828 to 1830. Josiah Quincy, 3rd, (1772-1864) was Member of Congress from 1804 to 1813, the first Mayor of Boston, 1823-28, and President of Harvard College, 1828-1845. George Sullivan (1771-1838) was a Member of Congress, 1811-1815, and Attorney General of New Hampshire for the twenty years succeeding. Roger Vose (1768-1842), Dennie's closest friend at college, was in Congress from 1813 to 1817, and thereafter a Chief Justice of the Circuit Court in New Hampshire. Of the class as a whole, Quincy wrote,[2] "My classmates were almost all successful in the professions to which they devoted their lives. Among them I recognize sound divines, good lawyers, skillful physicians—men who acted their parts well, filling the stations in life to which Providence assigned them with acceptable faithfulness."

Of his classmate, Dennie, the same writer has to say,[1] "The most talented, taking light literature as a standard, was Joseph Dennie, whose acquaintance with the best English classics was uncommon at that period. His imagination was vivid and he wrote with great ease and facility. . . . While at college he might unquestionably have taken the highest rank in his class, for he had great happiness, both in writing and in elocution;

1. Most of the ensuing data is from the unpublished records of the Harvard Quinquennial Office.
2. *Life of Josiah Quincy*, by his son, Edmund Quincy, pages 30-33.

but he was negligent in his studies, and not faithful to the genius with which nature had endowed him."

The chief source of information regarding Dennie's experiences, friendships, and antipathies at Harvard, however, besides the records of the college faculty, is to be found in the college correspondence, fortunately preserved, between him and his classmate, Vose.[1] This includes twenty letters written by Dennie and the replies of Vose. From them we learn that Dennie lived on the fourth or attic floor of Massachusetts Hall, which was then used as a dormitory. His roommate was Samuel Welles, son of Arnold Welles, long president of the United States Bank in Boston. Young Welles, who was a youth of pleasant disposition and irregular habits, three years younger than Dennie, was lost at sea in 1804. Among his other associates were "Tommy" Adams; (Rev.) Samuel Chandler, of Lexington; (Rev.) Thomas Gray of Boston; (Dr.) John C. Howard of Boston; Gilbert Hubbard of Boston; John Callender and Frank Withers, two young cavaliers from the South; and Roger Vose of Milton. Vose was an excellent classical scholar, a poet of some talent, an amorous and genial spirit, and withal an exemplary student. Their literary and convivial tastes soon drew him and Dennie together, and the friendship then begun lasted long after they had left Harvard.

The first letter of their correspondence, dated at Needham, 5 June, 1788, was written near the end of Dennie's first—the sophomore—year. Here he had been spending six enjoyable weeks of the spring term with his old teacher, Samuel West. His ostensible purpose in thus absenting himself from college was probably to recuperate in health:[2] his real one is made evident in the letter. He says that he has read through thirty volumes, chiefly poets and miscellaneous authors, and adds, "I have translated Virgil's first *Bucolic* into blank verse, have

1. Now in the possession of Miss Kate Vose Marcy, of Royalton, Vermont. Vose's letters and copies of Dennie's are in the keeping of Dr. Samuel F. Green, at the Mass. Historical Society Library.

2. The college laws regarding absences were notoriously lax. See Henry Adams. *Historical Essays*, "Harvard College in 1786-1787." At one time, from the middle of December, 1786, to 7 February, 1787, the college was closed, owing to lack of firewood.

written a full sheet of nonsensical prose upon Friendship,[1] and have scribbled a few poetical sentiments by way of introduction to '*Solvitur acris hyems,*' etc., a Theme with which I am much delighted.'' Already Dennie and his friends had begun to criticize the narrow unprogressiveness of the college and its government. He refers to his friend as ''buried in that rubbish of the school, that nonsensical syllogistical mode of reasoning which the united *wisdom* of the President and Tutors prescribes,'' and follows his remarks with unkindly comment upon several members of the faculty. At Needham, in the genial parson's library, and in the society of a ''rural fair'' named Betsey, Dennie spent some of the happiest days of his existence.

The first two years at Harvard seem to have been otherwise uneventful. By entering at once into the sophomore class he escaped the distasteful humiliations of the fagging system. Once, according to the faculty records, he was fined for participation in disorders at Commons on Thanksgiving Day, 1787, and once for ''going out of town without leave.'' He seems to have been generally regular in attendance upon prayers, lectures, and recitations, for neglect of which, fines or ''mulcts,'' were then imposed. His fines for this cause during the first two years aggregated only 4s. 5d. He and his set occasionally joined in the nocturnal larks, either in the dormitories or the taverns in Cambridge, at which, in spite of strict rules to the contrary, wine and song were indulged in by the students. His passion, however, was for literature. He writes,[2] ''Roger, when shall we again enjoy such rich evenings, as those in our Sophimore year, when we laughed in Concert over the page of Cervantes? That was the bright period of our College life. How often after feasting all night upon some literary banquet have we been ready to curse the rising sun for intruding upon our joys?'' Mathematics and sciences, however, he detested with equal fervor.[3] The former he called ''a barren speculative science

1. *Possibly* the essay of that name in the *Massachusetts Magazine*, Vol. I, No. IX, for September, 1789.
2. Letter from Groton, 9 Mar., 1792.
3. "In mature years he spent more than a day puzzling over his landlady's problem of the cost of seven and three-fourths pounds of mutton at five and one-fourth cents a pound, and finally assured the lady that 'the butcher was doubtless honest and she might safely pay her bill.'" Marble. *Heralds of American Literature*, p. 194.

that neither fills the brain nor ameliorates the heart."[1] In the semi-annual "Exhibitions" at Harvard, at which picked scholars displayed their skill in declamations, forensics and Latin composition, and for which he was naturally well qualified, he never took part. Though some of his letters indicate that he purposely avoided appointment to these honors, he later adduced his neglect by the faculty in this respect as an evidence of their discrimination against him. In this he was like many a spirited schoolboy who scorns to seek such little honors, yet is piqued when they do not come his way.

The great disappointment of his college life, however, came in his senior year. He was frequently ill, and in the spring of 1789 he left college on this account. Though the first term of the academic year following began in August, September was nearly gone before he returned. The succeeding events may perhaps best be shown by certain abstracts from the faculty records. The following one is dated 2 October, 1789:

"Whereas Dennie has been absent from the College from the last Spring vacation to the present time, and has not accounted for his absence agreeably to the laws of the College,

"Voted, that if he does not give reason in person, on or before the sixteenth day of October current, to the President, Professors, and Tutors, to their satisfaction, his chamber shall be taken from him, agreeably to the law in that case made and provided

"*Voted,* that when he appears, he make answer to a charge of contempt of the authority of the College, shown by him on Wednesday last past."

The nature of the contempt is explained in the record for 7 October:

"It appeared that one of the Governors of the College[2] having repaired to the room of Dennie and Welles in consequence of a disorder there, in the afternoon of the 30th of the last month, was treated by Dennie with great disrespect; that he remained covered in the presence of said Governor, until ordered to take off his hat; that when spoken to he replied to him in an insolent

1. Vose Letters, 16 Mar., 1790.
2. Amos Crosby, H. C. 1786, Tutor in Logic, Metaphysics, and Ethics from 1788 to 1792.

manner, that he positively refused to go with him to his chamber, when ordered, and persisted in his neglect to do so. All which conduct was a contempt of the authority of the College, is repugnant to the rules of order and decency, and subversive of the discipline and good government of the society: Therefore

"Voted and adjudged that Dennie be, and he hereby is degraded ten places in his class, and that he take his place in future between Moody and Quincy.

"Memo. the foregoing sentence was executed upon Dennie in the usual mode in the Chapel immediately after morning prayers October 8th."

Dennie did not accept with entire tameness this humiliation. He felt that he was being made the object of petty tyranny, and his bearing toward his instructors became defiant and "of ill tendency with respect to the other students," who sympathized heartily with him. In giving his motive for this conduct he later wrote to a classmate,[1] "I ever held it as a maxim that the bulk of the government, like the race of Jackasses, discharged their duty faithfullest, when most soundly beaten. Accordingly I was loud and bold in my censures, when anything censurable appeared." Such an attitude was not likely to soothe strained relations. On Thursday, 17 December, standing before his fellows in Chapel, Dennie delivered an oration of Lord Chatham's which, as Mrs. Dennie said, "was bitter," and which shadowed forth an obnoxious tutor in a manner which left no doubt of the speaker's meaning. The result was another—this time a crushing—faculty decree:[2]

"Voted, that Dennie be suspended the term of six months, and that he be placed under the care of the Rev. Mr. Parsons, of Amherst, or the Rev. Mr. Chaplin, of Groton, and that, during the time above mentioned, he prosecute the same course of studies which his class will pursue during the same term; and that, upon the expiration of the same, he shall be critically examined in the several branches of science he shall have studied during his absence," etc.

The fact that several other members of Dennie's lively coterie had undergone similar sentences did not lessen in his mind the

---

1. Unfinished letter to Gilbert Hubbard, April, 1790, from Groton.
2. Records of the Faculty, 21 December, 1789.

apparently unexpected disgrace. His bitter and surprised mortification at the temerity of the "race of Jackasses" in suspending him colors his letters to Vose. In the first one written after his banishment, he reviewed the three years of his college life and the governmental prejudices and severity by which "my moments have been embittered, my reputation tainted, and my improvement obstructed."[1] He wished to forget Harvard. "In that sink of vice, that temple of dullness, that roost of owls, I feel interested for none, except my worthy classmates, and Thompson,[2] who disgraces himself by descending from the height of his genius and virtue to associate with solemn blockheads." Later he wrote, "Whatever might have been my views in pronouncing that parliamentary speech in the manner I did, yet, as they never could prove my crime . . . such slight grounds did by no means justify my condemnation. With regard to the Government, I shall ever feel a rooted prejudice against them for their conduct towards me,—a prejudice which no time shall destroy."[3] Toward the tutor he had offended, however, he harbored no grudge. "My exceptions from College characters is too partial. I hope there are many Thompsons. Crosby at the bottom is benevolent, he is the sport of his feelings it is true, and am I not so myself?"[4]

Dennie elected to spend the period of his rustication at Groton, whither he set out in a chaise, 21 January, 1790, stopping a few minutes on the way to kiss a sweetheart at Concord. Though begun under inauspicious circumstances, his sojourn at Groton was to prove one of the happiest periods of his life. The first of his seventeen letters from that place to Vose gives an enthusiastic picture of the village as he drove into it at sunset one January day, sick and chilled through after his long ride in the piercing cold. He was impressed with the mountains to the north, the noble river, the variety of hill, dale and woods, and the air, "sweet and pure, sacred from the contamination

1. Vose Letters, 24 Feb., 1790.
2. Thomas Thompson (1766-1821), H. C. 1786, Tutor, 1789-1791, later a prominent lawyer of New Hampshire. M. C. 1805-07, Senate 1815-17. "A busy, active, kindly man," and the most popular member of his class. See Bell, *Bench & Bar of N. H.*, and the Diary of J. Q. Adams, *Mass. Hist. Soc. Proceedings*, Nov., 1902.
3. Letter to Gilbert Hubbard, April, 1790.
4. Vose Letters, 24 Feb., 1790.

of those spleen-inspiring blasts which at Cambridge used to harrass my enfeebled frame.''[1] Mr. Chaplin turned out a good friend and companion, ''a sensible priest, who has read Rabelais as well as Cruden's *Concordance*''—in short, ''a second *West*,'' which from Dennie was the acme of praise. Here he found also congenial associates, well educated, ''sensible, liberal and spunky,'' with whom he could spend all but the few hours he set aside for study. For his most intimate companion, Timothy Bigelow, just establishing a law practice at Groton, he expressed the warmest praise.[2] As an inmate of Mr. Chaplin's household, ''the little man'' was often invited to the homes of Colonel Prescott, of Revolutionary fame, and of Judge Oliver Prescott, where he was entertained with a liberality which accorded with his views of ''the noblesse.'' He immediately fell in love with Judge Prescott's charming daughter, Lucy, at whose birthday party he officiated as poet laureate, and ''produced an ode as dull as any of Colley Cibber's.''[3] It is pleasant to learn that Lucy Prescott was afterward happily married to Bigelow, Dennie's intimate friend.

Dennie's letters to his classmate are so spirited and vivacious, and reflect so well the irrepressible gaiety of his character that one would be tempted, did space allow, to quote largely from them. By his correspondence with Vose and other sympathetic spirits[4] he kept in touch with occurrences at Cambridge and with his Concord charmer. The following extracts are his reply to Vose's charge as to the inconstancy of his affections:[5]

''Jos. Dennie's grave advice is not the less valuable, because Jos. Dennie acts in opposition to his own sentiments. . . . Hear what I have to say respecting my attachment to the sex. . . . My constitution is inflammable, my sensibility exquisite. Hence a fine face acts upon me like electricity. Fur-

1. Vose Letters, 24 Feb., 1790.
2. Timothy Bigelow (1767-1821) H. C. 1786. As a boy he served an apprenticeship in the printing office of Thomas' *Massachusetts Spy*, at Worcester. He was a lawyer at Groton and Medford, and served his state, in the legislature, senate, and Governor's Council, almost consecutively, for thirty years.
3. Vose Letters, 16 March, 1790.
4. Letters are extant from Erasmus Babbitt, Gilbert Hubbard, Samuel Walker, Francis Withers, John Callender, Thomas Gray, J. C. Howard, and Samuel Chandler.
5. Vose Letters, 11 March, 1790.

ther, fickleness is a prominent feature in my character. Though I were enraptured with a fairer Venus than ever poet fabled, tho I were upon the point of matrimony with such a Goddess, yet let chance waft me to another region where I could see another beauty, my heart would immediately be pierced, and, forgetting perhaps the protestations and engagements to the old charmer, I would use my utmost endeavor to cultivate the good graces of the new. . . . I did not say that I ruined the sex, that I took advantage of an unguarded hour, no, . . . I ever behaved honorably to my favorites. I made no promises. I excited no romantic wish. I was candid, every conquest was fairly made in the open field.''

Three of the letters to Vose are taken up with a criticism, from the sentimentalist's point of view, of the relative merits of Hume and Beattie, as writers and philosophers.[1] The third letter follows:

Groton, May 24, 1790

Dear Friend:

In perusing Beattie, we immediately perceive that he possessed a rich, fertile and cultivated imagination. Such is the beautiful energy and dignity of his language, that the poet breathes in every page. His periods are correct in a high degree. He is happy both in the selection and collocation of words. His knowledge both of poetry and music is evinced by the melody and just balance of his sentences. Beattie is himself a poet, and one of high rank. He has in addition to many others, written a poem entitled the Minstrel, which the critics declare one of the best productions that has appeared since the demise of Queen Anne. In fine to close these observations, Hume and Beattie both received the same advantages from celebrated Scottish seminaries, both were students and both were scholars. But in genius, abilities and in the employment of their talents, essentially different. Nature has bestowed upon one the imagination of a poet, a bold, vehement, and creative genius. In imagination the other was deficient, but he was endowed with singular sagacity, a patient and plodding attention, subtlety, and a talent for disputation. He was master of every trick,

1. Printed in the *Report of the Council of the American Antiquarian Society*, October, 1889.

of every sophism in controversy. His mind was of that microscopic species that could disregard the vast and magnificent, and pore upon the obscure and the little. Beattie looked abroad, contemplated the wide expanse of nature, feasted upon her charms, and gratefully thanked the author of the feast. Hume pined in the dark cell of the sceptic, voluntarily obscured his optics, and then murmured because there was no light. The one could plod over the schoolmen's page, could trace the dreary mazes of Malebranche and Leibnitz, and wear life away among the reveries of Pyrrho. The delight of the other was to cultivate those valuable books, where truth and sentiment predominated, to roam over Fairy land with Shakespeare, to turn the moral page with Tillotson, and to imbibe the great truths of religion from the Gospel of God. Widely different, in fine, widely different did these great men employ their talents. The one labored in language indistinct as his perceptions, and dark as his designs, 'to cloud the sunshine of our belief.' The other pointed out a 'vista' to heaven, asserted the dignity of truth and common sense, and defended Christianity in a style resembling the cause which he advocated.

"From the perusal of Beattie I think, Roger, I have derived advantage. I have learned to make a just estimate of sceptics and scepticism. I have learned that time is wholly lost, which is spent in tracing the intricacies of such authors. I have learned that such writings, contrary to the objects of other performances, bewilder the reasoning power, darken the understanding and harden the heart. That prejudice, which I ever cherished against metaphysics, is now rooted. To cultivate this barren, unprofitable science is worse than wasting, it is murdering time. Let every scholar study and re-study select parts of Locke. We should be acquainted with the operations of our own minds. But let the works of Hobbes, of Tindal, Hume, and Bolingbroke sink into that oblivious dream, to which they are so nearly allied.

Sincerely yours,

Jos. Dennie, Jr."

Three of his friends, Vose, Withers, and Ellery, visited him at Groton during the spring. He studied little, but read assiduously, pestering his obliging friend for books from the college library, which were frequently sent back overdue. In May he sent an interesting account of train-band day at Groton. Classes at Harvard being over for the seniors, he began importuning Vose to join him. At Groton the two friends could lead an idyllic life together, in the company of Doctor Swift, Lord Chesterfield, Doctors Moore and Goldsmith, with Shakespeare and "*that clever young man,* Addison";[1] while at Harvard the last quarter would be spent in "unmeaning noise, racing from chamber to chamber, and swilling oceans of wine and punch." Vose, however, remained at Cambridge. With the approach of Commencement, letters of both friends begin to show a new sober tone. In several of them there is a serious discussion as to which of the three learned professions is to be adopted and whether both may not settle, or at least study, in the same town, possibly under the same roof. Dennie seems to lean toward medicine, and urges his friend to join him in studying with Doctor Oliver Prescott, at Groton. He intimates that he is giving two hours a day to deliberation on the matter. Vose's friends designed him for the ministry, but he confides that "Nature never intended us for ambassadors of Christ."[2] Another source of uneasiness is revealed by Dennie in a letter of May 24, in which he asks Vose to sound the students, and if possible the faculty, regarding the examination he will be obliged to take. "To be examined for a degree," he says, "after the treatment I have received, is too humiliating—I cannot brook the idea. They are acquainted with my abilities. They can have no other motive to examine, except to humble your friend."

Vose's report, however, proving unfavorable, Dennie, perhaps influenced by parental admonitions, renewed his studies in astronomy and natural philosophy and "*Bigelone favente,*" soon felt competent to "face Packard with boldness."[3] Studies done, he spent his remaining days at Groton with Bigelow and the Prescotts. At length his mother came on from Lexington, and in her company Dennie rode, in bitterness and dejection, to Boston. Upon presenting himself at Cambridge with cre-

1. Vose Letters, 28 April, 1790.
2. Vose Letters. Vose to Dennie, 2 May, 1790.
3. Vose Letters, 17 Aug., 1790.

dentials from Mr. Chaplin and passing his examinations successfully, Dennie was, on 8 July, reinstated in his class.[1] At the same time favorable action was passed upon his petition, running as follows:

"To the President, Professors, and Tutors of Cambridge University, the petition of Joseph Dennie, Junior, humbly showeth,—

"That your petitioner, in consequence of an insult to a member of the government of the University having incurred the displeasure of that body, was in the month of October degraded from his proper station in the Senior Class. Your petitioner, convinced of the impropriety of his conduct towards the gentleman insulted, would entreat his forgiveness, and pray that, influenced by his unfeigned contrition, the governors of the University would pass an act of oblivion with regard to the past unjustifiable behavior of their petitioner, and would generously restore him to that section from which by his own imprudence he has been excluded."

In this speciously humble document there is evident a degree of independence and a rather showy dignity which was conspicuously lacking in most similar petitions. In the Chapel where six months before he had delivered his defiant oration, Dennie now, after prayers on 9 July, standing up in his degraded place while his petition and the vote upon it were read, was formally restored to his proper rank in the class. This last humiliation over, he left in bitterness and wrath for Lexington, not waiting to attend Commencement and the graduation of his class. He says,[2] "The cursed impertinence of a mock examination being over, a lying petition read, and the last acts of pigmy despotism exercised, I forsook Cambridge with bitter execrations, and repaired to Lexington to snuff sweet air, to dine with Temperance and Co., that is upon Milk,[3] and to build up anew my tottering fame." And he adds significantly, "I study *Juvenal.* Verbum sapienti, etc." He never forgave Harvard for what he honestly believed to be an unwarranted injury and disgrace.

---

1. *Faculty Records*, 8 July, 1790.
2. Vose Letters, August 17, 1790.
3. A letter to his mother, 8 June, 1790, speaks of one instance of "florid expectoration." A milk diet was then prescribed for consumption.

Little has been said in these pages about Dennie's literary work at college. He was writing poetry and essays in 1788, and he had a high reputation among his classmates for ability in composition. The *Massachusetts Magazine*, for a time perhaps the best in the country, was established in 1789, and he probably contributed freely to it over various signatures. A verse *Panegyrick on Thomson,*[1] signed *Academicus,* and probably a few moral essays signed *Socialis,* in the volume for 1789 are his work. The style of his early letters is lively and charming. Of them he wrote, "Once for all, Roger, I tell you that I write carelessly that I may write easily and with sprightliness. You must not be surprised at frequent instances of faulty arrangement, wrong collocations, etc. I write not to old P[earson]."[2] The later letters especially foreshadow, in their ease and fluency, their little tricks of italics and quotations, and their inflated language, the *Farrago* and *Lay Preacher* essays to come.

A characteristic passage from one of the letters follows:

"With regard to myself, Roger, I am Jos. Dennie still. Sometimes too high, and sometimes too low. My health has been very indifferent since your return. My enjoyments have been much embittered by pain &c. I however support this evil as well as I can & am upon the whole a tolerable practical philosopher. Convinced more & more every day of the brevity and uncertainty of life, I deem it madness to lose in unavailing sorrow and repinings a single hour, for this plain reason, that I have not many to enjoy. I have quite done with Castle building in the air, and endeavor to enjoy what I have rather than indulge in chimerical wishes for what I have not."

Poor Joe Dennie! For twenty years more he was to go on, sometimes too high and sometimes too low, building castle after castle in the air, only to see them vanish, and indulging in chimerical wishes for what he could not have.

---

1. Feb., 1789. See Appendix C.
2. Vose Letters, 11 March, 1790. One of the letters is in Latin, written without grammar or dictionary, giving an account of his trip to Groton, and his surroundings there. It is a good schoolman's Latin, stilted and formal but smooth and correct.

CHAPTER IV

CHARLESTOWN, VGTJ-VGTC—LAW STUDENT AND LAY READER; "THE FARRAGO"

At Lexington Dennie remained, nursing his wrath at "the dark and hollow manoeuvres of a club of stupid pedants,"[1] and coaxing back some degree of health and strength to his enfeebled frame, from July to December, 1790. The last letters which passed between him and Vose, now teaching school at Milton, indicate their lively interest in contemporary periodical literature in Boston. Vose inquired, "What do you think of the *Yankee?* Who do you think is the author? . . . He wants the variety you laid so much stress on, as being essential to a periodical writer."[2] And, with college man's candor, he added, speaking of Mrs. Warren's poems,[3] "I think the old lady deserves praise, Joe. I believe she is no fool."

The pursuit of literature, however, in the United States of the 1790's, was not a gainful occupation, and it was considered necessary for the young graduate to turn his attention to one of the three learned professions. He had some leaning toward the practice of medicine, but his friends dissuaded him from that as too arduous for his physique, and unsuited to his temperament. Vose, whose judgment he valued, urged the ministry or the law, preferably the latter. "Your retentive memory," he wrote, "will soon give you an acquaintance with the principles of law; and your knowledge of history; your acquaintance with national policy; will entitle you, in case your health admit, to the first offices of the state. I will dare predict that, with tolerable fortune, you will be able to convince the southern states, that Massachusetts can produce a Madison. In the desk, likewise, you would undoubtedly shine, could you exchange a small quantity of the rake for an equivalent of pru-

1. Vose Letters, 17 Aug., 1790.
2. Vose Letters, Vose to Dennie, 28 Sept., 1790. The *Yankee* was the title of a series of essays in the *Boston Centinel*.
3. Mrs. Mercy Warren, whose *Poems, Dramatic and Miscellaneous* were published in 1790.

dence and gravity."[1] Counsels like these prevailed, possibly against Dennie's own desires, and it was decided that he should begin the study of law.

For this project no place or preceptor seemed more fitting than the office of Benjamin West, of Charlestown, New Hampshire. Not only was this gentleman a brother of the beloved instructor, the Reverend Samuel West, of Needham, but from Dennie's experience at Groton it was judged that the interior of New Hampshire, away from the harsh atmosphere of the coast, would be as healthful a location as could be found for him. Accordingly, after the necessary negotiations, he set out from Lexington at the beginning of December, 1790. The first two letters of a long series written to his parents from New Hampshire describes his trip, by way of Groton, Keene, Westmoreland, and Walpole, and his reception at Charlestown on the evening of 8 December.

From inquiries along the route he had become impressed with the reputation of Mr. West, who was pretty generally considered the foremost advocate of the Cheshire County Bar. He was the sixth son of the Reverend Thomas West, of Rochester, Mass. With the aid of his brother Samuel, he was enabled to graduate at Harvard in 1768, having first started at Nassau Hall.[2] After teaching school and studying divinity for a time, he took up the study of law, and in 1773 began practising at Charlestown. At the outbreak of the Revolution he went to South Carolina, became involved in the campaign there, and after six weeks' captivity, a long illness, and a sea voyage of seven months getting from Charleston, South Carolina, to Philadelphia, reached New Hampshire again in August, 1779. Here, after several years of competition and hardship, he achieved a considerable success in his profession. He refused election to Congress in 1781 and 1789, and to the Constitutional Convention in 1787, but being an ardent Federalist, accepted membership in the New Hampshire convention for ratifying the Constitution, and in the Hartford Convention of 1814. He was a simple, refined gentleman, witty in a quiet way and scrupulous in avoiding offense to others. It is said that he never overcame a certain

1. Letter to Dennie, Dennie Papers, 12 May, 1790.
2. Later the College of New Jersey, or Princeton.

tremor on arising to speak, but this over, his utterance was fluent and eloquent. He died in 1817,[1] at the age of seventy-one years.

Naturally a clerkship in Mr. West's office was much to be desired. Some of the youths who were students at the same time with Dennie, or just before, were Samuel West, Jr., son of the Reverend Samuel, J. C. Chamberlain, Samuel Hunt, Frederick A. Sumner, and Ebenezer Bradish. All but Hunt were Harvard graduates and all but Bradish and Sumner were later associated with Dennie's literary schemes; their legal apprenticeship together, therefore, was doubtless very pleasant. The office, in which most of their time was spent, was large, airy, and convenient, and Mr. West was courteous and genial. Dennie seems to have begun his studies industriously. In January, 1791, he wrote to his parents. "As Cervantes saith of writing, so it may be said of law, it is really hard work. However, I find the further you proceed in this thorny region, the clearer the prospects." Later his zeal began to lessen under the combined attack of distracting social pleasures, ill-health, and temperamental indolence.

Charlestown in 1790 was an enterprising village of about 1100 inhabitants, beautifully and healthfully situated on the west bank of the Connecticut river. It was one of the more important towns in the southwesterly county of Cheshire, which was still sparsely populated, and which had only just decided whether it belonged to New Hampshire or the newer and more sympathetic state of Vermont to the west. The inhabitants Dennie found sociable and communicative, and the air peculiarly healthful. With a readiness always characteristic of him, he soon made himself intimate with the most prominent and intellectual families in the town, and was not long in becoming admitted as a lodger to the household of Doctor William Page. At the large, well-kept house of Dr. Page, who represented his town in the legislatures of both Vermont (1780-1781) and New Hampshire (1781-1791), the best company in the village frequently gathered. Dennie's program of life was as follows:[2]

1. The chief sources for this sketch are Bell's *Bench and Bar of New Hampshire*, pp. 727-729; and Saunderson's *History of Charlestown*, N. H., pp. 596-607.

2. Letter to his parents, 31 May, 1791, Dennie Papers.

"I rise at Dawn, retire at eight or nine. Exercise considerably & enjoy better health now than when in Massachusetts. The morning, forenoon and beginning of the afternoon I devote to study & exercise. At four or five I go into the *best* company & enjoy social hours. This is my life."

In a later letter he described his amusements:[1]

"I chat upon politics with Dr. Page, on literature or miscellaneous topics with my brother Clerks at the Office; or play whist, mere games of Commerce, with Judge Olcott and family. Sometimes in the hour of glee I go with my companions to Willard's caravansary, where the strongest liquor I quaff is a cup of coffee. We sup, lounge, sing, &c. and retire at ten."

In February, 1791, Dennie made a short visit at home. In the late summer of the year, without the knowledge of his parents, he made a journey to Enfield, Hartford, and New Haven, Connecticut, as the escort of Mrs. Tryphena Olcott, wife of Judge Olcott, and her niece. He attempted the trip on horseback, but his physique was unequal to the jaunt, and he had frequently to change places with the niece and occupy a seat in the chaise. At New Haven he attended the Yale Commencement. As he had letters to President Stiles, he called upon him and was courteously entertained. The cost of hiring a horse and the sundry expenses of a gallant along the route brought Dennnie into debt, which was considerably increased by a prolonged and severe illness in March and April of the following year. Dr. Page happened to be absent, attending the session of the legislature, and the inexperience of the young doctor who was called in nearly brought matters to a fatal termination. With the return of Dr. Page in the spring, however, Dennie recovered slowly. He now discarded the milk and vegetable diet which had been prescribed by his parents as a safeguard against consumption, and took to beef, half a pint of red wine daily, and plenty of horseback riding as exercise. These modes of convalescing, however, still further diminished his credit; he had now been away from home for fifteen months, and calls for a visit to Lexington became urgent.

At last, in the middle of June, 1792, he started for home—a curious Goldsmith-like pilgrimage of a month. At Keene

1. Letter to his parents, 19 Oct., 1791, Dennie Papers.

he halted to attend the sessions of the Supreme Court. Here again he became ill, and falling into kindly hands, consumed several weeks in a leisurely recovery before continuing his travels. A memorandum in the elder Dennie's hand across the back of one of his son's letters states that the latter "Arrived at Lex Jul. 13. Sett out on his return to Charl Sep. 4, 1792."

Dennie returned to Charlestown with money enough to pay his debts, a keen sense of disgrace and regret for a year and a half wasted, and a plentiful supply of resolution for the future. He satisfied his creditors, adopted a more sober program of life, and applied himself with greater diligence to the study of law, though probably with a growing distrust of his fitness for it. He regarded it as "a nauseous pill, not to be poured down the throats of even the vulgar without gilding."[1] With sound self-analysis he wrote to his father:[2]

"I can appreciate my own talents. I never shall be profound. I never shall be a silent unenterprising lawyer. My talents to you I can freely confess are superficial, but they are *showy*, and the deficiencies of Judgment in the thought are in *vulgar* opinion compensated by the boldness and glitter of Fancy in the expression."

Superficial but showy! How many of the defects of Dennie's work are summed up in these words, and how clearly is the deficiency of judgment expressed in the very opinion that boldness and glitter of fancy, wholly divorced from judgment, could ever succeed, either in law or in letters.

His health, in spite of a mild winter, continued poor. "I am the sport of the elements," he once wrote,[3] "and at times they buffet me strangely. My cough is troublesome and my imagination is too often conjuring up spectres. I wish you would grasp the pen of erasure and strike out Consumption and Hectic from my vocabulary." His nervous system was too irritable and his sensibilities too exquisite for him "ever to be a *vulgarly* happy man." Yet he was never wholly without a fund of good spirits, "a bank which, in my sickliest hours, furnishes me with change to bribe evil spirits to depart. . . . Meanwhile let

1. Letter to his parents, 12 Oct., 1791.
2. Letter to his parents, 29 Dec., 1792.
3. Letter to his parents, 6 Feb., 1791.

the *Scabbard* moulder as it may, the *Blade* shall not lose its polish and become rusty."[1]

Another passage from the same letter hints at a new sphere of activity which Dennie was preparing to enter:

"The same irritation which sometimes hinders me from pronouncing my part on life's stage will enable me so to act at another as to challenge the spectator's applause. Pope, Dr. Watts, and Doddridge through life were combating with death in many of its forms, yet they were Men of Business, fulfilled their daily tasks, useful to others, and acquiring fame and fortune to themselves."

The two decades succeeding the close of the Revolution witnessed the rise of many village newspapers in the newly-settled portions of New England—in Maine, and along the Connecticut River in Massachusetts, New Hampshire, and Vermont. The country was, however, thinly peopled, readers were few, subscriptions were tardy and hard to collect, the transmission of news was irregular and slow, and as a result most of the papers had a mushroom existence. They were generally modeled upon the older, well-established papers, such as the *Independent Chronicle, Columbian Centinel,* and *Boston Gazette,* of Boston; the *Massachusetts Spy,* of Worcester, and the *Connecticut Gazette,* of New London. Three others of later origin, which probably also served as models, were the *Farmer's Journal,* of Danbury, Connecticut, the *Hampshire Gazette,* of Northampton, Massachusetts, and the *Connecticut Courant,* of Hartford. The perusal of any of these papers, many of which, in an excellent state of preservation, may be consulted in the libraries of Harvard University, the Boston Athenaeum, the City of Boston, and the American Antiquarian Society,[2] at Worcester, cannot fail to furnish amusement, and not a little instruction, to the reader of today. They consisted almost always of a single sheet, once folded, to make four pages of print, varying from 14 to 24 inches in height, and from 11 to 16 in width. The paper and ink used were considerably better and more lasting than

1. Letter to his parents, 6 Nov., 1791.
2. This library contains the fullest collections of early American newspapers. Our city dailies of twenty or thirty years ago are often nearly illegible, whereas copies of the *Boston Gazette* and its contemporaries of 1750 are almost as clear as when they were issued.

those used in the making of most papers of the present day. The titles, in the infancy of a republic with unlimited outlook and ambitions, seem often absurdly high-sounding or abstruse, such as the *Herald of Freedom*, the *Palladium*, the *Morning Ray*, the *Rural Repository*, the *Federal Orrery*, the *Scourge of Aristocracy*, etc. The news was often fragmentary and of old date. News from abroad, at this period chiefly concerned with the paroxysms of the French Revolution, and brought by letters or the testimony of none too veracious captains of slow-moving sailing vessels, was not available until from four to eight weeks after the events recounted. One learns that the good old Anglo-Saxon interest in narratives of murder and cruelty is not a morbid modern development. The display of credulity regarding freaks of nature and unfamiliar lands was somewhat greater than it is today. The decrees of kings, declarations of war and acts of Congress and legislature were a godsend to the editors, who printed them in full, often crowding out matters of local interest, which it was assumed could be learned by word of mouth, or might be reserved for later issues. The advertisements in the larger towns were numerous and remunerative. One of the most frequent insertions was for the apprehension of indentured servants who had run away from their masters.[1] Another, now banished from newspaper columns, was that of "a young woman with a good breast of milk," desiring a position as wet nurse. Proposals for publishing books, generally got out by subscription, to avoid risk to the printer, were frequent and detailed. Editorial writing had not reached a very advanced stage. The sentiments of the publishers are most evident in brief, pungent observations and in garbled news. In some papers items and articles of scientific interest were numerous. Among the inventions discussed are devices for aerial navigation by means of balloons, for the reproduction of the human voice,[2] and for the restoration of human life by means of electricity.[3] On urgent occasions an Extraordinary sheet—whence our "extra"—was issued.

To us at present, however, that part of the paper which in

1. The reward offered in most cases was one cent.
2. *Massachusetts Spy*, 13 Sept., 1792.
3. *Columbian Centinel*, 19 June, 1793.

most cases was set aside as a literary department, is of greatest interest. At the upper left-hand corner of the last page were generally to be found one or more poems, original or selected, usually occupying not more than half a column. This column bore some title indicative of poetic inspiration, such as the *Fount,* the *Aonian Rill,* the *Parnassus Packet,* the *Pegasus of Apollo,* the *Tongue of Apollo,* the *Galaxy,* or the *Muses.*[1] There appeared the effusions of local poets and poetesses, and when none of sufficient merit were offered, selections from British classic or contemporary poets. The commonest themes for native versifiers were translations from the Latin classics, especially, of course, Horace; satirical and humorous political poems; and odes, for various occasions and addressed to various persons objects, and states of being. The Fourth of July and New Year's Day were productive of most of the occasional odes, one established convention being the *New Year Address* supposed to be delivered by the carriers of the newspapers to their patrons. Besides the poetical column, most of the better newspapers attempted to present each week one or more essays, dealing in a pleasant fashion with some point of morals or manners. These were distinct from the political essays called forth in series or singly by various national or international crises, in which the ablest pens and minds were often employed. It is, in fact, only in the clear-cut, direct, and forceful writings of this kind, of which the *Federalist* papers are the best-known example, that American letters of the period can successfully vie with what was being produced on the other side of the ocean. In New England the tradition started by many able writers during the Revolution was maintained by John Quincy Adams,[2] Fisher Ames,[3] Benjamin Austin[4] and many others. Besides

---

1. These are to be found respectively in the *Columbian Centinel,* Boston, the *Eagle or Dartmouth Centinel.* Hanover, N. H., the *Guardian,* New Brunswick, N. J., the *Massachusetts Spy.* Worcester, the *Rural Repository.* Leominster, the *Federal Orrery,* Boston, and the *Farmer's Weekly Museum.* Walpole, N. H.

2. He attacked Paine and the sympathizers with France in three series of essays in the *Columbian Centinel,* signed *Publicola* (1791), *Marcellus* (1793) and *Columbus,* (1793).

3. Ames contributed several series of political essays over the signatures *Lucius Junius Brutus* and *Camillus* to the *New England Palladium.*

4. The *Honestus,* and *Old South* of the *Independent Chronicle.*

these, however, which first appeared only in the larger papers and on special occasions, there were between 1785 and 1800, perhaps a hundred short series of lighter periodical essays, contributed to various New England journals. Few papers were so poor as not to have one juvenile or clerical moralist contribute directly to their columns, but the more popular series were copied and recopied many times. Some typical representatives of this class were the *Neighbor* essays, in the *Massachusetts Spy:* the *Times,* in Noah Webster's *American Minerva,* at New York; the *Cordwainer,* in the *Western Star,* at Stockbridge; and the *Metabasist,* in the *Farmer's Journal,* at Danbury, Connecticut. These vary in quality from grave moralizing in the *Neighbor* and clear common sense and political argument in the *Times* and the *Cordwainer,* to racy satire on manners in the *Metabasist.* All, of course, were distantly or directly imitative of the *Spectator,* and the long line of English periodical essays which followed it.

The *Metabasist* essays, were reprinted, as regularly as they appeared, in a Vermont paper which was in many respects typical of its contemporaries. It had a high-sounding name, bore an optimistic motto, carried on the usual departments, was the product of journalistic pioneers, and had a brief existence. This was the *Morning Ray, or Impartial Oracle,* established at Windsor, Vermont, Tuesday, 15 November, 1791, by Judah P. Spooner and J. Reed Hutchins. Of Hutchins little is known. Judah Paddock Spooner (1748-1807) was a Connecticut man, who started out in life as carrier for the *New London Gazette,* published by Timothy Green, a distant cousin of Dennie's mother. He contributed to the *Gazette,* married a daughter of Nathan Douglass, of Douglass and Ely, publishers of the *Farmer's Journal,* at Danbury, and in 1773 opened a printing office at Norwich with his brother-in-law, Timothy Green, nephew of the Timothy already mentioned. In the Revolution he fought at Bunker Hill and later was for some time captive in a British prison ship at Brooklyn, while Green kept up the shop at Norwich. In 1780 the partners struck out northward and established a press and newspaper at Hanover, New Hampshire. The new state of Vermont was organized with definite boundaries in that year, and a bounty of 100 bushels of wheat was offered as an inducement for a printer to settle within the state. Green and Spooner accordingly crossed the Connecticut and set up a press at Westminster, whence the first number of the *Vermont Gazette: or Green Mountain Post Boy* was issued on 12 February, 1781. This was the first press and the first newspaper in the present state of Vermont. In 1783 the press was sold to George Hough, who moved with it to Windsor, further up the river, and established, with Alden Spooner, a brother of Judah, the *Vermont Journal and Universal Advertiser*, 7 August of that year. On the removal of Hough to Concord, New Hampshire, Spooner became sole owner. After a few years Judah P. Spooner came to Windsor, worked a while for his brother, then in a printing office of his own, and in the fall of 1791, commenced the *Morning Ray* with J. R. Hutchins. This paper has been fully described in the second sentence of this paragraph. The motto was "The Wilderness Shall Bud and Blossom as the Rose."[1] After 20 March, 1792, it was published by Hutchins alone until its discontinuance, a few weeks later. Spooner went next to Fair Haven, Vermont, where he was engaged from 1793 to 1798 in printing the *Fair Haven Gazette* and the *Farmer's Library,* for the famous Colonel Matthew Lyon,[2] and in publishing, in 1796, 1797, and 1798 the *Vermont Almanac and Register*. He was involved in the suits against Lyon for slander and sedition, and died, an unsuccessful and disappointed man, in 1807.[3]

The *Morning Ray* for 21 February, and 6 March, 1792, contains numbers II and III of a new periodical essay, the *Farrago,* contributed by Joseph Dennie. The issue for 14 February, which probably contained the first number of the series, is

1. An imperfect file of less than twenty numbers, from the beginning to 4 Sept., 1792, is to be found in the library of the American Antiquarian Society, Worcester, Mass.

2. Lyon had a remarkable career. He was an Irish indentured servant boy, who, by his own efforts and a prudent marriage, became a colonel in the Revolution, representative in Congress from Vermont and Kentucky, and a national figure in Democratic politics. His electoral vote from Vermont is said to have elected Jefferson in 1800. He was a virulent political writer, and established the first press in Kentucky.

3. This sketch is drawn chiefly from the *Records of William Spooner of Plymouth, Mass., and his Descendants*, pp. 150-158, and the *History of Fair Haven, Vermont*, pp. 96 ff. It has been given at length for the light it throws upon historical conditions.

missing from the extant file, but among the Dennie papers[1] I have found a manuscript copy of the essay in Dennie's own handwriting. It is a straightforward, well-written statement of the aims and probable reception of a periodical essayist. As the name indicates (Latin *farrago*,[2] "mixed fodder," hence "medley") the series was to treat of varied matters in varied moods, satirizing in a pleasing manner the foibles and faults of the times. Numbers II and III, the *Character of Meander*, and *Meander's Journal*, are among the best products of his pen. Though the type is a conventional one,[3] it is probable, as Hall suggests,[4] that many traits of Dennie's own character are painted into the portrait of the young lawyer who "studies Shakespeare at the Inns of Court," neglectful of his professional tasks; and the *Journal* probably approximates the pleasant, trifling life he enjoyed leading.[5] The *Morning Ray* for 13 March has the following notice, "*Farrago* No. 4 came too late for this day's paper. We would thank him to be more seasonable with his weekly 'Offering' in the future." As the paper for 20 March is missing, I have no means of knowing what Number IV was. With it, owing to Dennie's serious illness at that time, his contribution to the *Morning Ray* probably ended. Of this literary beginning he wrote to his mother:[6]

"In moments of dreary vacancy I have amused myself, and enlarged my knowledge of English style, by writing, at different times and in various vehicles, 'The Farrago.' This is a miscellaneous essay, which was first commenced in the winter of 1792, was printed originally at a village in Vermont, on the *Cumberland* calculation.[7] In the press of Obscurity I knew that I should risk nothing either in censure or praise. The public, however, saw or fancied, some merit; and as American essays

1. Presented by Miss Mary Dennie, of Boston, to the Harvard University Library. See bibliography, I. C.
2. Probably pronounced "farraygo" by Dennie. See the introductory verses to the essay, *Appendix A* of this paper.
3. See, for instance, *Spectator*, No. II.
4. *Philadelphia Souvenir*, page 76.
5. The third essay, for its biographical and illustrative value, and the first number because, so far as I can discover, it is not elsewhere accessible in print, I have included as an appendix to this treatise.
6. 4 January, 1794.
7. Sichard Cumberland (1732-1811), dramatist and essayist, author of the *Observer* essays.

have been hitherto unmarked, except for flimsy expression and jejune ideas, they have allowed me praise for reviving, in some degree, the Goldsmith vivacity of thought, and the Addisonian sweetness in expression."

In a letter to his parents, dated from Charlestown, 21 April, 1793, occurs Dennie's first reference to his law practice. "At an occasional court," he says, "I have *honestly* acquired two or three dollars," which Colonel Clapp naively calls,[1] "a small sum for such work, and less than lawyers now ask for ten civil words." His natural fluency was such, he wrote, that when he had a stock of ideas, words would of course follow. In the fall of 1793 he had discovered a new use for this fluency, which nearly led to a desertion of the law. His first announcement of it was made to his family in a letter of 4 Jan., 1794,[2] after a silence of five months. This direct and lively account of his transactions is characteristic of the letters, which are frequently more attractive and instructive than his more formal writings. His narrative follows:

"The clergyman[3] of the village died in July.[4] Of course, for a few weeks after his demise, the pulpit was vacated. That I could read, perhaps with more than mediocre propriety, was early suggested to some of the chief characters here by the partiality of those juvenile friends whom, amid the dullness of a winter's eve, I had amused with the scenes of Shakespeare. On a Sunday when, in the expectancy of a neighboring curate, the village had convened and were disappointed of their homily, Esquires Stephens and Hubbard,[5] at the request of the people, requested me to read the Liturgy of the Church and a sermon of Sterne. I diffidently complied, and was candidly heard. The inimitable union of grandeur and simplicity that Paley asserts is discoverable in the Church service, operating on ambition, induced such a degree of exertion in the reader as to gain, though perhaps not deserved, the applause of the hearers. A candid

1. W. W. Clapp, *Joseph Dennie*, p. 16.
2. This long and interesting letter is quoted almost entire in Col. Clapp's sketch, pp. 16-23.
3. Reverend Bulkley Olcott, pastor of the Second Congregational Church.
4. 26 June, 1763.
5. Hon. Samuel Stevens (1735-1803), for many years selectman and representative. Judge John Hubbard (1754——).

Claremonter, who, in Goldsmith's phrase, with open mouth swallowed my words, favorably reported to the wardens and vestry of a vacant church at his native village.[1] Accordingly the ensuing week I received an *official* message from Judge Kingsbury,[2] a leading member of the Episcopal Society, desiring me to be at the trouble of a visit there to read prayers on the next Sunday. This was the first moment that I conceived the project of rendering my talent gainful—of allaying in some *small* degree my thirst for independence, and *partially* relieving you from the *justly* intolerable burden of my support. I cheerfully conned my task on Saturday afternoon, and foreseeing from a knowledge of my ear-soothing powers and the blind admiration that *mob* has for sound,—foreseeing the probable issue of this business, on Sunday morning, I sallied forth on this clerical enterprise, like Haman, joyful, and with a glad heart. I read the popular sermon of Sterne on the character of the Good Samaritan. The next day, in full vestry meeting, it was *unanimously* voted, that a committee of the wardens should request me to contract for four months as a *Reader*, at the rate of 24 s. per Sunday. I obligated myself and regularly officiate.''

He goes on to defend himself from the criticisms of some of his Massachusetts friends, who have hinted at the incongruity of combining the legal and clerical professions:

''The revenues of the Church of these infant Republics are too scanty to lure from an avowedly lucrative profession a young man whose ambition is daring, and who, though despising *Pelf* for its own sake, loves it for the consequence that in these 'costermonger times' it procures. Nothing is more remote from my intention than a resignation of law practice. The task of Sunday does not in the least derange the study of Blackstone. The essence of the whole is this, that a day formerly passed vacantly on in miscellaneous reading, is now dedicated to a useful exercise in elocution, which, by accustoming me to the sight and criticism of the many, inspires confidence, furnishes me with energetic Biblical phrases, and fancy with happy allusions, and lastly furnishes a small stipend that pays my board and defies the mechanic's dun.

1. The pulpit of this church had not been regularly filled since 1791. Claremont adjoins Charlestown on the north.
2. Sanford Kingsbury (1743-1833), state representative and senator and judge of probate.

"The inhabitants of Claremont are very importunate that I should, in the spring, enter their church 'a priest forever after the order of Melchisedec'; that I should go to New London and receive ordination from Bishop Seabury. They have offered to settle me immediately, to allow me £80 per annum and the profit of glebe lands leased in Claremont and seven adjoining towns, and have pledged themselves that in ten years the profits of the glebe should rise in duplicate proportion, or an equivalent should be paid. . . . In your reply to this letter, therefore, which reply I will show them, insert a clause of refusal, that I may bid them in March an honorable adieu, and have my otherwise painful rejection of their proposals gratified by your positive denial.

"The Church of St. John's, at Portsmonth,[1] has indirectly sounded me on the subject of a settlement there, and has said that I should be remunerated with £200 per annum."

That this contingency was a very tempting one, and that he was becoming apprehensive regarding his calling for the law, in spite of his confident assertions, is indicated by the tone of the concluding paragraphs:

"I wish that you would, without reserve, communicate your sentiments respecting the affairs of the Church. Some of my friends here are of the opinion that I should appear to greater advantage myself, and benefit my friends more, as a church divine than an advocate. I confess to you that, were the emolument equal, I should not hesitate in choice. Undoubtedly *one* is the more *honest* vocation. I often witness a degree of oppression in a lawyer's office almost unavoidable; but to me, whose hands have not yet grown callous with the receipt of guilty bribes, there is something painful to the moral sense in wringing farthings from the poor misguided peasant. If liberty of election were fully allowed, my *superficial talents*—for . . . I am superficial—would have a better effect upon the eye of mob, surveyed rather from a pulpit than the bar. I have the ready faculty of speech, but I doubt whether *profound* thought keeps pace with volubility.

1. Portsmouth, New Hampshire, not Rhode Island, as stated by Hall. The account of Dennie's services as lay reader given in Marble's *Heralds of American Literature* is also inaccurate.

"Mr. West told me, that, amid the present discouragements to bar practice, he thought the Portsmouth benefice would be a fortunate exchange.

"Adieu, my dear friends: I'm just about launching into the turmoil of ocean life. Your best *pilotage* is necessary to the success of my voyage."

The contract, however, was not renewed in March. The project of turning to a new profession after three years of preparation for the law cannot have appealed to his parents, nor were the insufficient remuneration and restricted activities of a clergyman's life attractive to Dennie. The "candid Claremonters," moreover, may have found some faults in their candidate; Hall, in the *Philadelphia Souvenir*,[1] says they objected to his playing whist and smoking cigars on Saturday evenings. His short experience as lay reader, however, was a fruitful one, since it furnished him the suggestion and design of his celebrated *Lay Preacher* essays.

The three-years clerkship required by the New Hampshire law expired in December, 1793, but too late for Dennie to be admitted at the December term of court. He had originally intended, on the completion of his studies, to start a practice in Middlesex or Suffolk County, in Massachusetts, but following the advice of his friends in the profession, especially Rufus G. Amory, a well-known lawyer of Boston, he relinquished that idea. At Boston, Dennie told his parents, there were, besides Parsons, Sullivan, and Thatcher, a shoal of junior practitioners, occupying vacant offices, "mere barber shops, for the purpose of idle assemblage and chat, never darkened by the shadow of clients," and that these young lawyers were driven to seek support precariously at the gaming table or cringingly by marrying a fortune. "Now," says Dennie, "I would rather cut my throat with a penny razor than suffer even a plan of such a life to sweep across my mind."[2] The case being such, he decided to open an office in some part of New Hampshire, where, if there were inconveniences to be tolerated, living was cheaper, the climate was more healthful, and the legal profession was attended with greater distinction.

1. Page 34.
2. Letter to his parents, January, 1794.

Accordingly, when in March, 1794, he was admitted to practice in Keene, by the unanimous vote of the bar, he opened, with the consent of West, a law office at Charlestown. This was pleasantly situated, with a southern exposure, in the house of Mrs. Martha (Pomeroy) Olcott, widow of the Reverend Bulkley Olcott. To her four children, Theodosia Olcott Morris, Martha Olcott Smith, both of whom married lawyers; Theophilus Olcott, Dartmouth, 1800, himself a lawyer; and Lucretia Olcott, as to a large circle of young people of talent and taste in the village, he was an oracle and a delightful companion. This period he was afterward accustomed to call the happiest part of his existence. From his office, where he slept soundly, "unscared," as Pope says, "by the spectre of poverty," he announced to his parents[1] his determination "to assert and display my independence, to uphold and to defend causes with unspotted hands, and by an obstinate adherence to my office, to be ready for Business whether clients enter or avoid my doors." He naively adds, "I am worth about 4/6[2] clear and unencumbered," in spite of which, "I am determined, if I am poor, never to feel, much less look so,—to wear glossy coats, and shift them before they are threadbare," because—and here his ingrained distrust of the world at large obtrudes itself—"'Tis the disposition of the world, the Ass, to withhold benefit from those who want it, and give the sum of more to him that has too much."

Jeremiah Mason, who was in 1795 a young lawyer in the adjoining town of Walpole, says of Dennie's legal education:[3] "His legal knowledge consisted wholly in a choice selection of quaint, obsolete, and queer phrases from 'Plowden's *Commentaries,*' the only law book he had ever read with any attention, and this was read for the sole purpose of treasuring up these quaint phrases. These he often repeated in ridicule of the law, to the great amusement of his auditors." It should be remarked that Mason was fond of painting with high colors and his subsequent account of Dennie's fortunes is very inaccurate. A more just account is perhaps that by Dennie's friend, Royall Tyler, in Buckingham's *New England Galaxy,* for 24 July, 1818:

1. Letter to his parents, 2 Apr., 1794.
2. i.e. "four shillings sixpence (s. 4 d. 6)." Misread $416 by Clapp, and so copied by others.
3. *Memoirs of Jeremiah Mason,* by George S. Hillard, page 30.

"In his study he could read and admire the profound lucubrations of the English jurists; the theory was beautiful and interesting; but to carry his knowledge into practice—in the course of his professional business to encounter the gross familiarity of an illbred client, the vulgar sarcasm of an opposing advocate, and the unpolished prerogatives of the bench, his soul disdained—and it is entirely probable that his extreme irritability of the mental nerve would have caused him to abandon with equal promptitude any other profession or business which brought him into familiar contact with the coarse mass of common life."

Dennie's distrust of the world was fully verified on the occasion of his professional debut as an advocate. The case on which he was engaged was for the postponement of execution against the defendant in an action for non-payment of a promissory note. Dennie's conduct of his suit, and its fortunes, are thus described by Tyler, who was present:

"No young lawyer ever entered on practice with more favorable auspices. The senior members of the bar augured success, and he numbered all who were valuable among the jurors as particular friends. As it was generally known when he was to deliver 'his maiden speech,' by a kind of tacit agreement the gentlemen of the bar resolved to afford him the most favorable arena for the display of his eloquence. The opposing counsel had engaged to suspend all interference, although his statements deviated ever so far from the fact.

"The court opened, and as if by previous concert, all other business was suspended, and our young advocate, after bowing gracefully, assumed the air of an orator, and addressed the court.

"He began with a luminous history of compulsory payments, he showed clearly that as knowledge was diffused humanity prevailed even from the savage era, when the debtor, his wife and children, were sold into slavery to satisfy the demands of the creditor, and the corpse of the insolvent was denied the rites of sepulture, through the iron age of our English ancestors, when the debtor was incarcerated in *'salva et areta custodia,'* down to the present day, when by the amelioration of the laws, the statutes of bankruptcy and gaol delivery had humanely liberated the body of the unfortunate debtor from prison, upon the surrender of his estate. He observed, that in the progress of knowledge, the municipal courts had, by interposing 'the law's delay' between the vindictive avarice of the creditor and the ruin of the debtor, always to the honor of the judiciary department, preceded the Legislative in the merciful march of humanity. That the time was not far distant when the Legislative would repeal those statutes which provided for imprisonment for debt, and punished a virtuous man for a criminal merely because he was poor.

"But aside from these general considerations, he begged leave to lay the defendant's unhappy case before the court; he would 'a round unvarnished tale deliver.' His client was an husbandman, an husband and the father of a large family, who depended *solely* upon the labour of his hands for bread—he had seen better days—but his patrimonial farm had been sold for Continental money, and the whole lost by depreciation, whilst others had been getting gain—a deep scar in his side, occasioned by the thrust of a British bayonet at the battle of Bunker Hill, was all he had to remunerate him for his services as a soldier during the revolutionary war. Here the 'poet's eye began to roll in a fine phrenzy.' We saw the hapless husbandman 'plodding his weary way' through the chill blasts of a winter storm, and seeking through the drifting snow his log cottage, beneath the craggy side of an abrupt precipice; 'the taper's solitary ray' appears—vanishes—and again lights up hope in his heart—the door opens—children run to lisp their sire's return and climb his knees the envied kiss to share—the busy housewife prepares the frugal repast, the wicker chair is drawn before the spacious hearth, 'and the crackling faggot flies,' the labours of the day are forgotten and all is serenity and domestic bliss—the family bible is opened—the psalm is sung, and the father of the family rises in the midst of his offspring and invokes a blessing upon his country and his government and fervently prays that its freedom may last as long as the sun and moon shall endure—acknowledges his own trespasses and pours out his heart in gratitude, that in the midst of judgment God remembered mercy—that though despoiled of wealth the wife of his youth was continued to him. His children were blest with health, that they had a roof to cover them from the wintry storm, and that under his Divine protection they might sleep in peace with none to disturb them or make them afraid. But scarcely does the incense of prayer ascend from that golden censer, a good man's heart, when an appalling knock is heard; the wooden latch is broken, the door is widely thrown open—Enter the bailiff, 'down whose hard, unmeaning face ne'er stole the pitying tear,' with the writ of execution issued in this cause, he arrests the hapless father, and amidst the swoonings of the wife, the sobbings and imbecile opposition of his children, he is dragged 'through the pelting of the pitiless storm' to a loathsome prison.

"Was not this a case to be distinguished from the common herd of parties, which cumbered the court's docket? Was not some consideration to be had for a brave man who had bled for that Independence without which their honours would not now dignify the bench as the magistrates of a free people?—was rigid justice untempered with mercy to be found alone in the Judicial Courts of a people renowned for their humanity? and shall 'human laws, which should be made only to check the arm of wickedness,' be changed into instruments of oppression and cruelty?

"The orator ceased—mute attention accompanied the delivery, and at the close all were charmed and all silent; even the opposing counsel sat hesitating betwixt his fees and his feelings, and forbore to reply. This silence, which our young advocate seemed to notice with peculiar complacency, was broken from the bench. The judge, an unlettered farmer, who, by the prevalence of party, had obtained the summit of yeoman ambition, a seat on the bench of an Inferior Court, who knew only the technical jargon of the court, and to whom the language and pathos of Dennie were alike unintelligible, sat during the delivery of the address, rolling a pair of 'lack lustre eyes' with a vacant stare sometimes at the orator and then at the bar, as if seeking most curiously for meaning, and who was perhaps restrained only by the respectful attention of the latter from interrupting the speaker. The Judge broke silence.

"*Judge.* I confess I am in rather a kind of quandary, I profess I am somewhat dubus, I can't say that I know for sartin *what the young gentleman would be at.*

"*Counsellor V[ose].* My brother Dennie, may it please your

honour, has been enforcing his motion for an Imparlance on the part of the Defendant, in the cause of Patrick McGripinclaw *et alii*, Plaintiff, vs. Noadiah Chubber.

"*Judge.* Oh! Aye! now I believe I understand—the young gentleman wants the cause *to be hung up for the next term, duz he?*

"*Counsellor V.* Yes, may it please the court.

"*Judge.* Well, well, if that's all he wanted, why couldn't he say so in a few words, pat to the purpose, without all this *larry cum lurry.*

"Our advocate took his hat and gloves from the table, cast a look of ineffable contempt upon the Baeotian magistrate and stalked out of the court house."

Dennie had sense of humor enough to appreciate the situation and frequently afterward narrated his discomfiture to his friends with great effect, but one experience of the sort was enough. Shortly afterward Tyler sought to enlist his services in an action for seduction, before a classical judge, a case which offered an excellent opportunity for the exercise of Dennie's peculiar talents, but he refused. "It may do for you, my friend," he said, "to pursue this sordid business—you can address the ignoble vulgar in their own Alsatia dialect. I remember the Baeotian Judge, and it is the last time I will ever attempt to batter down a mud wall with roses."

The *Farrago* essays were destined to be varied not only in mood and matter but also in the vehicles in which they were published. The first four appeared in the *Morning Ray,* at Windsor. Of the fifth, sixth, and seventh I have found no trace, but they were probably published in the *Morning Ray,* Spooner's *Vermont Journal,* or the *Eagle,* between 20 March, 1792, and 19 Aug., 1793. Spooner's *Vermont Journal*[1] was the paper published at Windsor, Vermont, by Alden Spooner, brother of Judah P. Spooner, under various titles, from 1788 to 1818. Spooner was born in New London, Conn., in 1757, served in the Revolution, worked with his brother in the printing office at Norwich and at Westminster, Vermont, established himself

1. Only seven scattered members of the *Journal* for 1792, '93 and '94 are preserved at the American Antiquarian Society Library. They contain nothing of Dennie's.

at Windsor, and represented his town in the Vermont legislature in 1793, 1800, and 1802. He died in 1827.

On the 22nd of July, 1793, a new paper, the *Eagle: or Dartmouth Centinel,* was started at Hanover, New Hampshire, by Josiah Dunham, then Preceptor of Moor's Charity School, connected with Dartmouth College. He was a man of distinguished talents, ripe scholarship, and a noble presence, who had an interesting career as editor, soldier, orator, and teacher. He was born about 1769 at Lebanon Crank, now Columbia, Conn., the son of Deacon Samuel and Anna (Mosely) Dunham. He was graduated in 1789, at Dartmouth, where he later received the degree of A. M. After teaching at Hanover for three years, he edited the *Eagle* from its establishment until 6 April, 1796. Later he served a number of years in the army with the rank of captain. After resigning his command at Fort Mackinac in 1808, he went to Windsor, Vermont, where he started a flourishing female academy and edited the *Washingtonian.* He was Secretary of State for Vermont and aide-de-camp, with rank of Colonel, to Governor Martin Chittenden. At Lexington, Kentucky, whither he removed in 1821, he organized and conducted for many years another popular young ladies' school. He died there 10 May, 1844. Many of his orations and pamphlets were published.[1]

The Eagle: or Dartmouth Centinel sustained from the start a more distinctly literary character, as far as I have observed, than any of its country contemporaries. Besides its poetical department, the *Aonian Rill,* it frequently devoted several columns to literary essays, parodies, humorous articles, and moral speculations. A fairly large corps of youthful contributors, with such fanciful noms-de-plume as *Florio, Amintor, Monitor, Tim Pandect, Pastorella,* and *Laura* assisted in enlivening its pages. The services of the Charlestown essayist were soon enlisted, and in the fifth number of the *Eagle,* 19 Aug., 1793,[3] appeared the *Farrago,* No. VIII, the *Letter from Brown, Brick-*

1. This sketch is derived from the obituary notice of his widow, Mrs. Susan (Hedge) Dunham, in the *N. E. Hist. & Gen. Register*, 1857.
2. The most complete file is in the Am. Antiquarian Society Library, at Worcester.
3. Numbers 3 and 4 of the *Eagle* are missing from all the files I have consulted. The *Farrago*, Nos. VI and VII may have appeared there.

maker. After this the essays appeared at irregular intervals until 18 Sept., 1794, fifteen numbers in all. They are characterized by a vivacity and freshness which fades out to some extent from the later series of essays. The *Letter from Brown, Brickmaker,* tells the story of a man who was reported killed by the Indians, and whose neighbors and friends persisted in treating him as dead. The ninth essay describes the life of "strenuous idleness," which Dennie would have liked to follow. The tenth, *He Cuts a Dash,* introduces a satirical method frequently and effectively employed by Dennie. A series of types, prodigals, dandies, flirts, quacks, drawn with a few descriptive strokes, each type cutting his own little dash in life, is flashed before the reader's eyes as by a stereopticon. The same method is used in Farrago XVI, *My Aunt Peg,* directed against the shams of life, and in XVII, *The Happiness of Dupes.* These titles I have in general chosen myself, the essays bearing no individual heading, except, usually, an illustrative motto, such as "Now I have got a Ewe and a Lamb, everybody says, Welcome, Peter,"[1] or "How shall I compass the cash?"[2] The fourteenth number is a *Character of Charles Cameleon,*[3] the versatile man, less skilfully drawn than that of Meander. Occasionally a personal note is observed, as in XVIII, which is an apology for a long absence due to sickness and in XXII, *Much Study is a Weariness of the Flesh.* Other follies at which his laughing raillery is directed are tactiturnity, scandal, and overcaution.

Other wits were associated with Dennie in making the literary department of the *Eagle* a success. Mason[4] informs us that at this time a set of young lawyers in the towns along the Connecticut, from Greenfield, in Massachusetts, to Windsor, Vermont, were in the habit of holding gatherings at various taverns for purposes of amusement and recreation, at which much liquor and talent were set flowing. Among these he mentions as the chief, Dennie; John W. Blake, a fluent, graceful lawyer of Brattleboro, Vermont; William Coleman, of Greenfield, Mass., an able writer for the *Greenfield Gazette,* and later editor of the

1. *Farrago* XIII.
2. *Farrago* XIX.
3. Probably Roger Vose is the original of this sketch.
4. *Memoirs,* pp. 28-33.

New York Evening Post, perhaps the strongest of the Federalist papers in its day; and Royall Tyler, of Guilford, Vermont, who in 1794 entered into a long-lived literary partnership with Dennie, and of whom, therefore, some brief history must be given.[1]

Tyler was born in Boston, 18 July, 1757, the son of Royall Tyler, a prominent merchant there, who died in 1771, in the midst of the Stamp Act agitations, in which he bore a conspicuous part. He graduated at Harvard in 1776, after having been rusticated for an undergraduate prank. At that time, writes Mason, who was a Yale man, Harvard "was more distinguished for producing good fellows than good scholars," and Tyler shared in the gaieties and lighter dissipations of his fellows. At the beginning of the war he saw service under General Sullivan, but soon began to study law with Francis Dana at Cambridge. During his three years' clerkship he belonged to a talented coterie in Boston, which included Trumbull, the painter; Christopher Gore, Governor of Massachusetts and U. S. Senator, for whom Gore Hall was named; Rufus King, Congressman, Senator, and Ambassador to England; William Eustis, Governor, Congressman, and Secretary of War; and several others. In 1779 he was admitted to the Massachusetts bar, and began a practice of two years at Falmouth, now Portland, Maine. In 1781 he returned to Boston, where, and at Braintree, near by, he remained the next few years. In 1786 he served as Major under General Benjamin Lincoln, in suppressing Shay's Rebellion and pursuing the fugitive ringleaders in Vermont and New York. In April, 1787, his play, *The Contrast,* the first play distinctively American in authorship, setting, and spirit, and presented by an American company, was acted in New York, Wignall, a noted actor of the day, presenting the first appearance of the typical Yankee on the stage. His prologue began:

"EXULT, each patriot heart, this night is shown
A piece, which we may fairly call our own;
Where the proud titles of 'My Lord!' 'Your Grace!'
To humble Mr. and plain Sir give place."

---

1. The materials for the succeeding sketch were gathered chiefly from Burnham's *History of Brattleboro,* pp. 86 to 102, based upon the MS. *Memoir* of Judge Tyler by his son.

About the same time were written the less successful *May Day; or New York in an Uproar*, and the *Georgia Spec.; or Land in the Moon*. In 1789 he defended some of Dennie's classmates at Harvard in a suit for assault.[1] In 1790, having suffered in reputation and fortune at Boston, he removed to Guilford, Vermont, where he practiced law until 1801, when he removed to Brattleboro. In 1791 he verified a youthful prophecy by marrying Mary, daughter of Joseph Palmer of Framingham. While at Guilford, his practice extended to both sides of the river, and at Charlestown, New Hampshire, he had an experience similar to Dennie's, acting as substitute minister for a short period. He also wrote actively at Guilford, producing at this time, the *Comic Grammar* and *The Algerine Captive*. His muse was also fecund in odes for various occasions, prologues for dramatic performances, and conventional amatory addresses. He was appointed a Judge of the Supreme Court of Vermont in 1801 and was Chief Justice from 1807 to 1812, during which time he published *The Yankey in London, Reports of Cases in the Supreme Court of Vermont from 1800 to 1803*, and a series of periodical observations entitled *Trash;*[2] was awarded the degree of A. M. by the University of Vermont in 1811; and was elected Professor of Jurisprudence at Vermont in the same year. He later served six years as Registrar of Probate for Windham County, until he retired from active practice in 1820. He died at Brattleboro 16 August, 1826, full of years and father of eleven children, most of them distinguished preachers, lawyers, or teachers. A memoir of Judge Tyler, begun by his son, the Rev. Thomas P. Tyler, has never been completed and published.[2]

The similar tastes and talents of Tyler and Dennie brought them into the closest intimacy among their jovial fellows of the profession, and in 1794 they formed a literary partnership entitled the *Shop of Colon and Spondee,* which purported to offer for sale literary articles of all sorts, verse or prose, grave or witty, moral or political, parody or elegy, etc., etc. The long

1. Vose Letters. Vose to Dennie, 7 May, 1789.

2. The accounts of Tyler's literary work in Chambers' and Allibone's dictionaries, which give him credit, among other things for nearly all the *Colon and Spondee* productions, are greatly at fault.

and elaborate comic advertisement of the Shop[1] was printed in the *Eagle* of 28 July, 1794, and samples of its wares appeared in the *Eagle's* columns for nearly a year thereafter. In general Dennie, who was *Colon,* was to contribute the prose articles, and Tyler, who was *Spondee,* the verse. As a matter of fact, each supplied both prose and verse, at first signing their respective initials, "C.," or "S.," to their work. Their contributions to the *Eagle* consisted chiefly of brief and spicy satiric paragraphs, epigrams, anecdotes, cross-readings, and occasional poems. Dennie's verses include an address *To Laura, Occasional Prologue for "The Clandestine Marriage,"* presented at Charlestown, and *The Hypochondriac's Will,* with its grimly apprehensive couplet:

> Spleen whisper'd lowly in my ear,
> "Consumptive Joe, gaunt death is near!"

The revolutionists in France, Harvard College and the lotteries it frequently conducted for the raising of funds, the governors of Massachusetts, the Boston Democrats, and the New England agricultural shows are among the subjects of which fun, not always unmixed with vitriol, is made. The pointed paragraphs from the *Shop of Messrs. Colon and Spondee,* were, in fact, a very effective weapon on all occasions and were frequently reprinted by the Federalist papers of New England.

Another fellow-contributor with Dennie was John C. Chamberlain, who entered West's law office at Charlestown in 1793, before Dennie left it. He wrote a number of essays which were printed in the paper over the signature *Tim Pandect.* He may also have contributed some of the *Vigil* essays, which ran in the *Eagle,* succeeding the *Farrago* papers, from 19 September, 1794, to the spring of the following year. These essays were the work of several hands, among which Dennie's unmistakable style is evident in some of the best papers. Among these are *Vigil* I, the introductory essay; V, *Pigmies Are Pigmies Still;* VI, *They Fail for Want of Stock,* and VII, *Good Fellows,* three "stereopticon essays," in Dennie's best vein; and probably also XIV, *I Dreamed of Things Impossible,* and XVII, *Tomorrow.* The contributions of Dennie and Tyler to the *Eagle* ceased in March, 1795. In April the paper was taken over by John Mosely

1. This advertisement is given in full in Buckingham's *Specimens of Newspaper Literature,* Vol. II, pp. 204-205.

Dunham, probably the editor's brother, and his partner True. Josiah Dunham continued as editor until May, 1796, but the paper deteriorated as a literary sheet, more attention was given to news and advertisements, and the *Aonian Rill*, which had a habit of drying up intermittently, finally ceased to flow altogether.

Meanwhile, Dennie's literary reputation had begun to grow. People had noted in his essays a freshness and buoyancy of thought which, in combination with the classical expression of his century, had not characterized the work of any American essayist before him. In the letter to his parents of 4 Jan., 1794, from which I have so many times quoted, Dennie wrote, "The editor of the *Boston Centinel* has frequently republished these trifles, and twelve or fourteen of the most generally circulated gazettes have devoted a column to the *Farrago*." He might have added that the *Centinel* had accompanied its reprint with a flatulent adulation of his essays. The time had now arrived which our author thought opportune for turning his talents to some financial advantage.

CHAPTER V

BOSTON, MARCH-AUGUST, 1795—"THE TABLET"

The first warning of Dennie's intended descent upon Boston is discovered in a notice in Paine's *Federal Orrery*, 23 Feb., 1795, to the following effect:

"Messrs. Colon & Spondee request their brother *haberdasher*, T. P., to open an account with their '*shop*' at the foot of the Green Mountain, and as their junior partner served the concluding year of his literary apprenticeship in the same *warehouse*, of Apollo, clipped the tape of rhetoric with the same scissors, and handled the *yardstick* of sentiment behind the same counter, they doubt not of his ready compliance with the *credit* you require."

Paine, who changed his Christian name from Thomas to Robert Treat, Junior, to avoid the opprobrium that might come to him from confusion with the great Thomas Paine, author of *Common Sense* and *The Crisis*, was born in Taunton, Massachusetts, in 1773, the son of a distinguished lawyer and signer of the Declaration. Two years after Dennie's graduation, Paine received his degree at Harvard, where he enjoyed a considerable reputation for his verses. After making a false start with a mercantile house, he began, on the 20th of October, 1794, the publication of a semi-weekly newspaper, the *Federal Orrery*. This paper, which enjoyed from the start the most liberal support, was exceptional among its fellows for its literary quality. Besides essays and poetry of rather unusual newspaper excellence, it had a department called the *Attic Ordinary*, somewhat similar in nature to the *Shop of Colon and Spondee*. Among his contributors were Mrs. Sarah Wentworth Morton, the poetess, with whom as *Philenia*, he had conducted a laudatory Platonic courtship in the *Massachusetts Magazine*, under the signature of *Menander;* William Bigelow, alias *Charley Chatterbox;* and the Reverend J. S. J. Gardiner. Paine himself contributed vigorous and vitriolic Federalist editorials, verse lampoons on the Boston Democrats, and sensible theatrical criticism, a permanent theatre having, after strenuous efforts on the part of its advocates, been licensed in Boston in 1794. But Paine was indolent, and careless of the business management of the newspaper, and was obliged to relinquish the *Orrery*, in April, 1796, to Benjamin Sweetser, in whose hands it deteriorated rapidly. Paine now took up the study of law with Theophilus Parsons, in whose office John Quincy Adams and many other noted lawyers secured their legal education, and was admitted to the bar in 1802. Meanwhile, he had written in 1798 the famous Federalist ode *Adams and Liberty*, produced able criticisms of plays and players for the *Boston Gazette* and other papers, and by marrying an actress had brought upon himself the wrath of his father and the disapprobation of hypercritical friends, though his wife is said to have been an amiable lady of unblemished reputation.[1] Paine practised law in Boston for a few years, but his natural incapacity for work and his distracting love of the stage, despite the unmerited patronage of many friends, ruined his business, which he abandoned in 1809. He lived two years longer in the most abject poverty, and at his death, 13 November, 1811, left his family destitute. His works, in verse and prose, with a biography prefixed, were published the year after his death. In comparing him with Poe, Professor Trent,[2] who is not wasteful of praise, says, "He was probably on the whole a better scholar, speaker, conversationalist, and wit than the unfortunate genius whose name is now honoured in every land. But his talents lay on the surface and were not charming enough in their kind to attract posterity."

Dennie's contributions to the paper published by this somewhat kindred spirit were chiefly satiric paragraphs of the sort which had appeared in the columns of the *Eagle*. Such a one is the virulent attack upon Harvard, 9 March, 1795, wherein it was stated that, "the aggregate of the Dutch diligence of our university consists of centoed orations and vapid rhymes from the students; and from the presidents, professors and tutors of a whole century . . . dull discourses upon dull departed brethren, embarrassed essays on philosophy and exploded logic, and accounts of the variation and dip of the magnetic needle. . . . By the care of a few country curates, were not some

1. See Buckingham. *Specimens of Newspaper Literature*, p. 249.
2. *History of American Literature*, p. 199.

ethereal spirits taught to soar a nobler height, the majority of the students would soon degenerate into the annual A. M. of a president,[1] and be saluted masters of all arts without being proficient in one.''. To this diatribe Paine, being one of the ''vapid rhymesters,'' deemed it necessary to suffix the following disclaimer, ''Those who have heard the *natural* history of a Waterhouse, beheld the surgical operations of a Warren, witnessed the experimental philosophy of a Webber, or listened attentively to the philological lectures of a Pearson, may, perhaps, be inclined to doubt the *verity* of this statement.'' Dennie's strictures, however, were not based upon spleen alone, if we may trust the statements of as genuine an American as Noah Webster, who wrote, ''as to classical learning, history (civil and ecclesiastical), mathematics, astronomy, chemistry, botany, and natural history, excepting here and there a rare instance of a man who is eminent in some one of these branches. we may be said to have no learning at all, or a mere smattering;'' and further, ''our learning is superficial in a shameful degree, . . . our colleges are disgracefully destitute of books and philosophical apparatus . . . and I am ashamed to own that scarcely a branch of science can be fully investigated in America for want of books, especially original works. . . . There are not more than three or four tolerable libraries in America, and these are extremely imperfect.''[2]

In the *Orrery* for 19 March, ''Colon,'' weary of politics, announced that he would enter a new field and hazard a theatrical opinion. Then followed an article of extravagant praise for the acting of Miss Collins as ''Cherry'' in a play of Farquhar's, and Miss Hughes as ''Rosa'' in Reynolds's *How to Get Rich.* The few critical observations in the succeeding issues show only too well Dennie's lack of discrimination in matters of the stage. This period appears to have been the high tide of the literary excellence of the *Orrery,* approximately a third of each issue being devoted to letters. ''Charles Chatterbox''(William Bigelow) was contributing his fantastic *Omnium Gatherum,* and the Reverend J. S. J. Gardiner had commenced, 6 April, 1795, Part II of

1. It was then customary to award the degree of A. M., on application, after three years, to graduates of good standing.

2. Quoted by Henry Adams, *History of the U. S. during the First Administration of Jefferson.* Vol. I, pp. 62-63. Webster wrote in 1800.

his *Remarks on the Jacobiniad,*[1] whose venomous innuendos aroused so much party anger in Boston that Paine, in lieu of the anonymous author, was on one occasion publicly chastised on State Street for printing it. The publication later in the *Orrery* of a coarse and more vicious satire, *The Lyars,* directed at Jarvis and Austin, procured a second assault at the hands of a brother of Doctor Jarvis. Needless to say, these satires helped for a time to swell the subscription lists of the *Orrery,* and the *Remarks* were soon reissued in a duodecimo volume. The latest direct contribution of Dennie to the *Orrery* which I have identified is in the number for 13 April, 1795.

At home Dennie found conditions sadly altered. His father, whose health had been increasingly poor for several years, especially during the winter months, and who was at such times subject to depressing melancholy, had now lapsed into a dementia which was to last, with occasional intermissions, until his death. Mrs Dennie, herself frequently an invalid, had now to devote her life to the care of her helpless husband, a task which she fulfilled with tenderness and pious fidelity to the end. His father's loss of reason affected Dennie seriously. Though perhaps not so sympathetic as Mrs. Dennie with their son's literary leanings, the elder man had been the counsellor and correspondent, to whom Dennie in frequent letters had outlined his movements, hopes, and reverses. Mrs. Dennie was, at her age, a poor and infrequent correspondent, and from 1794 on, the exchange of letters was almost abandoned. The remaining records of Joseph Dennie, Senior, need not long detain us. On 18 September, 1792,[2] Joseph and Mary Dennie, of Lexington, deeded to James White of Boston, bookseller, for £60, one undivided eighth part of a brick tenement and a wooden store situated on Queen (now Court) Street, then occupied by White, Thomas Adams, publisher of the *Independent Chronicle,* and Russell and Clap,[3] printers. This had been left to Mary

1. This satire professed to be a review, in twenty-one papers, of an epic poem, the *Jacobiniad,* in which the ironical praises of the goddess Faction, and her followers, the Constitutional Society, alias Jacobin Club, in Boston, were celebrated. Long selections from this imaginary poem were quoted, attacking with bitter personalities prominent anti-federalists like Benjamin Austin, Dr. Jarvis, Perez Morton, and the town clerk, William Cooper.

2. Records of the Registry of Deeds, Suffolk County, Boston, Mass.

3. John Russell and Samuel Clap. Russell, who died in 1795, had been a partner of Green in the firm of Green & Russell.

Dennie by the will of her brother, John Green, printer, at his death in November, 1787. The will of Joseph Dennie of Lexington, merchant,[1] made 27 July, 1794, "being in full health and of sound disposing mind and memory, but taking into consideration the uncertainty of human life," bequeathed all his property to his wife Mary—in case of her decease, or marriage with certain conditions, to his son Joseph—except the sum of £50 to each of his esteemed friends, James White of Boston, bookseller,[2] and Harriet Green of Lexington. This young lady was a relative, probably a niece, of Mary Dennie. She, the "prudent Harriet" of Dennie's letters, was an inmate of the household from 1785 on, and endeared herself to the family by her patient and kindly ministrations in their distresses. Fortunately, by inheritance and by a bequest of £1500 in the will of William Dennie in 1783,[3] the family was freed from the fear of want. On 23 June, 1797,[4] Joseph Dennie assumed a mortgage to the sum of $5,333.33 on a wharf and adjoining flats in Boston, the property of Ebenezer Burdett, a lumber merchant of that town. A codicil added to Dennie's will, 8 May, 1804,[5] awarded an additional sum of $1,000 to Harriet Green, and a second, 19 March, 1807, bequeathed to her $500 more. Both of these codicils, written during periods of restored health, are signed in a firm, clear hand. Both were disallowed at the execution of the will, 14 January, 1812, since they did not "appear to be executed in due form of law."

Dennie's purpose in coming to Boston at this time was to put into execution some project by means of which he might raise money to eke out the scanty income from his law practice at Charlestown, which hardly served to meet expenses. "A law library, a horse, and a capital of 1 or 200 pounds are essential to that degree of Wealth and eminence at the bar which it is my first ambition to attain," he announced in an enthusiastic letter to his mother from Boston, 24 April, 1795. He had at

1. Probate Records of Middlesex County, Cambridge, Mass.
2. When the will was executed, 14 Jan., 1812, James White, on receipt of $1.00, discharged Mrs. Dennie from payment of the bequest.
3. Suffolk County Probate Records.
4. Registry of Deeds, Suffolk County.
5. Middlesex County Probate Records.

first sounded Paine, Russell,[1] and Thomas,[2] with regard to enlisting his pen in their services, but met with little encouragement. He had, however, made many admirers among those who had read his reprinted *Farrago* essays, and he made new friends of all with whom he associated now. His class and college mates in Boston welcomed him warmly, and his political orthodoxy was sufficiently evident from his *Colon and Spondee* articles to insure him the favor of the Federalist worthies at Boston. Some of his enthusiastic friends, remembering the success of Tyler's *Contrast,* urged him to write a comedy or an opera, but Dennie wisely refrained from undertaking a task for which his talents were so unsuited. After considerable planning and negotiating, a scheme was hit upon for the publication of a weekly miscellany, to serve chiefly as a vehicle for the *Farrago* papers. Suitable arrangements for publication were made, and liberal patronage was promised by the foremost people of the town, Mrs. Sarah Morton and the Rev. George R. Minot showing especial interest in the project.

The mention of these names, now doubtless forgotten except by those versed in the local history and literature of New England, makes necessary some remarks about literary Boston in 1795. Perhaps at no time since then has the term "literary Boston" been so completely a misnomer. The supremacy in letters which that town had held from its establishment until the second third of the eighteenth century had now passed to Philadelphia and Hartford. The disturbances occasioned by the Revolution and the establishment of a republic, the bustle of new commercial and industrial enterprises, the animosity of party bickerings, the dissensions induced by the breakup of the old Calvinistic theology, the backwardness of the chief seminaries of learning—all these were perhaps causes sufficient to explain why so little, if indeed anything, which the decade from 1790 to 1800 produced, has come down to us as worthy of being remembered. Add to these the ambitious belief that the works which were then being produced were great and lasting because they were ambitious and American, and the pious belief that they

1. Benjamin Russell (1761-1845), publisher and editor of the *Columbian Centinel.*
2. Isaiah Thomas (1749-1831), publisher of the *Massachusetts Spy* and the *Massachusetts Magazine.*

were great and permanent because they were pious and instructive, and the case becomes hopeless enough. The result of these causes was that many and ambitious books were written, because the Bostonians, like the Americans elsewhere, were obsessed by the pathetically laudable desire to outshine, or at least equal, their scoffing British cousins in letters as they had done in arms; instructive books, because Calvinists and Unitarians alike were still deeply concerned about their own and one another's souls; but books destitute of literary excellence for which they deserve to be read, except by the student and the historian. In general, however, the American mind, versatile by nature, was driven by internal distractions and external indifference, to exercise its versatile talents in other directions than that of letters. The result is a long list of jurists, divines, physicians, editors, and teachers, who achieved eminent or moderate success in their respective professions, and wrote books as an avocation.

In Boston and its vicinity in 1795 there were a dozen or so of such jurists, divines, and others whose local literary reputation was sufficient to require mention here. George Richards Minot (1758-1802) and Fisher Ames (1758-1808) were distinguished lawyers. The former, who was a Harvard graduate of the class of 1778, and Chief Justice of the Massachusetts Court of Common pleas, wrote a *History of Shay's Rebellion* and two volumes continuing Hutchinson's history[1] down to his own time. Ames, who graduated from Harvard in 1774, was a powerful figure in Congress during Washington's administrations. He wrote forceful arguments for the Federalists in the "Lucius Junius Brutus" and "Camillus" letters in the *New England Palladium;* and his speech in behalf of Jay's Treaty was long famous. Reverend Thaddeus Mason Harris (1768-1742), Harvard College, 1787, was pastor of the First Unitarian Church in Dorchester. He edited the *Massachusetts Magazine* in 1795 and 1796, after it had undergone a brief suspension, and wrote, besides poems, sermons and addresses, biographies, and biblical lore, a *Journal of a Tour into the Territory West of the Alleghany Mountains*—perhaps his best known work—in

1. *History of the Province of Massachusetts Bay*, by Governor Thomas Hutchinson. Vol. I, 1764; Vol. II, 1767; Vol. III, 1828.

1803. Reverend Jedidiah Morse (1761-1826), Yale, 1783, an Orthodox minister at Charlestown, was also a western traveller and a famous geographer. His *Geography Made Easy*, appearing in 1784, was followed by many abridgments which were used as text-books in the New England schools. His son, Samuel F. B. Morse, inventor of the telegraph, inherited his father's scientific curiosity. A third minister, the Reverend John Eliot (1754-1818), Harvard College, 1772, pastor of the New North Church, compiled a *Biographical Dictionary of Eminent Characters in New England*, in 1809. A fourth, the Reverend J. S. J. Gardiner (1765-1830), Rector of Trinity Church, was the reputed author of the *Remarks on the Jacobiniad.* A fifth was the Reverend Jeremy Belknap (1744-1798), Harvard College, 1762, author of the *History of New Hampshire*, 1784-1791; *The Foresters*, an allegorical romance in verse, 1796; and an *American Biography*, only two volumes of which were completed, in 1794 and 1798. He is more important, however, as founder of the Massachusetts Historical Society, in 1790. A sketch of Robert Treat Paine, Jr. (1773-1811), has already been given. Another minister, the Reverend John Murray (1741-1815), an Englishman, called the "Father of Universalism in America," published some *Letters and Sketches* in 1812. His wife, Judith (Sargent) Murray (1750-1820), was better known, on account of her *Gleaner* essays, published in three volumes in 1798, with an imposing subscription list, headed by President Adams. The essays in Vol. I had been contributed first to the *Massachusetts Magazine* over the signature "Constantia." Three other women, Hannah Adams (1755-1832), Sarah Wentworth (Apthorpe) Morton (1759-1846), and Mercy (Otis) Warren (1728-1814), deserve, perhaps, more praise than any of the preceding. The first, daughter of a bookseller of Medfield, educated herself and supported her family, first by weaving bobbin lace, and later by writing a *View of Religion*, 1784, which ran to several editions; a *Summary History of New England*, used in a revised form as a school text-book; a *History of the Jews*, 1812; *Letters on the Gospels*, 1826; and other works. Sarah Morton, wife of that Perez Morton who was satirized in the *Remarks on the Jacobiniad*, contributed, under the pseudonym of "Philenia," Della Cruscan verses to the *Massachusetts Magazine*, which were greatly admired. In 1790 she published *Ouabi, or the Virtues of Nature,* which was a verse romance of idealized Indian life, and a book of prose and verse entitled *My Mind and Its Thoughts* in 1823. Mercy (Otis) Warren, daughter of James Otis, the Revolutionary orator, and wife of James Warren, a patriot of Plymouth, was a correspondent and intimate associate with John and Samuel Adams, Elbridge Gerry, Henry Knox, and other leaders of the Revolution. Before the Revolution she had produced two comedies, *The Adulator,* 1773, and *The Group,* 1775, satirizing the British. Two dull tragedies, *The Sack of Rome* and *The Ladies of Castile,* followed in 1778, and *Poems, Dramatic and Miscellaneous,* in 1790. Her *History of the American Revolution,* in three volumes, 1805, derives its importance from her intimate acquaintance with many of the chief actors in the scenes described. A more interesting writer was Susanna (Halswell) Rawson, who had not yet settled down to her long and quiet life as teacher in a ladies' academy at Newton after a romantic career in England, at Nantucket, and on the English and American stage. She wrote almost constantly, publishing many novels and miscellaneous works, besides contributing to the *Boston Magazine* and other periodicals. But her fame rests chiefly upon her novel, *Charlotte Temple,* 1790, a tale of seduction, whose only close rival for popularity with sentimental female readers at the beginning of the last century was *The Coquette: or the History of Eliza Wharton,* by another Massachusetts woman, Mrs. Hannah Foster (1759-1840).

Besides these there was the group of younger men, not yet come into prominence, who in the Anthology Club, and its organ, the *Monthly Anthology,* were to bring about the beginning of better things for New England. Among them were William Emerson, John Thornton Kirkland, Abiel Holmes, Josiah Quincy, Sidney Willard, Joseph Buckminster, William Tudor, and others, most of them Harvard graduates and nearly contemporary in age with Dennie. Other patrons of Dennie's project were the Reverend John Clark, pastor of the First Church, and the Reverend Samuel West. The members of the legal profession, especially Christopher Gore and Samuel Dexter,[1] who passed around subscription papers, were also enthusiastic in their support.

The idea of a magazine was not a new one to the Bostonians. According to the lists[2] prepared by Mr. Albert Matthews, no fewer than eleven had been published in the town at various times between 1743 and 1795, and one, the *Massachusetts Magazine,* was even then appearing monthly, after a short period of quiescence. These periodicals were all short-lived, only the *Massachusetts Magazine* lasting longer than four or five years, and were imitative, in form and content, of English publications, notably the *Gentleman's Magazine.* The earliest was the *Boston Weekly Magazine,* of which only three issues appeared, 2, 9, and 16 March, 1743. This had a lead of only three days over its nearest rival, the *Christian History,* which lasted, however, until 23 February, 1745; and of six months over the *American Magazine and Historical Chronicle,* September, 1743-December, 1746. Three others followed before the Revolution. In the year of peace, 1783, the *Boston Magazine,* a substantial publication by no means devoid of merit, made its appearance. It contained the usual department for original essays and poems, scientific articles, summaries of news and necrology, a gazetteer of the towns of the state, and occasionally the account of a revolting murder. Jeremy Belknap, G. R. Minot, James Freeman, and several others, later members of the Historical Society, contributed to its support. It lasted from October, 1783 to December, 1786. From May to December, 1786, it competed with the *Gentleman's and Lady's Town and Country Magazine,* which soon subsided, but reappeared—or another magazine of the same title—from February, 1789, to August, 1790. The *American Apollo,* 6 January-28 September, 1792, was a weekly paper published by Belknap[3] and Young. For nine months it was the vehicle for the collections of the Massachusetts Historical Society, and when that society commenced the publication of

1. Hon. Samuel Dexter, H. C. 1781, of Charlestown, later Senator from Massachusetts.

2. *Lists of New England Magazines, from 1743 to 1800* by Albert Matthews, Cambridge, 1910. Reprinted from *Colonial Society Pubs.* Vol. XIII.

3. Joseph Belknap, son of the Rev. Jeremy Belknap.

its own *Collections* the *Apollo* continued as a weekly newspaper with an uneventful history. The *Massachusetts Magazine,* already several times named, which began its career in January, 1789, was the first to secure anything like a permanent footing. From 1789 to 1795 it was published by Isaiah Thomas and Ebenezer T. Andrews, who carried on an important publishing business in Newbury Street, at the sign of *Faust's Head.* It was a miscellany of sixty-four pages, containing "Poetry, Musick, Biography, History, Physick, Geography, Morality, Criticism, Philosophy, Mathematicks, Agriculture, Architecture, Chymistry, Novels, Tales, News, Marriages, Deaths, Meteorological Observations, etc.," a list so complete in its details as to make us wonder what *etc.* could possibly have been. It was a fairly faithful reflection of its British models, and offered a good opportunity for the display of local talent. So far as I can learn, no study of its history and contributors has been written. After being discontinued for a while in 1795, it was revived in April by Alexander Martin, with Thaddeus M. Harris as editor. In July, 1796, William Bigelow became editor and Benjamin Sweetser and James Cutter, successively, publishers. The magazine ended with that year.

The newly projected magazine, however, was to be different in nature from its predecessors. The original scheme is outlined by Dennie in the letter to his mother of 24 April, 1795. A small weekly literary miscellany was proposed, of which a *Farrago* essay should form every week the principal piece. It was thus modeled upon the periodicals in which the *Spectator* and *Tatler* papers and Johnson's *Rambler* and *Idler* had appeared, but it was to contain "no tiresome news or advertisements." The idea was accordingly novel to the Bostonians. Dennie's name was not to be used; the editorship was to be undertaken by "one of the correctest scholars here, who is one of our literary society."[1] The publisher who was engaged, William Spotswood, a bookseller and publisher at 55 Marlborough Street, agreed to assume the whole financial risk, and to share the profits equally with Dennie, an arrangement very agreeable to the latter, since it would enable him to live and carry on his law practice at Charlestown, and would bring him, it was

1. The identity of this proposed editor is unknown.

expected, an additional income of £150 annually, in return for a single weekly *Farrago*, of which, he says, "I have twenty-five numbers already written." At the end of the year, moreover, Spotswood promised to publish the *Farrago* essays for him in a duodecimo volume, an offer sufficiently appealing to the vanity of a young author.

The arrangement appears to have been only partially carried out. Dennie remained in the vicinity of Boston, probably as an associate editor, until mid-summer. The announcement of the forthcoming *Tablet*, probably written by him, in the *Federal Orrery*, 18 May, states:

"The Editors, gratified for a liberal and respectable subscription, and eager to begin the discharge of their public engagements, have anticipated the period of publication; and give a specimen of their work, on a much earlier day than Hope and Industry could have promised."

THE TABLET,—*A Miscellaneous Paper, devoted to the Belles Lettres,* made its first appearance the following day, Tuesday, 19 May, 1795.[1] It was a four-page sheet, eight inches by twelve, and bore the motto, "As a Stranger, Give It Welcome.—*Shakespeare.*" The first page was devoted to the *Farrago*, and the fourth chiefly to the *Parterre,* composed of verses, original or selected, anecdotes, levities, and epigrams. The intervening pages were taken up with departments of Original Criticism, Biography, Miscellany, and Literary Intelligence. The whole was as a general thing well written and attractively ordered, and made an interesting and entertaining miscellany.

The *Farrago* paper with which the series commenced, announced the author's intention to follow the literary fashion, "which requires variety and high seasoning." He calls himself a literary adventurer, a follower of the great Spectator, who, though juvenile, has observed the world. His mornings he gives to books, his evenings to men. Timidly, he asks the indulgence of patrons for his non-partisan and non-sectarian sheet. The quotation from Peter Pindar with which the essay begins, denotes his method of essay-writing:

1. A complete file of the *Tablet* is in the Boston Public Library.

"A desultory way of writing,
A hop, step, jump mode of enditing."

Of the twelve essays which followed, seven were reprinted from the *Morning Ray* or the *Eagle;* the rest were new. Numbers IV and V deal with favorite subjects of his satire, inconsistent censure, and the study of mathematical sciences. *Farrago* VI, *Two Cheats Make an Even Bargain*, and XII, on the abuse of the word *Royal*, are good examples of his stereopticon method. Perhaps the most diverting of all is X, *Praise of Dulness*, with its ingenious device for preventing the rise of geniuses. This series completed the production of the *Farrago* essays. Spotswood's offer was not fulfilled, and though most of them were reprinted in Dennie's later publication, the *Port Folio*, they were never published as a volume.

The chief contribution to the *Tablet* outside of the *Farrago* was a series of criticisms on the English poet Churchill, by the Reverend John Sylvester John Gardiner. This gentleman, whose name has occurred frequently in this chapter, was born in Wales, in 1765, and was sent to Boston about 1770, to be educated by his grandfather, Dr. Sylvester Gardiner. The latter, when the proscription of the Loyalists occurred in 1776, took the boy with him to the West Indies. It is said that the father of J. S. J. Gardiner, John Gardiner, a Boston lawyer and patriot, was disinherited by his Tory father, and in turn disinherited his Tory son. During the war the boy was educated in England by the noted Samuel Parr. In 1783 Gardiner returned to Boston to study law and later theology. From 1787 to 1791 he had charge of an Episcopal church at Beaufort, S. C., and from 1791 until his death was Assistant Rector and Rector of Trinity, in Boston. Here, in addition to delivering and publishing vigorous and intellectual sermons, he conducted a classical school from 1792 to 1805, advocated the theatre, was a founder of the Athenaeum and President of the Anthology Club, and editor of the *Monthly Anthology*, and contributed to numerous periodicals. He was noted for his literary and scientific interest, his intense loyalty to England and the Episcopacy, and his equally intense aversion to French and Democratic principles. This characteristic is voiced in the *Remarks on the Jacobiniad*, modeled on the English *Rolliad*. He died while on a tour for his health, at Harrowgate, England, 30 July, 1830. In his introductory essay on *Philology or Criticism* in the *Tablet*, he deplored the lack of any important English critic except Johnson. Blair,[1] he said, was too general in his method, Dryden insincere, and Dennis malignant; therefore, in criticizing, as he proposed to do, all the poets not touched by Johnson, he would follow the analytic method of Ruffhead.[2] The six discussions which follow, form a sufficiently analytical discussion of Churchill. The criticism was not completed.

Besides the contributions of Gardiner, there were a few *Colon and Spondee* items, recopied from the *Eagle*, a series of Biographies of English orators and other worthies, probably reprinted from English publications, though not acknowledged, and a few amusing essays, signed *Proteus*, in the department of Miscellany. Other contributors of prose signed themselves *Meddler* and *A*. The *Parterre* included poems, original or selected, of little merit, by the poet-laureate, Pye, and other commonplace scribblers.

As the editor of a promising periodical paper and a writer of established local reputation, Dennie doubtless found his residence in Boston a pleasant one. Many of his college friends lived in the city and he was an intimate visitor in many homes there. A picture of his life at this time is found in Edmund Quincy's *Life of Josiah Quincys*[3]

"Mr. Dennie was a most charming companion, brilliant in conversation, fertile in allusion and quotation, abounding in wit, quick at repartee, and of only too jovial a disposition. My father used to tell of the gay dinners which celebrated the not infrequent visits Mr. Dennie made him when he was keeping house with his mother. On these white days he would summon the flower of the youth of Boston to enjoy the society of their versatile friend, and the festivity which set in at the sober hour of two would reach far into the night before the party were willing to break up."

Dennie probably did not return to Charlestown until July. A letter to his mother from Boston, 5 June, 1795, announces

1. Hugh Blair (1718-1800), author of the *Lecturer on Rhetoric*, 1783.
2. Owen Ruffhead (1723-1769), author of the critical biography of Pope, 1769. Johnson said Ruffhead "knew nothing of Pope and nothing of poetry."
3. Page 31.

his intention to visit Lexington on his return to New Hampshire, *via* Worcester. The postponement of the June term of court, he said, had enabled him to delay at Boston. Meanwhile Samuel West, Jr., was acting as his attorney at Charlestown. He expressed his hopes and fears regarding the *Tablet*, and his satisfaction at the approval of the clergy, "the best educated class" in America. Not long after, Colonel Clapp states,[1] "Mr. Dennie received his share of the first quarter's payments and returned to Charlestown." What then happened was told by Dennie himself two years later.[2]

"Returning in the summer of 1795, animated with expectation of realizing fortune and fame from '*The Tablet*,' I sat down to the desk of composition, and was making extensive arrangements, when an unexpected and mortifying billet from Spotswood announced the death of my *child!* I had never felt the inconvenience of being poor, and the anguish of disappointment, till then. For if I had been in the possession of property, neither the waywardness of the times, nor the dulness of the Bostonians, would have repulsed the growth of my miscellany. I was obliged to submit; and with a little purse, and spirit nearly as diminutive, began to conceive that my ill-luck was to be a *life-estate*, and that I was one of Dryden's unfortunates, who had but an *hour*, and lost even that."

Whether, as Dennie sincerely believed, the discontinuance of the *Tablet* after the thirteenth number, 11 August, 1795, was due wholly to the dulness and parsimony of the Bostonians, to whom a miscellany devoid of news, solid instruction, and remunerative advertisements, may not have appeared worth the price of three dollars annually, or whether, as was equally likely, strictures like those against Harvard in the *Farrago* paper on Mathematics cooled the ardor of their approval, he was bitterly disappointed at the outcome. Humiliated at college, and laughed out of the law-courts, it is little wonder that the failure of this darling project, so sanguinely conceived and so auspiciously begun, should strike him into a bitter dejection which was almost despair.

1. *Joseph Dennie*, p. 25.
2. Letter to his mother, 26 April, 1797.

CHAPTER VI

WALPOLE, 1795-1799—"THE FARMER'S MUSEUM"

The volatile spirits of the young author, however, could not long remain depressed: the disillusioned castle-builder soon selected a fresh site for his airy fabric and commenced his labors anew. In late September or early October, 1795, Dennie moved his law office from Charlestown to Walpole, a town of about 1,500 inhabitants, some ten miles farther down the river, where the high road from Keene reached the Connecticut. Mason, in his *Memoirs*,[1] gives a sketch of the place in 1794, when he moved hither:

"This was a brisk, active village, with several traders, and many industrious mechanics, and two or three taverns. . . . Walpole was, at that time, a place of more business than any in that vicinity, and was much resorted to by the people of the neighboring towns. There was also a considerable travel from a distance, passing on what was called the great river road. . . . The inhabitants of that part of the Connecticut river valley were then just passing from the rude and boisterous manners of first settlers to a more civilized, orderly, and settled state. There was more motion, life, and bustle than in the older parts of the country."

He adds that a little later Joseph Dennie came to the village "under the pretence of practising law." Since there were already three lawyers at Walpole,[2] Dennie's prospects in that profession cannot, indeed, have seemed very substantial. The presence of his college comrade, Roger Vose, who had settled in the town in 1793 or 1794, was undoubtedly a stronger incentive for Dennie's change of scene. Moreover, he was less interested in the law that in another field of activity represented at Walpole.

This was the *New Hampshire Journal: or Farmer's Weekly Museum*, a newspaper published by Isaiah Thomas and David Carlisle, Jr. The former was the veteran printer of the *Massa-*

1. *Memoirs*, page 28.
2. Namely, Jeremiah Mason, Roger Vose, and Samuel West.

chusetts Spy, at Worcester, founder of the American Antiquarian Society, and author of the *History of Printing in America.*[1] Besides his Worcester establishment, he owned presses and bookstores in Boston, Newburyport, Brookfield, and Walpole. Carlisle was a native of Walpole who, after completing his term as apprentice in the *Spy* office, had entered a partnership with his former master in his home town, under the firm name of Thomas and Carlisle. From their printing office and bookstore were issued several books and, beginning 11 April, 1793, the *Farmer's Weekly Museum.* This was a sheet eighteen by eleven inches in size, printed on coarse paper, and bearing the motto, *"Where Liberty is, there is my country." Franklin—The Liberty of the Press is Essential to the Rights of Man.*

Under Carlisle's management it compared favorably with its New Hampshire contemporaries. He had a taste for literature, and devoted a large part of his paper to essays and poems culled from other journals or from English authors, as well as to original productions by contributors of his own. Among the latter were the *Religionist* essays, by the Reverend Thomas Fessenden, and others signed *Monitor, Interpreter* and *Friend.* The *Neighbor* essays were frequently copied from the *Massachusetts Spy, The Times* from Noah Webster's *American Minerva,* and, from July, 1795, on, a series of "Citizen of the World" papers from the *New Jersey Chronicle,* entitled *Tomo Cheeki, the Creek Indian in Philadelphia,* by Philip Freneau. Five of Dennie's *Farrago* essays and several numbers of the *Vigil* were reprinted from the *Eagle* in 1793, 1794 and 1795. In March, 1794, Dennie had contributed the initial number of a series called the *Saunterer,*[2] the product of several pens, which appeared in the *Museum* at irregular intervals till September of that year. Royall Tyler and John C. Chamberlain were the chief contributors.

On 12 October, 1795, the first of a new series of essays, entitled *The Lay Preacher,* made its appearance in the *Museum.* The conception of the series is thus told by Dennie himself in a letter to his mother from Walpole, 26 April, 1797:

1. He also published, with Ebenezer Andrews, the *Massachusetts Magazine,* from 1789 to 1795.
2. Letter to his parents, 2 April, 1794.

"Musing on the fate of my paradoxes, and a vagabond like George Primrose, I sat out one evening for this place, without the merit or the consolation of being a philosophic adventurer like him. On the road I formed that plan which I have since realized, and which has attached *some* success. There was a press here conducted by a young man, honest, industrious, and then a partner of Thomas. I determined, by the agency of my pen, to convince him that I could be useful, and then—my humble knowledge of human agency taught me—I was sure he would encourage me when his own *interest* was the prompter. Without saying a word respecting a stipend, I wrote and gave him an essay on *Wine and New Wine*, and called it the *Lay Preacher*. It had been objected to my earliest compositions that they had been sprightly rather than moral. Accordingly, I thought I would attempt to be useful, by exhibiting truths in a plain dress to the common people."

The sermon, *Wine and New Wine*,[1] was immediately accepted and printed, and a *Lay Preacher* appeared in the *Farmer's Museum* weekly thereafter until 24 May, 1796. Dennie's letter referred to above goes on to add, "Persisting in this and various other tracks of newspaper composition, at the expiration of six months my Printer made me pecuniary proposals which I accepted." The "other tracks of composition" mentioned were chiefly summaries of Foreign and Domestic Intelligence, interestingly and pungently written, in which he took care, like Doctor Johnson, that the Whig dogs got the worst of it, and which became one of the most attractive features of the *Museum*. He also contributed items called Literary Intelligence and political satires attacking democrats in New England. In fact, the paper, which had been impartial in politics, became henceforth vigorous in its support of the Federalist administration. That Dennie practically conducted the literary and political departments of the *Museum* after October, 1795, is shown not only by the testimony of its pages, but also by his own statements.[2] He seems to have done this, however,

1. This sermon is reprinted in Clapp's *Joseph Dennie*.
2. Letter to his mother, 6 Aug., 1796. "I have conducted it, *others* say, with propriety, for nearly a twelvemonth." Also, *Gazette of the U. S.*, 15 Aug., 1800. "To Readers and Correspondents." "From October, 1795, when that responsible position was taken, until the September of 1799, when it was relinquished," etc. These dates have never before been definitely determined.

without recompense and without formally becoming editor, until April, 1796, when, Isaiah Thomas having relinquished his partnership and turned the paper over to Carlisle,[1] Dennie was given the direction of it. That some bargaining may have preceded this arrangement is suggested by the absence of the *Lay Preacher* from the issue of 22 March, 1796. The sermon, *A Good Wife,* which may have been originally written for that week, Dennie sent to his old friend, Dunham, who printed it in his *Eagle*, on 4 April, 1796.[2]

Dennie's salary as editor of the *Farmer's Museum* was £110, payable annually, the first day of April.[3] In addition he had, in 1796, an income of about £90 from his law practice, but this must have diminished with his increased attention to journalistic pursuits. That the law had become irksome to him is evident from the testimony of Mason, and from an incident told in the *Life of Josiah Quincy:*[4]

"One day one client strayed in, but the interruption he caused to the leisure and favorite occupations of his counsel learned in law was so great that a repetition of the annoyance was carefully guarded against. Mr. Dennie thenceforth kept his office-door locked on the inside."

Under Dennie's management the *Farmer's Museum* speedily became the best and most popular country newspaper in New England, as far as literature and politics were concerned. He cared little for local items of news and the cataloguing of deaths, marriages, and prices; and left advertisements to the care of Carlisle. *Colon and Spondee* re-opened their shop, supplying the paper with political and satirical paragraphs and parodies on the poetry of Charlotte Smith and the Della Cruscans. In August they began a series of political satires on the antifederalists in Congress and elsewhere, called *The Runner: or Indian Talk.* Several new contributors of essays or poems came to the editor's assistance within the year, all, of course, under assumed names, which are difficult, often impossible, to

1. Thomas retained his interest in the Walpole bookstore. See the *Farmer's Museum* for 29 March and 5 April, 1796.
2. This is the only instance in which a *Lay Preacher* was originally published outside of Dennie's own periodicals.
3. Letter to his mother, 6 Aug., 1796.
4. Page 31.

identify. Chief among these were *Simon Spunky* (T. G. Fessenden), the *Hermit* (J. C. Chamberlain) and the *Meddler,* who has not been ferreted out. The best articles, however, were Dennie's own. One of the most interesting departments was that addressed to Readers and Correspondents, crisp comments on rejected and accepted contributions, statements of the editor's designs, apologies, and promises. These items, it is said, were often written at the last moment, and expanded or cut down to suit the demands for space. In September, 1796, Dennie tried his hand, somewhat diffidently, at formal literary criticism, in a series of articles entitled the *Country Critic.* The series dealt in an unsatisfactory manner with the *Epistles, Domestic, Confidential and Official,* of Washington. It was against Dennie's principles to copy from contemporary American periodicals except in cases of exceptional merit, but he occasionally printed selections from the better known British poets and published a series of critical Biographies, taken from English reviews. Among the authors thus treated were Shakespeare, Milton, Chaucer, Spenser, Pope, Cowley, Jonson, Waller, Drayton, Donne, Suckling, and others.

The most notable articles in the *Farmer's Museum,* however, were the *Lay Preacher* essays. These ran from April to 13 September, 1796, with exception of the number for 31 May and 21 June, and irregularly after that, once or twice a month, until the end of Volume IV, April, 1797. In a *Lay Preacher* written considerably later[1] Dennie stated that the idea of a series of essays in the guise of lay sermons was suggested to him by a "Shandean" discourse he found and read in the study of a divine whom he was accustomed to visit during vacations at college. Although influences of the *Sermons of Yorick* of Lawrence Sterne, a favorite author of his, are easily traceable in the homilies of the New Hampshire moralist, Dennie's own services as lay reader at Claremont undoubtedly furnished him with the chief inspiration of his design, which was most happily suited to his temper and experience. As a preacher he could appropriately censure the follies, crudities, and shortcomings of his countrymen; as a *lay* preacher he was not debarred from rambling into politics, literature, and occasionally frivolous

1. *National Gratitude,* 1 July, 1799.

satire on manners and society. Each "sermon" was preceded by a motto, or text, generally from Scripture, and the outline was that of a sermon in little. Strictly, they were not sermons at all, but periodical essays similar in scope and purpose to the long line of such works, from Addison down, which they continued. The subjects were as varied as the writer's moods could make them, and the treatment was always attractive. Nothing to equal them in vivacity, range of subject, and classical flavor had yet appeared in America,[1] and they were widely copied in newspapers throughout the country.

In the *Farmer's Museum* for 8 December, 1795, the following notice was printed under the heading *Literary Intelligence.*

"We hear that the first attempt at vivacious and periodical Essay writing, in America, will be exhibited, during the winter, under the title of 'The Farrago,' with additional essays by Zachery Beauclerc, Esq.,[2] to be published a volume at a time, that the public taste might be tried and its encouragement proved." This plan to publish the *Farrago* papers was never carried out. In August, 1796, however, a small volume entitled *The Lay Preacher, or Short Sermons for Idle Readers,* was issued from David Carlisle's printing office and offered for sale at his bookstore in Walpole. The book contained about forty of the essays, which had already appeared in the columns of the *Farmer's Museum.* It had a fairly large sale and served as the foundation of Dennie's national reputation. The English traveller, John Davis, writing in 1803, considered it "the most popular work on the American continent." Letters complimenting Dennie upon his performance, from John Fenno, editor of the *Gazette of the U. S.*, Mrs. Sarah Morton ("Philenia"), and Noah Webster, are contained in the Dennie Papers. Best of all is a letter from his old preceptor, Samuel West, in which praise is mingled with fatherly warning. He wrote, "I never entertained ye least doubt, my friend, with respect to your abilities for making your way in ye world, much to your own honor and ye advantage of society—but genius is invariably connected

1. Their only close rivals were the sober *Essays* of Noah Webster, published in 1790, clear-cut, straightforward and not uninteresting compositions, but deficient in brilliancy and elegance.
2. So far as I know, this pseudonym was never used by Dennie.
3. John Davis. *Travels in the United States of America*, page 204.

with strong passions, and from that source arises ye dangers."

It may be useful to compare the literary output of America for 1796, when the *Lay Preacher* was published, with that of England for the same year.[1] In 1796 Burns died and Prescott was born. In America there appeared Joel Barlow's *Hasty Pudding,* written three years earlier, Thomas Paine's *Age of Reason, Part II,* Susannah Rowson's *Americans in England, The Lay Preacher,* the *Essays* of Count Rumford (Benjamin Thompson), and Washington's *Farewell Address,* with two or three other works which can hardly claim to be literature. In England, to offset this, there are listed, besides Burke's *Letters on a Regicide Peace,* Fanny Burney's *Camilla* and minor works by Peter Pindar and George Colman the younger, the first published work of Walter Scott, the first volume of *Poems* of Coleridge, and the *Joan of Arc* of Southey, of whom at least two were to become more notable writers than any American then living. Whether one considers the historical significance or the intrinsic value of these works, the American output appears pitifully light in the scales.

With congenial friends and pursuits, a growing literary reputation, and an income sufficient to enable him to live as he desired, Dennie's sojurn at Walpole during 1796 and 1797 was comparatively happy. He lived in the household of the Reverend Thomas Fessenden (1739-1813), H. C. 1758, for forty-six years the Presbyterian minister there. He was a liberal-minded, jovial preacher, who contributed to the *Museum* and produced in 1805 a lengthy work called the *Science of Sanctity.* From his diminutive size, his cocked hat, and a fancied resemblance to the Jack of Clubs, which played an important part in their favorite game of *Palm Loo,* he was affectionately nicknamed *Old Palm,* by Dennie and his associates. The dress and manners of the eighteenth century held on longer in New England than in New York or Philadelphia. An excellent account of Dennie's costume and demeanor at this time is given by Joseph Buckingham, the noted printer and editor, who as a boy served a brief apprenticeship of six months in Carlisle's office in 1796:[2]

---

1. See Ryland's *Chronological Outlines of English Literature,* and Whitcomb's *Chronological Outlines of American Literature.*

2. Buckingham. *Specimens of Newspaper Literature,* Vol. II, pages 196-197.

"I have a vivid recollection of Dennie's personal appearance, in 1796, when I began my apprenticeship in the printing office of David Carlisle. In person he was rather below than above the middle height, and was of a slender frame. He was particularly attentive to his dress, which, when he appeared in the street on a pleasant day, approached the highest notch of the fashion. I remember, one delightful morning in May, he came into the office dressed in a pea-green coat, white vest, nankin small-clothes, white silk stockings, and shoes, or *pumps,* fastened with silver buckles, which covered at least half the foot from the instep to the toe. His small-clothes were tied at the knees, with ribbons of the same color, in double bows, the ends reaching down to the ankles. He had just emerged from the barber's shop. His hair, *in front,* was well loaded with pomatum, frizzled, or *craped,* and powdered; the *ear-locks* had undergone the same process; *behind,* his natural hair was augmented by the addition of a large *queue* (called, vulgarly, the *false tail*), which, enrolled in some yards of black ribbon, reached half-way down his back. Thus *accommodated,* the Lay Preacher stands before my *mind's eye,* as lifelike and sprightly as if it were but yesterday that I saw the reality.

"Among his familiar acquaintance, and in the company of literary men, Dennie must have been a delightful and fascinating companion. In the printing-office, his conversation with the apprentices was pleasant and instructive. His deportment toward them was marked with great urbanity and gentleness. Being the younger apprentice,—in vulgar phrase, the *printer's devil,*—it was my lot to call upon him for copy, and carry the proof to him. Thus, for seven or eight months, my intercourse with him was almost daily, and was as familiar as propriety would sanction between an editor and an apprentice. I never saw him otherwise than in good humor.

"Dennie wrote with great rapidity, and generally postponed his task until he was called upon for *copy.* It was frequently necessary to go to his office, and it was not uncommon to find him in bed at a late hour in the morning. His *copy* was often given out in small portions, a paragraph or two at a time; sometimes it was written in the printing-office, while the compositor was waiting to put it in type. One of the best of his lay sermons was written at the village tavern, directly opposite to the office, in a chamber where he and his friends were amusing themselves with cards. It was delivered to me by piecemeal, at four or five different times. If he happened to be engaged in a game when I applied for copy, he would ask some one to *play his hand for him while he could give the devil his due.* When I called for the closing paragraph of the sermon, he said, '*Call again in five minutes.*' 'No,' said Tyler, 'I'll write the improvement for you.' He accordingly wrote the concluding paragraph, and Dennie never saw it till it was put in print."

Buckingham, who was a Connecticut boy of rigid morals, and brought up in extreme poverty, was scandalized, and nearly made bankrupt, by the custom of the *Museum* apprentices, that a newcomer in the office should "treat" with wine, brandy, sugar, eggs, and crackers.[1] He soon left Walpole and sought employment at Greenfield, Mass. He was a great admirer of Dennie's talents and after the latter's death wrote a series of essays in the *New England Galaxy*, called the *Preacher*, in imitation of him.

Jeremiah Mason, like everybody else who has described Dennie, states that he was a charming companion. He says,[2] "He was the most aerial, refined, and highly sublimated spirit it has ever been my hap to meet with. . . . With a good share of native genius he had a delicate and accurate taste, much cultivated by an ardent study of the English classics, with which he was thoroughly imbued. His language in common conversation, without any appearance of stiffness or pedantry, was always pure and classical. He early determined on the life of an author, and he deemed it necessary to avoid the use of low or vulgar language in conversation, in order to be secure against it in writing. . . . His powers of conversation were of the highest order. He had a slender and feeble frame, and was often depressed by bad health; but when in good health and spirits, I think have never known a more eloquent and delightful talker."

The commencement of Volume IV of the *Farmer's Museum*,

---

1. Buckingham. *Personal Memoirs and Recollections.* Vol. II, pp. 24-26.
2. *Memoirs*, pages 30-31.

4 April, 1797, was marked by a noteworthy innovation. In the first place, the name was changed to *The Farmer's Museum and the New Hampshire and Vermont Journal.* More important, however, was the setting apart of the last page of the *Museum* as a separate literary department, surmounted by an elaborate flower design and headed *The Dessert.* The remaining three pages were devoted to "Politicks, Biography, Economicks, Morals and Daily Details." An increasing amount of attention was given to politics. Dennie was kept in touch with occurrences at Philadelphia and with negotiations abroad by communications from Gen. Lewis R. Morris (1760-1825), of Springfield, Vermont, and Jeremiah Smith (1759-1842), of Peterboro, New Hampshire, both Federalist members of Congress. Occasionally, too, the great Fisher Ames furnished a hint or a paragraph which could be used by the *Museum.* Morris was a member of the famous New York family whose seat was at Morrisania, but had moved into the newly settled district of Vermont after the close of the Revolution, and had married Theodosia, daughter of widow Martha Olcott, with whom Dennie had lived at Charlestown. He was one of the most prominent men in Vermont, and served in Congress from 1797 to 1803. Smith was perhaps better known. He was an excellent scholar and a polished gentleman, a graduate of Rutgers in 1780, an associate of Webster, and Congressman from 1791 to 1797. His contributions were frequently in the form of hurried notes and scraps of information which he sent to Dennie to be expanded and polished for publication. The Daily Details were almost confined to the two weekly summaries, *Incidents at Home* and *Incidents Abroad.* The Biographies included, besides English authors like Burns, Warton, Surrey and Goldsmith, orators and statesmen like Fox and Burke, and foreign worthies like Bonaparte, Wieland, La Fontaine, and Schiller.

The year 1797 marked the high tide of the fortunes of the *Farmer's Museum.* On 24 July, Dennie announced that he had subscribers in all the states except Georgia, Kentucky and Tennessee, and that 1,000 new ones had been gained within eighteen months (i. e. since January, 1796). By December he had 2,000 readers, including some "in Georgia and on the banks of the Ohio," a circulation larger than that of any other village paper in the United States. The editor was also "honored with the patronage of some of the most prominent characters in the Union."[1] Letters have been preserved, from Fisher Ames, the Reverend Samuel Eliot of Boston, G. R. Minot, Richard Alsop, Thomas B. Adams, and many others, praising Dennie's paper and his Federalist politics. The literary department, too, was flourishing. In February, 1797, Dennie had written, "With peculiar satisfaction the Editor informs his classical readers that most of the writers in his late miscellany, *The Tablet*, will resume their pens and employ them for the *Farmer's Museum.*" Chief among these was J. S. J. Gardiner, whose long-promised continuation of *Original Criticism* appeared tardily the next year. The break-up of the *Massachusetts Magazine* in 1797 brought some new correspondents to the *Museum,* and in the same year Isaac Story, a prolific essayist over various signatures, was won over from the Newburyport *Political Gazette.* Other new correspondents used the names "Common Sense in Dishabille," the "Congregationalist," "Charles Chatterbox," and the "Peddler." In the winter of 1797 "Colon and Spondee" issued from their shop a series of *Shreds of Criticism* on several authors, short paragraphs, for the most part, dealing with small matters of technique, versification and diction, in the work of contemporary poets.

Aldrich's *Walpole as It Was and as It Is* gives an interesting account of the Literary Club, whose members contributed to the *Farmer's Museum,* and held frequent and jovial meetings at Major Bullard's famous Crafts Tavern at Walpole. "His house," says Aldrich, "was the resort of a *coterie* of wages, wits, and literati from all the surrounding country. . . . The old tavern, in those days, at those gatherings, was turned into a *literary pandemonium;* wine drinking, late suppers, card playing, joke cracking, and the like formed the programme for frequent meetings during the year; and the 'wee hours of the morning' were the only acknowledged signals for breaking up. The good cheer of Maj. Bullard's house was known far and wide."[2] The members of the coterie were for the most part representatives of the legal profession and graduates of Har-

1. 14 March, 1797.
2. *Walpole as It Was and as It Is*, page 81.

vard or other colleges. Dennie, sociable, generous, witty, an excellent declaimer and story teller, well informed and keenly enthusiastic about literature, was easily the central figure. Others who aided in making Walpole, tiny and remote, a literary center of some fame were the Harvard men, Royall Tyler, '76, of Guilford, Vermont, Roger Vose, '90, John C. Chamberlain, '93, of Alstead, N. H., and Samuel West, '88; Thomas Green Fessenden, Dartmouth, 1796; and Samuel Hunt, of Charlestown. Besides these, Jeremiah Mason, Yale 1788, Colonel Alpheus Moore, Harvard 1783, of Westmoreland, Doctors Heilleman and Spaulding, and Major Bullard occasionally took part in the festivities.

Jeremiah Mason (1768-1843), Y. C. 1788, was a Connecticut man, who practised law at Walpole from 1794 to 1797, and afterwards at Portsmouth and Boston. He was a shrewd, witty, and intelligent lawyer and served as U. S. Senator from New Hampshire, 1813-1817. In 1795 he started the Walpole Library Association, the forerunner of the present public library of the town. He was the first librarian, and Dennie was the second. His Connecticut principles are evident in the pages of his *Memoirs*, in his criticism of his more frivolous Harvard friends.

Tyler was in 1797 a man of forty, with a growing family, and a considerable reputation for legal, as well as literary ability. His contributions to the *Farmer's Museum* were all from the *Shop of Messrs. Colon and Spondee;* he was *Spondee*, and wrote patriotic odes, amatory verses and parodies of various sorts, Dennie supplying most of the prose articles. Tyler's novel, *The Algerine Captive, or The Life and Adventures of Dr. Updike Underhill*, was published in two volumes by Carlisle at Walpole in 1799. It is said to have been the first American novel republished in England. To the present-day reader the incidents of the first volume, narrating Dr. Underhill's experience as a country teacher and a country physician when quackery was the rule rather than the exception, and his practice in the slaveholding states, are decidedly more interesting than the subsequent narrative of adventures among the Algerines, laden as it is with geographical and moralizing observations, since the avowed purpose of the work was to instruct as well as amuse.

Roger Vose (1763-1842), Dennie's classmate, settled and married at Walpole and spent the rest of his life there, except for four years, 1813-1817, when he was a representative in Congress. He was an able but not brilliant lawyer, fond of fun and quick at repartee. His poetical abilities were lavishly praised by Dennie in their correspondence, but his output in the *Farmer's Museum* was probably small. I have been able to identify only a few humorous poems, including an epistle from *Frighted Fanny's Faithful Friend to Frederic, Fictitiously Fond.*

John Curtis Chamberlain (1772-1834), a native of Worcester, was a fellow-student with Dennie in the office of Benjamin West, at Charlestown. While here he contributed to the *Eagle or Dartmouth Centinel,* essays over the signature of *Tim Pandect.* On being admitted to the bar in 1796 he settled in practice at Alstead, adjoining Walpole on the east. He served in Congress in 1809-10. He was an excellent advocate, but was given to an excess of conviviality. Though not a member of the Literary Club, he belonged to Dennie's fraternity of writers and contributed in collaboration with him most of an interesting series of essays in the *Farmer's Museum* called *The Hermit.* These began appearing in the summer of 1796 and continued for a year or more. Chamberlain's most important literary work, however, was *A Narrative of the Captivity of Mrs. Johnson,* printed at Walpole by David Carlisle in 1796, and generally supposed to have been written by Mrs. Johnson herself.[1] The work aroused great interest and was several times republished, both in America and in England. Chamberlain moved in 1826 to the state of New York, where he died, at Utica, in 1834.

Samuel West (1771-1810) was a son of the Reverend Samuel West of Needham, and nephew of Benjamin West of Charlestown. In the latter's office he was a fellow-student with Dennie for two years, after he had graduated at Harvard. He was ad-

1. Mrs. Susanna (Willard) Johnson (1729-1810), with her husband, James Johnson, her sister Miriam, her three children, a hired servant and a neighbor, were captured by Indians at Charlestown, 30 Aug., 1754, and taken through the woods, with great hardships, to Canada. After long negotiations she and her husband joined each other at Charlestown, 1 Jan., 1758, and the whole family was later reunited. Saunderson's *History of Charlestown* has a full account of her captivity and of J. C. Chamberlain.

mitted to the New Hampshire bar in 1792 and spent the next six years practising law at Walpole. After that he removed to the county seat at Keene, where he enjoyed a reputation as "a most brilliant advocate and eloquent lawyer."[1] I have not identified any of his contributions to the *Farmer's Museum.*

The life of Thomas Green Fessenden (1771-1837) is an unusual example of Yankee resourcefulness. A son of Parson Fessenden, of Walpole, he paid his way through Dartmouth by teaching during the vacations and by conducting an old-time singing-school. While in college he occasionally contributed poetry to the *Eagle,* at Hanover, and the *Farmer's Museum* at home. His best production at this period was a humorous dialect ballad entitled *Jonathan's Courtship.* He next studied law, was admitted to the Vermont bar, and practised a few years. In 1801 he was sent to London as agent for a Vermont company which had patented a new hydraulic machine. Here, when it developed that a defect in the patent made the project worthless, he set about and invented one which *would* work. Failing to interest patronage in this, he invested what money he had left in a new machine, and lost all of it through fraud. Penniless in London, he decided to make use of his poetic talents. Another Yankee inventor, named Perkins, had devised what were called Perkins' Metallic Tractors, one of the earliest electrical appliances for medical use. These tractors had been introduced into England, where they had an extensive sale, but were opposed by most of the English medical profession. Fessenden now came to his countryman's defense in a long poem called the *Terrible Tractoration,* by "Christopher Caustic, M. D., A. S. S." This ironical tirade against the offending tractors, in which the footnotes, laden with scientific lore, far outweighed the text, purported to be the utterance of a disgruntled quack, driven out of practice by the innovation, who calls upon his profession to assist in their destruction. The work, in spite of its imitative nature and its poetic demerits, ran through two editions in England, and three more in America. He returned to the United States in 1803, where his *Poems* in 1807, and a malignant satire on Jefferson and the Democrats in 1805, entitled *Democracy Unveiled or*

1. See Bell's *Bench and Bar of New Hampshire,* which contains sketches of most of the characters mentioned in this chapter.

Tyranny Stripped of the Garb of Patriotism, permanently secured for him whatever credit may attach to the title, "the American Butler." In 1805 he began the publication of a weekly paper, the *Investigator,* in New York City. The rest of his quiet and useful life was spent in practising law and publishing agricultural papers in Bellows Falls, Vermont, and Boston. His later works were *Pills, Poetical, Political, and Philosophical,* in 1809, and the *Ladies' Monitor,* in 1818. His only really permanent work was the establishment, in 1822, of the *New England Farmer,* an agricultural weekly, which is still published. He died in Boston, 10 November, 1837, and is buried at Mount Auburn. A well-written biographical sketch of him by Nathaniel Hawthorne, who as a young man knew him rather intimately, appeared in the *American Monthly Magazine* for January, 1838. His principal contributions to the *Museum* were humorous ballads, verse satires on the Democrats, and occasional poems, such as the long *New Year's Ode* for 1798, all over the signature of "Simon Spunky."

Samuel Hunt (1765-1807), of Charlestown, a young lawyer who had retired from his profession after a few years' practice, was a member of the Literary Club and a contributor to the *Museum,* but his output was small. After a few years spent in foreign travel and two terms in Congress, he led a small band of colonists from Charlestown to the Ohio country, where he perished, with most of the rest, near Gallipolis, Ohio, 7 July, 1807.

Several of the most frequent and ablest writers of the *Farmer's Museum* were not connected with the Literary Club. The contributions of J. S. J. Gardiner, Jeremiah Smith, and Lewis R. Morris have already been noticed. Another who contributed political articles was Samuel Barrett, a Boston lawyer, who died in 1799. Thomas Day (1777-1855), Yale 1797, brother of President Jeremiah Day of Yale, and later a noted lawyer and judge of Connecticut, while a tutor at Williams in 1798 and 1799, sent a few poems to the *Museum.* His principal literary effort was *The Suicide,* a blank verse dialogue exhibited at the Yale commencement in 1797. James Elliott (c. 1775-1839), of Brattleboro, Vermont, was the author of a series of critical essays called the *Rural Wanderer,* in the *Museum,* 1799 and 1800. His *Poeti-*

cal and Miscellaneous Works were published at Brattleboro in 1799.[1] William Bigelow (1778-1844), H. C. 1794, school-teacher, preacher, editor, historian, and proof-reader, contributed to the *Museum* in 1797 and 1798, a *melange* of light and witty prose and verse called *Obi,* while teaching school and studying theology at Lancaster, Mass. He used the nom-de-plume "Charles Chatterbox," over which he had written for Paine's *Federal Orrery* and the *Massachusetts Magazine,* which he edited during its last days, from June to December, 1795.[2]

Of greater importance to the *Farmer's Museum* was the work of two young lawyers, David Everett of Boston[3] and Isaac Story of Marblehead. Everett is remembered, or rather not remembered, as author of the well-known lines,

"You'd scarce expect one of my age
To speak in public on the stage."[4]

While studying and practising law in Boston, from 1795 to 1802, he contributed prolifically to the *Boston Gazette,* to a literary paper called the *Nightingale,* and to the *Farmer's Museum,* besides publishing, about 1796, a blank verse tragedy, *Daranzel, or the Persian Patriot.* For Dennie's paper he wrote in 1797 a series of witty essays entitled *Common Sense in Dishabille,* which were followed by other miscellaneous articles signed "Peter Pencil." Everett was from 1797 to 1799 one of Dennie's most faithful correspondents.

In 1797 Isaac Story,[5] then practising law at Castine, Maine,

1. He was a Gloucester boy who went to Vermont, worked in a grocery store at Guilford, enlisted and served under Anthony Wayne in the Northwest Campaign, 1793-96, and later became a prominent lawyer in Brattleboro, and member of Congress in 1803-1809.

2. Several collections of his verse were published, and a sketch of his life, with illustrative selections, may be found in Buckingham's *Specimens of Newspaper Literature,* Vol. II, pages 276 to 293.

3. David Everett (1770-1813), Dartmouth, 1795, was a native of Princeton, Mass., and died in Marietta, Ohio, a few months after his removal thither, in 1813. From 1802 to 1807 he practised law at Amherst, New Hampshire. On returning to Boston he started and conducted successively the *Boston Patriot* and the *Pilot.*

4. Written in 1790, at New Ipswich, N. H., where he was teaching school.

5. Isaac Story (1174-1803), H. C., 1793, was a native of Marblehead and cousin of the noted jurist, Joseph Story. Besides his contributions to Dennie's and Barrett's papers, he wrote the *Traveler* essays for the *Columbian Centinel* and conducted, at Castine, the *Castine Journal and Eastern Advertiser* in 1798-99. After 1799 he practised law at Rutland, Mass., where he died, aged 29, in 1803. Three volumes of his verse and

began contributing to the *Museum* occasional humorous poems by "Peter Quince," in imitation of "Peter Pindar," (John Wolcot). These continued his contributions to William Barrett's *Political Gazette,* started at Newburyport in 1795 and discontinued as an independent paper in 1797. The same is true of a series of prose essays, *From the Desk of Beri Hesdin,* which appeared in the *Farmer's Museum* at intervals from the summer of 1797 to the end of 1799. They were well-written moral essays, modelled on the *Lay Preacher,* a little more serious in tone and marked by less vivacity.

Doctor Elihu Hubbard Smith (1771-1798), one of the Hartford Wits who contributed to the *Echo,* a friend of Charles Brockden Brown, and compiler of the first American Anthology,[1] corresponded with Dennie and advised and criticized freely. Apparently he did not contribute anything directly to the *Museum,* but several of the biographies of American men of letters reprinted from English reviews were the product of his pen, notably the sketches of his friends, John Trumbull, Colonel David Humphreys, Lemuel Hopkins, and Timothy Dwight. In answer, probably, to criticisms for thus republishing articles from British periodicals, Dennie printed, 18 February, 1799, the following rather illuminating defense:

"It is necessary to apprize *many* of our readers, that *all* the articles which we copy from British publications are of so *recent* composition that, with the exception of a very few persons who are in the habit of importing the newest publications, they are in fact *original,* to all intents and purposes, to a great majority of persons. . . . Every department in this paper, which is not furnished from the brain of the editor and his correspondents, is supplied from works, *which have not been more than three, six, or twelve months in America.* . . . Every man, unless tumid with the most ridiculous pride and confidence in American genius and literature, must be sensible from the newness of our country, from the deficiency of our seminaries,

---

essays were published, at Marblehead, 1792, at Boston, 1795, and at Salem, 1801. A narrative poem, *Epistle from Yarico to Inkle,* published anonymously at Marblehead in 1792, has also been ascribebd to Story.

1. Published at Litchfield, Conn., 1793.

from the comparative paucity of books, and from the almost total want of patronage, that many *literary* articles can be furnished in perfection, *only from Europe*. . . . The silly vanity of a self-complacent American may be wounded at this blunt, but notorious *truth*. Let him deny it if he can."

In spite of the unnecessary sneer in these lines, their boasted truth must impress an impartial mind. After all, Joel Barlow, Noah Webster, and Timothy Dwight, even Dennie, Freneau, and Charles Brockden Brown, do not loom very large beside Wordsworth, Coleridge, Scott, Burns, Doctor Johnson, Sheridan, and Goldsmith, whose works were either then appearing or fresh in the minds of men in England.

One of Dennie's infrequent letters home during this period refers feelingly to his father's insanity.[1]

"If my unhappy Parent enjoys a lucid hour, for God's sake express my duty and affection and let him be assured how I suffer in this rude buffetting voyage of life, the want of a Father's guidance. You, my dear Mama, are a real friend and tender mother, but a young Man requires some counsels which woman, timid and inexperienced, cannot bestow."

In August and September of the same year, 1797, Dennie visited his home and spent several weeks in Boston,[2] while *Beri Hesdin* occupied the pulpit of the *Lay Preacher*. He seems to have stayed most of the time at the new and palatial home of his old employer, James Swan, at Roxbury. Two letters to his friend, Mason, just settled at Portsmouth,[3] give an idea of his social pleasures, his familiarity with literary men and women, and his sentiments toward the Bostonians. In the first, dated 6 August, 1797, he wrote:

---

1. 26 April, 1797. Letter to his mother.
2. Dennie's probable purpose in visiting Boston is indicated by an entry in the *Diary of the Reverend William Bentley, D. D.*, of Salem, Vol. II, 29 Aug., 1797:

"Mr. Nancrede, editor of the American edition of St. Pierre's *Studies of Nature*, was with me. . . He tells of an intended Magazine under Dennie of Walpole, the editor of the *Farmer's Museum*. This Gazette has gotten him great fame. He has above 2,000 subscribers, and a considerable number even in Salem are upon the subscription list at Dabney's."

Joseph Nancrede was a Frechman, a bookseller, teacher, and editor in Boston. Several letters from him to Dennie are preserved, but they do not bear upon the magazine mentioned above.

3. Published in the *Mass. Hist. Soc. Proceedings*, 1880. Vol. XVII, pp. 362-65.

"I have arrayed myself in sables and prattled history with Belknap. I have spoken softly to Miss Buck and loudly to Miss Knox. I have lounged on the sofa of Philenia[1] and have darted Federalism at her French spouse."

The second letter, 25 August, gives his comments on the intellectual and social activities of Boston:

"I pass most of my time at M's., and visit George Cabot and J. Swan. Jews and Gentiles you will say; true. Men of all party colors; but no low people, Jere, no hewers of wood or drawers of water.

"I have had the honor of making two bows to the President[2] and receiving three. About three hundred guests were bidden to the feast, and I am sorry to say that the toasts were followed by clamorous hootings, and applause quite in the French style. All this is suited to the taste of the Bostonians, who are unquestionably the merest boys at all kinds of play.

"I find strong sense, urban manners and *Ellsworth's* energy in Cabot. He amuses me by his political zeal and instructs me by his worldly wisdom. Moreover, he giveth good dinners, and, sinner that I am, I think partridge at least as palatable as politics.

"There is here a kind of would be literary-club.[3] It meets each Wednesday, and consists of certain lawyers, quacks, and merchants. I have seen these people, who are mostly fools; Minot, Clarke, and Kirkland are exceptions. *Our* historian, Belknap,[4] appears to be buried in plethora, and his genius is as much palsied as his limbs. They are all lazy; and reversing the usual order, they convene rather to *eat*, than *talk*, together." He closes his letter with a playful remark about one of Swan's daughters, who had momentarily captivated his vagrant heart:

"She looks and talks exquisitely, has a strong mind, and some fortune, *if her mother please.* Now could I cheat the last

---

1. Philenia was Mrs. Sarah Morton. Her "French spouse" was Perez Morton, a prominent Democrat.
2. John Adams.
3. The Wednesday Evening Club, founded in 1776, predecessor of the Century Club. A historical and biographical sketch of its early members is contained in the *Centennial Celebration of the Wednesday Evening Club.* Boston, 1778.
4. He wrote the *History of New Hampshire.*

and gain the first, I think it would be a summary way to be rich and happy."

The remaining history of the *Farmer's Museum* may be briefly told. In December, 1797, a series of paragraph criticisms of the style of different authors, entitled *Shreds of Criticism*, appeared from the *Shop of Colon and Spondee*. Bigelow's *Obi*, and the *Pedlar* essays began in March, 1798. In May a projected "new and very elegant edition of the *Lay Preacher*, with very copious additions," was announced, but like many such projects, before and afterward, nothing came of it. In June, after an absence of nearly a year, the *Lay Preacher* returned, with a cheerful sermon on the text, *Here Am I, for Thou Didst Call Me*.[1] The essays appeared regularly until 17 September, and after that at intervals again until the last, 26 August, 1799. During the latter part of the year 1798, while Dennie's attention was directed toward other affairs, the *Museum* showed a marked decline in quality. The ablest contributors fell away and the amount of "exotic verse" and borrowing from British sources in the *Dessert* increased. An appeal to his old supporters, and added efforts on Dennie's part in the beginning of 1799 brought the paper back to its pristine excellence. Elliot's *Rural Wanderer* now made its appearance, as did the few poems of Thomas Day. Another contributor was John Davis, then at Coosawhatchie, South Carolina, an erratic English traveller and scribbler, of whom more will be said later. Most of the prose and verse not contributed by Dennie, however, at this period, was the work of Alexander Thomas, a relative of Isaiah Thomas, who succeeded Dennie as editor. Little or nothing appears to be known about him, but in 1798 and the succeeding years he kept the *Dessert* bright with witty and sentimental verses and witty and sententious essays. In partnership with Isaiah Thomas he conducted the *Museum*, with a brief intermission, for several years. In February, 1799, "Colon and Spondee" issued two new varieties of literary goods from their shop. One was a series of *Political Applications*, parodied passages from Shakespeare and other

1. Reprinted in Buckingham's *Specimens of Newspaper Literature*, Vol. II, pages 181-183. The sermon for 1 April, 1799, on *April Fool Customs*, is also to be found there, pages 188-191.

authors, to apply to American political situations. The other was a long-lived series of critical miscellany, entitled *An Author's Evenings.* These were in general composed of short and cursory comments on different authors, illustrated by copious extracts from their works. The most that can be said for the series is that they are interesting reading. At the beginning of Volume VII, 1 April, 1799, the name of the paper was changed, for business reasons, to *The Farmer's Museum, or Lay Preacher's Gazette.* In the same year a series of American biographies and criticisms of American works was undertaken.[1] It is interesting to find that Dennie immediately recognized the worth of Wordsworth and Coleridge's *Lyrical Ballads,* and that in spite of violent political differences, he praised the better poems of Freneau.

Meanwhile, the finances of the *Museum,* in spite of its large circulation, were in a bad way. Frequent appeals to delinquent subscribers appeared in 1797, and in December of that year the price was raised from $1.00 to $1.50 a year, to cover postage from distant points. Carlisle is said to have made three failures within a few years,[2] in one of which Dennie lost heavily. In the *Museum* for 2 January, 1798, Dennie, after outlining a number of improvements to be instituted, made the following appeal to his readers. "If the community think that this paper is of any service to the cause of government, virtue, and literature, let them encourage a man, who has devoted some years, vacated some gainful pursuits, and outwatched some lamps, to qualify himself as a literary and political herald." With the number for 20 February, 1798, Isaiah Thomas took possession of the *Farmer's Museum* again, Carlisle remaining the printer.[3] Dennie, with a reduced salary of $400, continued as editor. In June Alexander Thomas took the general management of the paper, leaving the editorship of the literary and political departments to Dennie. The latter's dispassionate account of the whole procedure, together with his subsequent ac-

1. The only work criticised was Dwight's *Conquest of Canaan.*
2. Marble. *Heralds of American Literature,* page 204.
3. That Dennie suspected Carlise's business honestly in these failures may be inferred from a letter to Roger Vose, 7 Feb., 1800, in which he speaks of the "curious and convenient bankruptcy of Carlisle." The latter remained printer of the *Museum* several years and later moved to Boston, where he printed Fessenden's *Democracy Unveiled,* in 1808.

tivities, is contained in a letter to his mother from Walpole, 6 September, 1799:

"Soon after my return from my visit to Massachusetts my Printer failed. In consequence of this bankruptcy, I lost my whole property in the sale of my little book,[1] and about 500 dollars, fairly and laboriously earned by editing. To have the whole profits of my pen, the *honorable* and *liberal* source of my support, thus snatched away, you may easily conceive to be not only mortifying, but an embarrassing event. I persevered, however, with my usual spirit, and cherished hope, in spite of my continued disappointments. With a reduced salary of 400 dolls. I have been obliged to work hard, and *remain at home*. Let no complaints, therefore, be heard on this subject. A journey to Boston would have incurred expense, unsuitable to the deranged state of my fortune, and I have not a friend in that Jewish, peddling and commercial quarter, who is disposed to render me service, even should *I descend* to ask it.

"In consequence of my perseverance in the cultivation of letters, I have greatly advanced my literary reputation, and by my success and popularity in *Lay Preaching*, have, in my obscurity, been slowly and silently, but I hope surely, fixing the basis of future character. My attention to political topics and my known zeal for administration have conspired to advance my hopes for fame and fortune. A year since I endeavored to secure a seat in Congress. My friends here were active and partial in my behalf, and besides much newspaper recommendations, etc., I had a handsome number of suffrages from unbiased citizens. But I pitted myself against a gentleman already in the representation of the State, and of much merit, and an older man. I was found guilty of being too young and inexperienced and I lost the election."

Dennie's name had, indeed, been put forward by some of his admirers, who had set forth his claims in the *Farmer's Museum* on 31 July, 13 August, and 20 August, 1798. He had responded to two toasts at the civic celebration on 4 July, and was probably the best known of the young lawyers in and around Walpole. His candidacy, however, does not seem to have been

1. *The Lay Preacher*, published in 1796.

taken very seriously by the electors.[1] Dennie's disappointment at the downfall of this new castle was doubtless keen, and his attitude after it was characteristic.[2] "I was disgusted with the levity and weakness of the *people*, and concluded, I believe very soundly, that promotion from them would be given very late, if given at all."

Accordingly, baffled by popular indifference, in his design to batter down the mud wall of Democratic opposition in Congress with the roses of Federalist oratory and satire, he next sought office through the patronage of the administration. His political reputation outside of New Hampshire was probably greater than at home. His consistent and vigorous attacks upon the Democrats of New England had brought upon him the counter-attacks of opposition papers such as the *Independent Chronicle*, of Boston, and the *Bee*, of New London, Connecticut. He proudly announced, on 16 January, 1798, "Since the editor has been splashed with the mud of *Chronicle* obloquy, he has gained upwards of 700 subscriptions." He was called "the erudite Walpole Fire-brand,"[3] and was classed with such prominent Federalist editors as John Fenno, Noah Webster, Benjamin Russell, Caleb P. Wayne, and William Cobbett ("Peter Porcupine").[4]

A parody on Shakespeare's Apothecary, in *Romeo and Juliet*, entitled *Retaliation, or the Editor*, was widely printed in the Democratic papers:

> "I do remember well a fed'ralist,
> And he in Walpole dwells, whom late I noted,
> With bloated cheek, red nose, and fiery eyes,
> Coining fell despotism. . . .
>
> . . . .

1. The figures at the town meeting at Walpole, 27 August, 1798, kindly furnished me by the town clerk, Mr. J. W. Hayward, follow:

"Votes for the Representatives of the State in the Congress of the United States were given as follows: Jonathan Freeman, Esqr., 124; Abiel Foster, Esqr., 120; Thomas Bellows, Esqr., 101; Peleg Sprague, Esqr., 86; William Gordon, Esqr., 63; Joseph Dennie, Esqr., 6; Oliver Peabody, Esqr., 2."

2. Letter to his mother, 6 Sept., 1799.

3. Buckingham. *Specimens of Newspaper Literature*, Vol. II, page 304.

4. Editors of the *Gazette of the U. S.*, Philadelphia; *American Minerva*, New York; *Columbian Centinel* and *Federal Gazette*, Boston; and *Porcupine's Gazette*, Philadelphia, respectively.

Noting this lordling, to myself I said,
If love of England, monarchy, or gold,
Could bribe a native to betray his country,
There sits a pampered wretch would sell her to him.'"[1]

The charge of excessive fondness for England contained in this satire is not unjust, as is frequently shown in his published articles and still more frankly in his letters. After repeated disappointments he had become obsessed by the idea that under the patronage of a royal government he would have received the recognition which he thought was due to him, and ascribed to the churlishness of a democracy much that his own indolence and depressed spirits were responsible for. In other respects, he was more aristocratic in his views even than John Adams, who wished to exalt "the rich, the well-born, and the able," above their fellows.[2] Dennie's ideas coincided with those rather of Alexander Hamilton, who answered a democratic sentiment with the heated remark,[3] "Your people, sir,—your people is a great *beast!*"

As early as 1796 Dennie had entertained hopes of political preferment. In a letter to his mother from Walpole, 6 August, 1796, he wrote:

"The upright and Federal politics, I have aimed to inculcate, have procured the attention of Government, and in letters from members of Congress, I have been warmly thanked for my services. . . . If Mr. Pickering's secretary in his late embassy, had not chosen to go with Mr. King, I should have been nominated as Secretary to the Court of London."

It is interesting to conjecture what effect upon Dennie's literary fortunes such an appointment might have had.

At the beginning of 1799, tired of his stay, in reduced circumstances and in obscurity, among the rustics of New Hampshire, desirous of a wider field for his literary and political activities, and disappointed of obtaining it through the electorate, he began to look about for a change. The outlook was encouraging. Letters are preserved offering him the editorship of influential newspapers in Boston, New York, Philadelphia,

1. *Independent Chronicle*, 11 Dec., 1797.
2. Channing. *Student's History of the U. S.*, page 280.
3. Henry Adams. *The First Administration of Thomas Jefferson*, page 85.

Baltimore, and Halifax, on terms which must have seemed attractive to the penurious editor. One of these offers was from James White, a prominent bookseller of Boston, a Federalist, and an intimate friend of the Dennies. He had bought the *Independent Chronicle* in May, 1799, and intending to conduct it as a non-partisan paper, offered Dennie the editorship, with a salary of $1200. The latter's remark about the matter is characteristic. He wrote, "I was really sorry that I could not assist Mr. White. But it was absolutely impossible, even if I had not received my appointment, unless, which would have been destructive to *his* interest, he had *wholly* changed the politics of the *Chronicle.* If he had allowed me 12 millions of dollars annually, I must have refused the offer. It would have belied my feelings, my habits, my principles, my conscience."[1]

Several circumstances, however, impelled him to go to Philadelphia. First, as the capital of the United States it offered a chance to make his literary fame national. Second, William Cobbett had offered to publish the *Lay Preacher* at Philadelphia and pay him $1,000 for the copyright.[2] Third, John Ward Fenno, who had succeeded his father as owner of the *Gazette of the United States,* had offered Dennie the editorship of the paper at a salary of $800, plus a percentage on all new subscriptions.[3] Finally, through the mediation of Lewis R. Morris and other friends at Washington, Dennie had secured an appointment as private secretary to Timothy Pickering, Secretary of State. The negotiations leading to that appointment are preserved in the *Pickering Papers,* at the Massachusetts Historical Society Library, in Boston. Pickering's letters have the studiously deferential tone of a man of affairs, conscious of rendering a favor to a man of "artistic temperament." Dennie's are filled with enthusiasm, vanity, and consciousness of having been useful to the administration. His purpose was divulged to his mother in these words, "In February last, I gave that official to understand . . . that I thought I could prove useful at his Bureau; that I wished a head station at his desk, for a few months that I might acquire the diplomatic

1. Letter to his mother, 6 September, 1799.
2. Dennie Papers. Letter from William Cobbett, 30 Jan., 1799.
3. Dennie Papers. Letter from John Ward Fenno, 12 Feb., 1799.

style, and that if, by the success of my pen, and by the confidence of the Govt., I should be found worthy, my objects were, either a Secretaryship to a Foreign Legation, or a Consulship.'"[1] After accepting the appointment on 26 May, 1799, Dennie stipulated for a delay of three months before starting to assume his duties, owing to a promise made to Thomas to give him a notice of that length of time before relinquishing his connection with the *Farmer's Museum.* Pickering granted the request, the more readily because a residence in Philadelphia during the summer was in those days a formidable matter for a man of habitually poor health. Dennie accordingly remained at Walpole some days longer than his terms required, writing for the *Museum Lay Preachers* ebullient with anticipations of fame in the city. He set out from Walpole about the second week in September, 1799, without having visited his parents at Lexington. He probably never saw them again.[2]

1. Letter to his mother, 6 Sept., 1799.
2. This neglect probably cannot be ascribed to indifference. The increasing decay of his father's mind was a spectacle almost unendurable to Dennie's sensitive mind, as is indicated in his letters on the rare occasions when he adverted to it.

CHAPTER VII

PHILADELPHIA, 1799-1800—THE "GAZETTE OF THE UNITED STATES"

During the unhealthful summer season of 1799, the government offices were removed from Philadelphia to Trenton, New Jersey, and thither it was that Dennie turned his steps, about the middle of September of that year. Behind him he left Walpole, remembered by several unpaid bills and some regrets; before him, he hoped, was at last fame. "I lingered in N. H. *rather* too long," he wrote to Vose from Philadelphia,[1] "but enough of mortal time is left, I hope, both for some fame and some fortune." If he made haste, as his friends who knew his dilatory habits urged him to do, he probably covered the distance from Walpole to Trenton, travelling by stage-coach, in six or seven days, of which four or five would be consumed in reaching New York, and two more in journeying from that place to Trenton.[2] To the considerable discomfort of traversing in a slow-moving coach the disreputable roads of that period, was added the pain of a sprained thumb, which deprived him of the use of his right hand for some time after his arrival, as he informed his mother in a letter some months later.[3]

He soon gave an account of himself, however. An interesting indication of his presence in New Jersey is to be found in the pages of *The Guardian: or New Brunswick Advertiser*, published at New Brunswick, during the months of October and November, 1799. This had been a serious and rather dull Federalist paper, devoted, as its name indicates, chiefly to advertising and to political news, and conducted by Abraham Blauvelt, a Rutgers graduate of 1789. Suddenly, on 15 October, the paper blossomed forth with a new literary department, entitled the *Parnassus Packet*, on the last page. The chief piece under this heading was an essay on *Slander*, the first of a series to be called *The Lecturer*, and signed "Orlando," but exhibiting, in its frequent italics, quotations, and highflown language, the usual

1. Vose Letters, 7 Feb., 1800.
2. See Adams. *History of the U. S., 1801-1805*, Vol. I, p. 11.
3. 20 May, 1800.

style of Dennie. The essay was headed by a characteristic bit of verse,

> " . . . My business in this State
> Made me a constant observer of the times,
> Where I have seen corruption boil and bubble
> Till it o'errun the stew; laws for all faults,
> But faults so countenanced," etc.

The next number, 22 October, has a second *Lecturer* essay on *Calumny*, very rambling and pointless, as Dennie's hasty writings frequently were. The Harvard Library file lacks the papers for 29 October and 5 and 19 November; those for 12 and 26 November have poems and short prose pieces from the *Farmer's Museum*, but no *Lecturer*. By 17 December, and perhaps earlier, the *Parnassus Packet* was discontinued.

In the latter part of October the government returned to Philadelphia, and Dennie took up his residence at the capital of the Nation. Philadelphia, with a population of 70,000 in 1800, was the largest, most beautiful, and in many respects most advanced city in the United States. Its market, prison, and water and lighting systems were models for the rest of the country. As a center of national communication, being the chief starting point for western traffic, *via* the Cumberland road, it had not begun to be rivalled by New York. Its manufactures were extensive and important. Under the leadership of men like Franklin, Rittenhouse, and Rush, it had long been preeminent in scientific investigation and in medicine. It had the only important public library in the country. As a literary center it then excelled Boston, New York, and Baltimore, and contained a number of gifted young men who, with true American versatility, were beginning successful professional careers, and writing verse, essays, satires, or plays as a diversion. Three short-lived magazines of considerable merit, the *Columbian Magazine* (1786-1792), the *American Museum* (1787-1792), and the *Weekly Magazine* (1798-1799), offered an outlet for their effusions. The two important American men of letters, Charles Brockden Brown and Philip Freneau, were intimately connected with Philadelphia. The city has always attracted to itself the brilliant talents of other cities and lands, whose accomplishments have reflected credit upon it. Franklin, Robert Morris,

Mathew Carey, Thomas Paine, and Jared Ingersoll, are only a few examples of this class during the eighteenth century. Moreover, as the national capital until July, 1800, Philadelphia was thronged with temporary residents representing the wit, eloquence, and sagacity of the entire country, together with a number of brilliant foreigners, like Talleyrand and Lafayette, who gave a cosmopolitan air to the city. It was, then, truly the political, intellectual, and social center of the United States, into which, from a quiet rural hamlet in New Hampshire, Dennie found himself transported in the autumn of 1799.

As Pickering's secretary Dennie probably had a pleasant life, though he must have been sadly unfit for the assiduity and attention to routine duties which the position required. Pickering was, however, a scholar and a gentleman, an intense Federalist, whose advocacy of the extreme views of Hamilton, rather than the more impartial course of President Adams, procured his dismissal from the Cabinet, in May, 1799; and their community of tastes and political sentiments made him and Dennie close and lasting friends. Dennie's position, too, as well as his personal acquaintance with the President and several of the New England members of Congress, gained for him ready access to the official and diplomatic circles of the capital. His income of $1,000 a year, secured for him by his friends by a special grant of Congress,[1] entitled him to live elegantly and to pay his Walpole debts.[2] In addition he had a small income from the *Farmer's Museum*, for which he had agreed to write. His contribution, beyond political items from the seat of government, was, however, probably small. He wrote the introductory essay of a series to be called *Proteus*, which appeared in the *Museum* 23 December, 1799, and gives some account of his education as a child at home. The two or three essays which followed were from another hand.

A third source of income was Fenno's *Gazette of the United States*, to which Dennie began contributing political articles during the last week in October. The following month, on 8 and 16 November, appeared the *Lay Preacher of Pennsylvania*, in two remarkable sermons on the devastations of the yellow

1. Letter to his mother, 6 Sept., 1799.
2. Letter to Roger Vose, 7 Feb., 1800.

fever in Philadelphia, using the texts, "Their widows are increased to me above the sand of the sea; I have brought upon them against the mothers of the young men a spoiler at noonday," and "These be the days of Vengeance"; in which the distresses and afflictions of the city, and indeed the world at large, were declared to be the result of men's sins, and especially of the frantic madnesses of the advocates of "liberty, equality, fraternity." Seven more sermons by the *Lay Preacher of Pennsylvania* appeared before the end of the year, including one on fathers, one on mothers, and two on marriage. That of 21 December, 1799, on the text, "Who is left among us that saw this house in her first glory? and how do you see it now? is it it not in your eyes, in comparison of it, nothing?" voices the sentiment of a bereaved nation, mourning for the dead Washington.[1] Together with these were published a number of his old sermons, for the purpose, he stated, of acquainting the Philadelphia public with their merits, with a view to issuing later a weekly pamphlet, to contain the essays, together with much and various literature, derived from original writers, at home, or from the purest sources abroad.[2] In the same announcement he told of the success of the *Lay Preacher* in New Hampshire, and enumerated a number of imitators, using the titles *Occasional Preacher*, *Gay Preacher*, *Itinerant Preacher*, and others.[3] Occasional items appeared also from the "Shop of Messrs. Colon and Spondee."

During the first year at Philadelphia, Dennie lived with William Meredith, a young lawyer of excellent connections, taste, and breeding. He was a Federalist in politics, an Episcopalian in religion, a college graduate and a lawyer, and a lover of letters, in all of which respects he was qualified for Dennie's esteem and affection. Simpson's *Lives of Eminent Philadelphians* describes his deportment as courteous and conciliating, his hospitality as refined and gracious, his opinions as firm

1. The *Washingtoniana*, published by Christopher Sower, at Baltimore, 1800, quotes this sermon from the *Lay Preacher*, "couched in words so energetic and expressive, that among the different tributes paid to the memory of Washington, this deserves particular notice."
2. *Gazette of the U. S.*, 12 Dec., 1799.
3. I have not unearthed any of these "Preachers," which may have been fictitious. The *Old Colony Lay Preacher* appeared in several numbers of the *Columbian Centinel*, Boston, during the early part of 1799.

but tolerant. "His language was clean, chaste, and elegant, his person commanding and graceful, and there was finish in all he did or said." His equally admirable wife was Gertrude Gouverneur Ogden. Robert Walsh, a Philadelphia writer, has said of her,[1] "She was a mother, capable of fully educating her children of both sexes—a wife, serving as the efficient counsellor and partner of her husband in all his duties and cares—a friend, anxiously reflecting, judging, feeling, acting, for those whom she honored with her regard." William and Gertrude Meredith were perhaps Dennie's most constant friends during his life in Philadelphia, even after their increasing family made it inexpedient for him to remain an inmate of their household. Though he was never to be a father, Dennie must have loved children. Mrs. Meredith in writing to Mrs. Dennie, 13 June, 1814, about an intended visit of her daughter Gertrude to Massachusetts, said: "You will see in her one of his little darlings—the prattling companion of his solitary hours fifteen years ago, and a child whose education he more than half directed—one whose musick and song always chased his melancholy for the last years of his life."

Dennie's circumstances at this period may perhaps be best expressed by quoting entire a long letter to his parents, summarizing his life in Philadelphia from the time of his arrival there. It was written during one of his father's brief intervals of sanity. The letter is rambling and not carefully written, and lacks already the vivacity and light spirits of his earlier correspondence.

Philadelphia, May 20, 1800.
Office of the Secretary of State.

My dear Friends,

Your letter of the 28 April, indited by a *Father* and *Mother*, was gladly received, and was doubly dear to my heart.

The urgency of affairs prevents the writing of letters to my best friends. Since my establishment here, I have been much occupied. You read in the public papers of last Autumn that I was appointed "*Inspector of Records.*" This was a curious example of the absurdity and inaccuracy of Gazette statements. No such office exists. Private and confidential Secretary to the

1. In his *Didactics*, Philadelphia, 1836.

Secy. of State is my designation, and my official duty demands the indispensable attendance of six hours daily in the ordinary routine of business; and, on special occasions, the service of the day, nay that too of the evening is required. I submit it to your reason whether or not much leisure is left for private purposes. Agreeably to my engagement, I should certainly have written to you on the road, but, by a sinister accident, I sprained the thumb bones of my better hand and was incapable, for some time after my arrival at Trenton, of tracing a legible character. To atone, in some measure, for this epistolary silence, so unpleasant to you and so binding on myself, I directed Fenno to send you regularly his Gazette. Hence you would perceive that I was in health, and in action.

I fairly and honorably by my *own spirit* and by my *own exertions,* without patronage of *friends,* as the *cant* of this world miscalls them, and without servility and sacrifices of my own, rose from the mud and dust and ashes of village obscurity to my present situation. Col. Pickering, who was my Principal, gave me a liberal employment and the highest degree of his confidence. We are intimate friends. He is suddenly displaced, but my Situation remains unaltered provided a Federal administration continue. If Mr. Jefferson come into power, it will then be time for a man of my feelings and principles to abandon public life, and, perhaps, even my country. It is uncertain, at present, who will succeed to the Department of State, in the room of the shamefully and fatally banished Pickering. A man singularly well principled; of a pure heart, a clear head, direct views, a faithful and laborious servant and an ancient gentleman! The office is now in Commission. Its duties are executed by the Atty. General of the U. S.[1] The President immediately on the dismissal of Col. P. requested all the officers of the bureau to *continue* and *discharge their duties as usual.* Therefore I shall hold my place and emoluments, at least for the present and until next Autumn or Spring I see what turn the politics of our Country take.

I have a large and airy office to myself, and pleasantly situated in the centre of this City. My duties though claiming much time, and of a dry and diplomatic character, are useful and honorable. I am well accommodated with lodgings at the house of William

---

1. Charles Lee, of Virginia.

Meredith, Esq., a lawyer of distinction and unsullied reputation here. His family is small and correct. I have convenient apartments, and the comfortable aid of a servant man, and, as you perceive, still retain some hankering after those agreeable Gypsies, the Muses. My *works* will appear, in the course of Six months, and in great pomp, as Swift says. I, at length, after various literary mortifications and disappointments, have the satisfaction of publishing my books in the *Capital,* and of guarding myself *absolutely* against risque and some *small hope* of a partial remuneration of my labour. Had not the *Revolution* happened; had I continued a subject to the King, had I been fortunately born in *England* or resided in the City of London for the last 7 years, my fame would have been enhanced; and as to fortune I feel a moral certainty that I should have acquired by my writings 3 or 4 thousand pounds. But, in this *Republic,* this region covered with the Jewish and canting and cheating descendants of those men, who during the reign of a Stuart, *fled away* from the claims of the Creditor, from the tithes of the Church, from their allegiance to their Sovereign and from their duty to their God, what can men of liberality and letters expect but such polar icy treatment, as I have experienced?—

My health is such as you would expect to find in the descendant of infirm parents and in a man of *quick vibrations,* as Dr. Hartley calls them, and of a studious life. My body is, as of yore, rather feeble, but I trust that my mind has rectitude, and displays useful energies, and I *reverently hope* that the Supreme Source of Intelligence will still furnish those mental gifts, with which he has been generously pleased to endow me. It will be agreeable to you, I presume, to listen to these minute details, and to make these miniature pictures of my private habits and history. I am still a Bachelor, of 32, and, I believe, a *determined* one. I have no attachments, nor no intentions. I believe I may justly call myself an *old* bachelor; as I wear my hair short, in the form of the clerical tonsure, I can with propriety say, like Father Jerome in the drama

> "Few the locks that now I own,
> And the few I have are *grey.*"

For my *Mother's* sake, who I thought would be pleased with the possession of this memorial of me, I sat at Trenton for my

Picture. I have made various attempts to forward it. But the transportation is difficult. I hope soon to send it to Lexington. It is executed in Crayons, by a *British* artist of reputation, and gives a tolerable resemblance of my features—I am treated here with much attention and respect, and, known as a professed man of letters and as *Commis* of the Bureau, I have a ready passport into good company—

On Sundays, when not too fatigued with the labor of the week or not occupied in writing Lay Preachers, or political essays, I go *conscientiously* to *Church* and listen to a *perfect* Liturgy and sound Sermon from the lips of Bishop White— You will be happy to know, what I can *truly*, and *religiously assert*, that my long and assiduous habit of investigating the Sacred writings has ended with me, as with Mr. Locke, and Grotius and Sir William Jones, in a perfect and settled conviction of their Divine origin, and matchless utility to mankind. In a concluding number of my Essays I shall add the testimony of one more *Layman* to the verity, beauty, and use of the Christian Religion. The Bible is truly a blessed book and happy and safe is that man, whose conduct, as far as mortal imbecility will allow, comports with that most salutary doctrine contained in the Gospels. The regular fulfilment of the prophecies is, particularly at the present hour, a mighty proof of Isaiah and his associates being divinely inspired. He, who adverts to the horrible convulsions of *subverted* France; the downfall of the Papal power; the moral darkness of whole nations; the total eclipse of whole orders; the "gold, that has become *dim*," and "the most fine gold that is *changed*"; *Kings* bound in chains, and their *Nobles* in fetters of Iron; the *Keepers* of the house trembling, and the *Strong men* bowing themselves; the Pitcher broken at the *fountain*, and the wheel broken at the *Cistern;* He, I repeat, who does not perceive that all this has been foretold by Ancient Holiness and Wisdom is blinder, than

"The poor beetle, that we tread upon."

I pass from topic to topic, in a desultory and miscellaneous style, because Matter presses upon me, and because I am anxious to etch as many little views and sketches of my situation and feelings, as possible. I wish, if I may employ metaphors from the Art of the Painter to *crayon out* an extensive view, and to *group* many objects.

During the intervals of official duty, I have found time to acquire a tolerable knowledge of the French language, and a smattering of the Spanish. I have, by very assiduous application to official dispatches, made the diplomatic style familiar, and have improved myself in the knowledge of our political relations, Foreign and Domestic. Amid these grave cares, I have found time, subjected to all the deductions of delicate Health, and flagging spirits, to read and write considerably, and sometimes to go into company and "see the Dolphins play." I have dined and talked much at the table of Sir R. Liston, the British Ambassador here. He is a courteous and well informed Man, conversant with most of the Courts of Europe, fertile in anecdote, and of various and well disciplined Knowledge. As he adds affability to his acquirements his conversation, of course, was very pleasant to me. Mrs. Liston is a plain Scotswoman of manners simple, and air unconstrained, as those of Mrs. Parkhurst or any of the Parish ladies, in your neighborhood. She has the strong understanding, and clear sighted Sagacity, for which *my Countrymen*, the natives of North Britain, are so remarkable. I have been much amused both by her *Provincial* dialect, which to my ear is very sweet, and by her shrewd and good humored observations.

Though I repair often to the houses of our officers, and of people of fashion, and briefly amuse myself with the pageantry of parade, and the prattle of an evening party, yet not *much* of precious Time is *sported* with in this way. I seek learned Strangers and Men of Letters, and wherever Information is exhibited, I am a Spectator. One of my frequent associates is Parson Abercrombie, the Rector of St. Peter's Church, a Scholar, Gentleman, and Christian. Dr. Andrews, the Vice Provost of the University, frequently gives me a Supper in his Convent, and a Mr. Edward Pennington, of Quaker connexions, sound principles, plentiful fortune, and in literature a sort of Mecenas, is very kind and hospitable to me. The British merchants are attentive to me and I find them very sensible and honest men. Indeed, I take this opportunity, if you do not already know this prejudice, to express my strong, well grounded, and settled attachment to

Englishmen and English principles. Independently of my family benefits and favours, I can declare with emphasis, that the best friends I have proved for many years are either Englishmen, or men of British attachment, partialities, generosity, and humor. Therefore for a selfish and Pharisaical reason I have a strong motive to love the Nation. Putting this aside, the English character, abstractly considered, is the most honest, the most generous, the most frank and liberal, and foul is that day in our Calendar, and bitterly are those *patriotic,* selfish and Indian traitors to be cursed who instigated the *wretched* populace to declare the 4th day of July, 1776, a day of Independence. We are now tasting the bitter fruit of that baleful tree, which our "forefathers at Plymouth" planted, which Sam Adams and Deacon Newell watered, and to which the natural malignity of our rascal populace has given the increase. Our government is so weak that it is powerless to hold out much longer against the assaults of Faction; and another war with Great Britain, and civil commotions are now near at hand. To your deluded *True* Americans, to your Picarooning pedlers, and to the simpletons, who believe that a republican government can subsist in this extensive region, a political Paul might indeed stretch forth his expostulating hand, and again rear his warning voice, with a "Sirs, ye should have listened to me, and not have *loosed from Crete,* and gained all this *harm* and loss." But I shall weary you with these political reflexions, and, therefore, return to my narrative. By the information of a friend, just returned from the East Indies, I learn that my "Tablet" has been reprinted at Calcutta and Madras, and thus I, and I trust you, have the satisfaction of understanding that my writings have reached Asia. I shall soon make trial of their fate in *Europe.* Some knowledge of my books has already been conveyed to England and at the bar of London Criticism they will soon appear, and, in the clerkly words of the old law, "Stand upon their deliverance." I have strong reason to anticipate a mild and equitable Sentence, from the concurrent opinions of Englishmen in America to whom it is just and grateful for me to ascribe much of the encouragement and approbation they have received here.

During the winter, I used to go, sometimes, to the Theatre and recreate myself with the mimic scene. But to this place of amusement I resorted less than you would suppose. The Comedians here are in the main, very indifferent, and were so much in the habit of acting the vile trash of one Kotzebue, a Jacobin German philosopher and atheist, that I shunned the stage. Whenever, and that was seldom, they selected a play of my favorite Shakespeare, or any drama, the offspring of British Sense and Virtue, I went with alacrity and listened to Cooper and Mrs. Merry with delight.

Pray write a few lines as soon as convenient. Mark any thing that is memorable. Live happily as you can in this unpleasant world. Cherish *Hope* and tranquil emotions. Believe that I love and respect you, and that, though wayfaring through the wilderness I have "to fight with beasts at Ephesus" I shall "overcome at the last" and that though "naked in the amphitheatre of life" I shall not dishonour myself or you.

Most affectionately yr's

Joseph Dennie.

A little older, surely, is the man who writes this, prematurely gray about the temples, his New England wig and breeches discarded for a more commonplace tonsure and attire, a little more soured upon the world, a little more rigid in his opinions, religious, political, and literary, and more caustic in his expression of them; yet still hopeful, still witty, and upon occasion gay, still a delightful companion to divines, diplomats, and ladies alike.

His political surroundings, and his conception of the political situation of the country are better expressed in a letter to his old friend, Vose, dated 7 February, 1800:—

"I frequently resort to the President's, a good man but somewhat obstinate, and, growing old, a sort of political dimness has ensued, which prevents his discernment from perceiving the miserable delusions and dangerous folly of any connexion with deranged France.

"Of Mr. Jefferson I know nothing; and in this I am not singular. From his sullen and retired habits, few know more than myself. I have frequently listened to the sophistry and watched the Montoni[1] features of the Genevan Gallatin. He

1. Montone, a character in Mrs. Anne Radcliffe's *Mysteries of Udolpho.*

is flattered and followed by a desperate crowd, whose names are too obscure, and whose bodies and minds are too contemptible, for the pen to describe. The Connecticut members form a sort of phalanx by themselves. They are gregarious, and despise or neglect most of their compeers. These men are not meanly furnished with the gifts of wit and wisdom; there are others of the Southern and Middle Interests who are able and active, but the brute mass, the men, who are told by the head, like all populace, are despicably mean, weak, and miserable. Such is the filthiness of some of their persons, and such the stupidity of some of the faces in the lower house of your National Assembly, that one would expect to see them following a dust cart, or rising from a chimney, and not even admitted into a scene of legislation.

"I think it by no means an improbable event that some civil convulsion will be felt in the heart of our republic. The ground is sometimes in motion under our feet, and the Federal edifice is not so stable but it may be racked if not overthrown. Should your political castle totter or decay you will find that those British builders which we have rejected, may yet be found necessary to repair our work, perhaps lay the first stone of a new corner. If the people discourage *royal* establishments, become *habitually* jealous of rulers, divide into factions, and pant for 1776, I would not give, Sir, a pinch of snuff for as much good Federalism as 16 or 32 *States* can furnish."

Dark and distrustful sentiments were these, bordering upon treason, but such were entertained by many sober-minded and conscientious Federalists in the North. The deep suspicion and bitter hostility with which the two parties then regarded each other is hard to comprehend now. Today the Republican who goes to the polls knows that the Democrats are not leagued together in secret to overthrow the government and betray the power into the hands of an ignorant and malicious rabble. The Democrat likewise realizes that the Republicans if they are victorious will not turn over the resources of the nation to British hands or endeavor to set up a monarchy on American soil. Whichever wins, the republic is too well established to be greatly shaken. Such was not the case in 1800. After only eleven years of existence under the Constitution, the government was still decidedly an experiment. For three administrations the power had been in the hands of "the rich, the well-born, and the able." To most of those who had supported these administrations the very probable contingency of the control going over to "the desperate crowd" who followed Jefferson, Gallatin, and Madison seemed nothing less than a national calamity. So thought the Social System which dominated New England, the consolidated lawyers, divines, educators, and merchants who made up the class from which Dennie came. The frightful excesses attendant upon the French Revolution made the law-abiding property owners of the northern states shudder with horror and dread, and to them the Democrats were American Jacobins and revolutionists, a belief fostered by the avowed mutual friendliness of France and Jefferson's party. On the other side the distrust of English and aristocratic influence was equally intense and equally well—or ill—grounded.

At Philadelphia, the seat of government, the conflict of divergent views was waged with most bitterness. In the House of Representatives, on 22 January, 1798, in the heat of debate, Matthew Lyon, Representative from Vermont, spat in the face of Roger Griswold, of Connecticut, and several physical encounters between the two ensued. Political duels and affrays of a more serious nature were of frequent occurrence. Such a one was that in Fourth Street between Benjamin Franklin Bache, editor of the *Aurora*, and John Ward Fenno, son of John Fenno, editor of the *Gazette of the United States*. A later editor of the *Aurora*, William Duane, for criticizing the troops engaged in suppressing the so-called Fries Rebellion, in Northampton County, was attacked at his home by a party of the officers concerned, and severely beaten, after having fought until he "could neither see nor hear nor stand."[1] A savage newspaper war, in which the bitterest personalities, the most unfounded charges, and the most pointed coarseness were freely engaged in, had been waged for some time, chiefly by Bache's *Aurora* and James Carey's *Recorder* on the Democratic side, and Fenno's *Gazette of the U. S.* and Cobbett's *Porcupine's Gazette* on the Federalist. Such coarseness and savagery of invective were partially justified by the usage of the British

1. Letter from Duane to Stephen R. Bradley, 10 Nov., 1808.

press; in fact most of the men engaged had had their training abroad. Duane and the Careys, James and Matthew, were Irishmen; and Cobbett, perhaps the most virulent of all, was an Englishman. The Fennos, father and son, were New England men, nearly the first of a long line who were to exert a powerful influence on the newspaper press of Philadelphia, New York, and Baltimore.

The death of Bache and the elder Fenno of the fever in 1798 left Duane, John Ward Fenno, and Cobbett the principal figures in this newspaper warfare. William Duane (1760-1835), whose interesting life has recently been sketched in a very poorly written and peculiar book,[1] was the son of Irish Catholic parents, born in northern New York, and educated in Ireland. After some experience as a printer in London, as editor of a newspaper at Calcutta—whence he was forcibly transported for injudicious criticisms—and as parliamentary reporter for the *General Advertiser* (now the *London Times*) he came to Philadelphia in 1796, and for a short time conducted the *True American,* an Anti-federalist paper. Soon he became one of the editors of the *Aurora,* which he conducted with great vigor and spirit. In 1801, three years after the death of his wife and Mrs. Bache's husband, the two survivors married, and the paper passed into Duane's hands. Under Bache and Duane it had attacked the administration at every point, and was considered the most sensational sheet in the country, though in no respect except partisan virulence could it compete with the refined sensationalism of the modern press. With 7,000 subscribers it had in 1802 the largest circulation in the country, and it was long a powerful factor in national politics.[2] Duane was constantly engaged in libel suits and political quarrels, as was William Cobbett (1762-1835) better known as *Peter Porcupine.* Cobbett, the son of a Surrey farmer, self-educated, after spending eight years in garrison in Nova Scotia, and another year in London agitating an advance in the pay of British soldiers, appeared in Philadelphia in 1792, in the capacity of tutor in French and political pamphleteer. He was violently pro-British and anti-French, and his utterances, such as the *Observa-*

1. *William Duane,* by Allen C. Clark, Washington, 1905.
2. James Wilson, grandfather of President Woodrow Wilson, was for some time employed with Duane on the *Aurora.* See William Bayard Hale, *Woodrow Wilson: The Story of His Life.,* pp. 4-11.

tions on Priestley's Emigration, were praised by the *Anti-Jacobin* in England. In 1796 he started a bookstore and issued a monthly pamphlet, the *Censor.* Some idea of the pugnacity of the man may be gained from his custom of exhibiting in his bookstore windows the pictures of nobles, princes, and kings, not excluding George III—"in short every picture that I thought likely to excite rage in the enemies of Great Britain." In March, 1797, he began the publication of a daily Federalist and pro-British paper, *Porcupine's Gazette and United States Daily Register.* In this for three years he carried the free utterance of the press to its full extreme in his bold and not always truthful attacks upon all persons and things democratic and un-British. The savagery and license of these writings won him many enemies among Federalists as well as Democrats. He went out of his way to attack the bleeding practices of Doctor Rush, was sued by the doctor, and in 1799 was compelled to pay damages of $5,000. His property was seized for payment and he left Philadelphia. At New York he delivered a few parting shots in the *Rush-Light* before departing for England in June, 1800. John Fenno (1751-1798) was a native of Boston and for several years a school-master there. He moved to New York, and when that city was the capital of the country, established there the *Gazette of the United States.* He moved with the seat of government to Philadelphia the following year. The *Gazette,* which was a semi-official organ, supported the Federalist administrations of Washington and Adams. After his death his son, John Ward Fenno (1778-1802), U. of P., 1795, then only nineteen, carried on the paper in his stead. Though he inherited his father's principles and abilities, the paper declined for a time, for which reason the successful young editor of the *Farmer's Museum* was asked to co-operate in its management.

For Dennie the years 1799 and 1800 were years of plans and prospectuses. The *Gazette* for 26 December, 1799, announced that, if the wealthy and wise would lend their support, the paper should appear in a revised and enlarged form, as "*The Gazette of the United States,* etc. A paper auxiliary to sound principles, by *Oliver Oldschool, Esq.*" The size of the New Year's subscription list was to determine whether or not the project should be undertaken. At the same time a small weekly pamphlet for the breakfast table, to contain "moral and amusing essays, and elegant literature in general," and be called the *Lay Preacher's Magazine,* was proposed, if sufficient encouragement were shown. The subscription list did not show the required increase, and neither project was carried out.

Dennie contributed extensively to the *Gazette,* however, and entered merrily into the war with Duane and the Democrats. The paper, which was a daily, and rather dull, with the habit still preserved by some Philadelphia publications, of covering the outside pages with advertising matter and printing the news on the inside, became decidedly more brisk, as well as literary. As an example of newspaper repartee in 1800, the following remark about the editor of the *New York Sun* may be quoted,[1] "The Editor of the *Sun* is a blockhead, and an ass and a True American.[2] I would have the sapient animal thrown at once into the *Poultry Compter* for his better information." Duane was "the gin-drinking pauper who is said to conduct Bache's paper,"[3] and of one of his writings it was observed, "This is a paragraph *such as* a fool would write, and *such* as Duane writes, whenever he is urged by the enlivening influence of GIN to write at all."[4]

The Lay Preacher of Pennsylvania continued to republish his old sermons and to write occasional new ones. Two of the latter, for 25 January and 15 March, voice Dennie's disapproval of the vanities of fashion, cosmetics, and other feminine follies of the capital. The *Political Portraits* and other squibs from the *Shop of Colon and Spondee* which had appeared in the *Farmer's Museum* were continued here, as were *An Author's Evenings* and the department of *Literary Intelligence.* Under this heading occur frequent references to Charles Brockden Brown, novelist, praising his *Edgar Huntly,* lamenting his ill-health and poverty, and censuring him for following the German romanticists and William Godwin. Tyler's *Algerine Captive,* which had appeared in 1799, is also praised, but for most American writings Dennie had nothing but scorn.

The right and wrong sides of Dennie's contemptuous attitude

1. *Gazette of the U. S.*, 27 Nov., 1799.
2. A name adopted by one faction of the Democratic-Republicans.
3. *Gazette of the U. S.*, 2 Dec., 1799.
4. *Gazette of the U. S.*, 27 Mar., 1800.

toward American literary productions can, I believe, be determined by the perusal of a couple of extracts. The first appeared in the *Columbian Centinel,* Boston, 19 October, 1799, and was entitled, "To the Editor of the *Farmer's Museum and Lay Preacher's Gazette.*" It was mentioned in the *Gazette of the U. S.* as an "illiberal and scurrilous attack upon the celebrated *Dennie,*" but it appears to be rather a dispassionate and sensible statement of facts. The following passages are quoted:

"I conceive that a great part of your uneasiness arises from this circumstance—that you have *written a book.* This book was neither printed so well, nor circulated so rapidly, as you could have desired. I wish, in my soul, that Spotswood, Dobson or Thomas would give us an elegant edition: Or, if this should not be done, that it might be reprinted in England, and a whole cargo sent over, in judgment for our neglect. However, that we may not be too severe upon our country, I would ask you, Sir, whether with all your literary talents and labors, you would have been sure of acquiring more fame and patronage in England than you have in America? Has it never been the case that geniuses as great as yours have been exhausted in cheerless poverty, even in that country to which you refer us as a pattern of everything that is generous and noble? Authors do talk of living in garrets—of feeding on cobwebs, etc. This phraseology, if I mistake not, originated in London. At least it has been frequently used there.

"On the whole, I am convinced, that if our country be erroneous either in religion or politics; or deficient in literary taste and patronage, the time is not far distant when she will be more correct, even should you abate something of your zeal and perseverance. Sarcasm will never convert dullness into ingenuity, nor will genius be bullied into exercise."

This sets forth the wrong side of Dennie's attitude, the pique, the disappointed vanity, the illusion that elsewhere all things are as they should be, and the resultant unthinking condemnation of things American. The partial justification of his censure, however, is well set forth in a paragraph from the *Gazette of the U. S.,* 29 April, 1800. The following ridiculously florid and stilted account of the launching of the frigate *President* at New York was reprinted verbatim from the *New York Advertiser:*

"Yesterday morning, at 10 o'clock precisely, the Daughter of the Forest and the Heir of the Ocean, embraced, in peerless Majesty, her destined element. The order, beauty, and godlike simplicity of the scene, the pen of man cannot depict. The beholders alone can know the mingled sensations of Pleasure, of Joy, and of National Glory, that the scene excited. The harbor on both sides for some distance was thronged with vessels whose decks were covered with admiring beholders. The neighboring hills, housetops, and even the shores of Long Island were crowded with spectators whose acclamations echoed the Glory of America. Several Artillery and Volunteer Companies, according to the arrangements of General Hughes, paraded near the shore, and after she entered the water, closed the scene with a feu-de-joie. On the whole, we think it the most noble scene ever exhibited on this side of the Atlantic. Her construction, timber, and workmanship reflect much honor upon her builders, and great merit is due to the judgment of Mr. Cheeseman, under whose direction she moved with the most perfect ease and harmony, and with a noble Bow, bade the Land ADIEU."

A very clever mock-serious criticism of this paragraph, line by line, occupied two columns of the *Gazette* and concluded with the following paragraph:

"After having, at some length, in a style of burlesque and banter, thus analysed this curious paragraph, it may seem impertinent to close the subject gravely. But the subject is of importance, and deserves the sober consideration of all, who aspire to write and converse with purity and simplicity. This paragraph was not selected for the purpose of *exclusive* animadversion. We have no particular spleen against this individual composition. It was picked up from a similar mass of writings in America, as a type of a very common, current and utterly vicious style, at once the fashion and disgrace of the family. Criticism is useful, and shall speak, though her voice 'grate harsh thunder' to the ear of the *true patriots*, bombastic editors, fustian orators, college boys and *id genus omne*. Our reproach and ridicule are intended to reform. America has indulged this rant too much. It is time it should be ridiculed and reasoned away. We *must choose this day whom we will serve*. We have the 'Moses and the Prophets' of language. We have Dean *Swift,* Dr. *Robertson* and Sir William *Jones.* We have too the miserable remnants of Cromwell's Puritanism, the Babylonish dialect of 'forefathers at Plymouth,' the red lattice phrases of acquitted felons, and the 'hissing hot' speeches from many a *town meeting.* Of these deformities let us be ashamed, and strive to emulate a diction pure, simple, expressive and English."

The most inchoate and at the same time exuberant period of our national history produced a great amount of blatant verbiage such as that quoted from the *Advertiser,* which, to a man of classical instincts and training, seemed worthy only of uncompromising censure. The defect of Dennie's criticism of it is that in his nervous irritation and his settled spite against republican institutions, he often overshot the mark and became as ridiculous as were the objects of his satire.

In the meantime Dennie's literary ambitions were active enough. By the advice of Cobbett,[1] the intended publisher of the long-desired edition of the *Lay Preacher,* the publication had been deferred until the winter of 1799. By the winter Cobbett had lost his suit and relinquished his printing and bookselling trade; so the scheme fell through. In the *Gazette of the U. S.,* 30 April, 1800, however, there appeared proposals for "An Original American Work, *The Lay Preacher,*" to appear in two volumes, royal octavo, to be published by subscription, price, four dollars, two payable upon signing. It was to be issued by John Ward Fenno, and sold by William Cobbett, New York, James White, Boston, and many other booksellers in various places, including London and Edinburgh. Earlier than this, on 29 March, the *Gazette* had informed its readers, under the heading of Literary Intelligence:

"It is understood that the Author of the *Lay Preacher* proposes to publish a liberal translation of the works of Sallust, the Roman historian."

Since the Americans were too much engrossed with other affairs to study "the beautiful reliques of ancient wisdom," he proposed to have it published by Strahan, Cadell & Davis, booksellers, London.[2] On 27 May appeared proposals for a

1. Contained in a letter to Dennie, 30 Jan., 1799.
2. I have found no further mention of this project.

third work, *The Farrago, or Essays Gay and Grave,* by the author of the *Lay Preacher,* to be published by a third bookseller, Asbury Dickins, of Philadelphia, at a price of two dollars. With these three promising irons in the fire, Dennie's outlook must have seemed to him very promising indeed, but he was doomed, as he had been so often before, to bitter disappointment. Except in a limited classical and diplomatic circle, he was not widely known in Philadelphia; Americans were interested in other matters, rather than letters; and his subscription lists were not filled. When one considers the relative merit of Dennie's essays and his repeated disappointments in the patronage of his countrymen, one realizes the element of justice in the chagrined castle-builder's later tirades against the American system of publishing literary works by subscription.

Cobbett's judgment was perhaps right when he inquired impatiently, "Why will you, then, continue to 'chop block with a razor'?"[1] Three letters from Cobbett dated from New York, 14 April, 1 May, and 7 May, as well as the long letter to his parents, 20 May, 1800, are interesting as indicating that Dennie had considered leaving America for England with Cobbett in June. The latter was urgent in his invitation, painting radiant pictures of Dennie's literary future in the British metropolis, but Dennie hesitated, waiting to hear from the results of his proposals for the *Lay Preacher.* Cobbett wished him to publish it in Europe. "The doubts which you appear to entertain," he wrote, 14 April, "do, I must confess, astonish me. The prospect is so fair; the offers I make so advantageous, that your hesitation makes me fear that you are still too much attached to home, to be prevailed on to leave it." His third letter accepts Dennie's decision as final, assures him of his friendship, and promises to sell the *Lay Preacher* in London. He sailed from New York in the beginning of June, 1800.

On 12 May, Pickering was removed from office as Secretary of State by President Adams, and John Marshall replaced him in the cabinet. At Adams' request Dennie and other subordinates of the department retained their places, but the young secretary's incapacity is shown in a letter from Pickering to Marshall, 27 June, 1800:[2]

---

1. Letter to Dennie, 1 May, 1800.
2. *Pickering Papers*, Mass. Hist. Soc. Collections, Vol. XIII, No. 557.

"Mr. Dennie will have the honor to present to you this letter. Desirous of being at the seat of government, and to be relieved from the drudgery of editing a newspaper for a very inadequate compensation, his friend Gen'l Morris recommended him for a place in the department of State. But I cannot, because I ought not, to conceal from you, that Mr. Dennie's habits and literary turn—I should rather say, his insatiable appetite for knowledge, useful as well as ornamental, render his service as a clerk less productive than the labours of many dull men.

"He still wishes, however, to renew his attendance in the department of State, to make a fresh essay to serve his country, provide for his support, and promote his ultimate views of rendering, in another line, more important benefits to his fellow-citizens and to mankind. He therefore, being a perfect stranger to you, has asked of me a letter of introduction. You will be gratified by the proofs he will give you of an enlightened mind, and with his admirable manners; and I am sure you will be inclined to the most liberal indulgence of his laudable proposition."

Dennie's connection with the Department of State, however, at the new offices in Washington, was probably not renewed. In April Fenno advertised the *Gazette of the U. S.* for sale, and in May it was bought by Caleb Parry Wayne. About the time of the transfer[1] a long announcement in Dennie's well-known style, declared, "The editor of this *Gazette* is happy to inform his Subscribers, and the Public, in general," that the paper would continue in its upright Federalist principles, an implacable enemy to Jefferson and Jacobinism. Wayne is said to have been a printer in Philadelphia. In January, 1798, he had appeared in Boston as the publisher of a Federalist paper, known successively as the *Daily Advertiser* and the *Federal Gazette*, which lasted only four months.[2] A paper conducted by him was sure to be violent in its partisan attitude and scurrilous in its attacks. On Saturday, 21 June, the office of the *Gazette* was removed to 65 South Front Street, probably the site of Wayne's printing house. On the preceding day it was announced that, "The Literary and Miscellaneous department in the *Gazette of the U. S.*

1. 14 May, 1800.
2. Buckingham, *Specimens of Newspaper Literature*, Vol. II, pp. 301-307.

will, for the present, be conducted by the sometime Editor of the *Farmer's Museum and Lay Preacher's Gazette*. Care will be employed to procure insertion of papers and paragraphs auxiliary to Government, Morals and Learning." Federalist statesmen, men of liberal and literary leisure, and gentlemen of the bar were asked to render their aid.

The position of literary editor of the *Gazette of the U. S.* Dennie probably retained during the year, and in spite of the large amount of space given to political news during the excitement of a national election, much attention was also paid to literature. The various literary and miscellaneous departments were continued in an interesting manner. Second-hand *Lay Preachers, Colon and Spondee* comments, the *Moral Dispensary* and *Epigrams from The Chirping Cobbler* enlivened the sheet, and a small body of occasional correspondents, using the pen-names "Seneca," "Tristram," "Viator," "Annette Toothbrush," "Manlius," the "Looker-on," and "Lucy Lackaday," was collected. On 9 August, 1800, the ballad *We Are Seven* was printed and its "inimitable simplicity and tenderness" were praised, the supposed author being Mr. Coleridge. Frequent allusions to the "asinine blunderer," Duane, occurred, the cleverest of which follows:[1]—

"The *modest Duane* tells his readers, that he receives letters praising the ABILITY (Quiz) with which the *Aurora* is conducted! This equals Hopkins' Razor Strops."

Attacks were also made upon Joseph Priestley, the English scientist and divine, founder of English Unitarianism, who, after his house was destroyed by a Birmingham mob, had ėmigrated to Pennsylvania, and had begun issuing his *Letters to the Inhabitants of Northumberland*, which advocated principles similar to those of Jefferson.

In the summer of 1800 there appeared anonymously in New York a little-known political pamphlet of some sixty pages, entitled *Desultory Reflections on the New Political Aspects of Public Affairs in the United States of America since the Beginning of the Year 1799.*[1] It bore a long motto beginning,

1. 25 August, 1800.
2. The only copies of this pamphlet and of *Part II* known to me, are in the library of the Boston Athenaeum. In both parts the name of John Ward Fenno has been written in as the author, but the librarian, Mr. C. K. Bolton, does not attach much significance to this fact.

"Keep watch! Make thy loins strong, fortify thy power mightily"; was prefaced by a short *Advertisement* of the writer's purpose, and was "printed for the Author by G. & R. Waite, and Published by J. W. Fenno, No. 141, Hanover Square." It is ascribed by Sabin's *Bibliotheca Americana*, on what authority I know not, to Dennie; and the literary style, the biblical and classical phraseology, and extravagant political ideas stamp it as probably Dennie's work. The action of the southern legislatures in appointing presidential electors pledged to Jefferson, thus precluding a contest and making his choice practically certain, was the cause for alarm. The remedies proposed by the author were as much out of accord with the historical conditions as might be expected. He desired to secure a more centralized government by abolishing the states and replacing them by counties governed by lieutenants. The individual power of the president was to be lessened and an immediate declaration of war against France, with whom naval hostilities had for some time been in progress, was urged. A *Second Part* of the *Desultory Reflections,* with the same signature and in the same style, appeared later in the same year. The motto this time was even more formidable, "And I looked and beheld a pale Horse; and his name that sat on him was Death, and Hell followed with him." The thirty-eight pages of this pamphlet form an arraignment of a federal government as a failure, and a demand for a Constitutional Party and a consolidated government. While most of the contents of these works must seem to us quaint, if not absurd, Dennie should be given credit for seeing the real weakness that existed in a confederation of states, the danger which threatened in 1814, and again in 1832, and eventually tore the Union apart in 1861.

The impending national election was the signal for the appearance, in the *Gazette* and other Federalist papers, of articles like that of 27 September, entitled:

THE GRAND QUESTION STATED

God—and a Religious President: or Jefferson and No God. The likelihood of the election of a Democratic president to succeed Adams stirred the Federalists to the bitterest vituperations against the Jacobin opponents of law, order, and property.

Parson James Abercrombie, of St. Peter's Episcopal Church, an intimate friend of Dennie, spoke from the pulpit in August on the danger of electing "an irreligious chief magistrate," and in answer to criticism, declared that "as a Christian minister he conceived it to be his duty, when the interests of religion and morality were involved, in the prevailing discussions of public policy, publicly and professionally to declare his opinion."[1] In November Jefferson and Burr received seventy-three electoral votes to sixty-five for Adams; and after some Federalist machinations to seat Burr, Jefferson, the arch-Democrat, was elected. Dennie and the Federalists of New England and the North truly believed that "some civil convulsion in the heart of our republic"[2] would follow. "History and their own experience supported them," says Henry Adams. "The clergy and serious citizens of Massachusetts and Connecticut, assuming that the people of America were in the same social condition as the contemporaries of Catiline and the adherents of Robespierre, sat down to bide their time until the tempest of democracy should drive the frail government so near destruction that all men with one voice should call on God and the Federalist prophets for help. The obstinacy of the race was never better shown than when, with the sunlight of the nineteenth century bursting upon them, these resolute sons of granite and ice turned their faces from the light, and smiled in their sardonic way at the folly or wickedness of men who could pretend to believe the world improved because henceforth the ignorant and vicious were to rule the United States and govern the churches and schools of New England."[3]

1. Scharf and Westcott, *History of Philadelphia*, Vol. I, p. 506.
2. Letter to Vose, 7 Feb., 1800.
3. Adams, *History of the U. S., 1801-1805*, Vol. I, pp. 86-87.

CHAPTER VIII

PHILADELPHIA, 1801—"THE PORT FOLIO"

In the *Gazette of the United States*, 16 October, 1800, appeared the first suggestion of a proposed new magazine, to appear shortly. In a long article headed "Literary Intelligence," Dennie recalled his plans at the beginning of the year and their ill success. The projected magazine, he said, was relinquished because only *two subscribers*, in Boston, presented themselves. The concluding paragraph follows:

"But the spirit of literary adventure is not easily quenched, and to the pursuit of his plans almost every projector, whether sanguine, or cautious, is generally constant. Though neither a Gazette *enlarged* nor a Magazine *intended* have seen the light, yet the scheme of a politico-literary miscellany has been silently pursued and perseveringly fostered. In a few days, Mr. ASBURY DICKINS, bookseller of this city, will publish a PROSPECTUS of a new weekly Paper, to be conducted on an extensive and liberal plan, combining, in the manner of the TATLER, Politics with Essays and disquisitions on topics scientific, moral, humorous, and literary. It will appear every Saturday under the title of

The PORT FOLIO."

Asbury Dickins was the son of John Dickins, a noted Methodist preacher, who had been editor of two magazines at Philadelphia, the *Arminian Magazine*, 1789-1790, and the *Methodist Magazine*, 1797-1798. The younger Dickins was a bookseller and publisher at Philadelphia for some time and later for twenty-five years Secretary of the United States Senate. He had become interested in Dennie's projects and had undertaken to publish the *Farrago* for him. The contract for the *Lay Preacher* was probably also turned over to him when the publisher, Fenno, left the city, since a notice in the *Gazette* of 13 October, 1800, directed that all subscription papers for both books be sent to him on or after 1 November. Apparently the subscriptions did not warrant publication, and the works never appeared.

The case of the *Port Folio* was different.[1] The season was auspicious for the establishment of a new well-conducted magazine. The *Weekly Magazine of Original Essays, Fugitive Pieces and Interesting Intelligence*, an ably managed periodical, in which Brown's *Arthur Mervyn* first appeared, came to an abrupt end in June, 1799. Between this date and January, 1801, only two short-lived and unimportant magazines, the *Philadelphia Magazine and Review*, 1799, one volume, and the *Ladies' Museum*, 1800, five numbers, are listed in Smythe's *Philadelphia Magazines and their Contributors, 1741-1850.* Professor Smythe knew thoroughly the gossip, history, and glory of literary Philadelphia, and his work in cataloguing and analizing the periodical writings and writers of the city is a service not lightly to be forgotten—one which has not been adequately done for New York, Boston, or Baltimore. His book is the first source for much of the biographical data of a study such as this. Outside of Philadelphia his interest waned, and his statements are frequently misleading,[2] but the real value of his work should not be lost sight of in discounting the possible overestimation of the literary greatness of his city.

Not only was there no competition for the moment, but there were at hand a large number of enthusiastic lovers of literature eager to contribute to his columns. Philadelphia was, for the time being, the literary as well as the political and social center

---

1. The *Gazette of the U. S.* and the *Farmer's Museum* published in November the following notice, (*Farmer's Weekly Museum*, 10 November, 1800):

"Mr. John West of Boston, bookseller, has issued proposals for publishing a magazine monthly, to be entitled *The Cabinet.* The names of several gentlemen respectable for literary talents are published as contributing to the proposed publication. . . . The names of the literati, who are to furnish the literary part of *The Cabinet* are the Rev. Dr. Morse, Rev. John S. J. Gardiner, Rev. T. M. Harris, George Blake, Esq., Joseph Dennie, Esq., and David Everett, Esq."

No magazine of this title ever appeared.

2. On page 92 of the work named above, for instance, he says, "Fessenden was the last to maintain the fame of the 'Hartford Wits'; and the glory of 'McFingal,' and the 'Conquest of Canaan,' and the 'Anarchiad,' and the 'Political Green-house,' and the 'Echo' faded with the failing of the *Farmer's Museum.*" The Connecticut poets, however, like the Conecticut statesmen, were gregarious. They stood and fell by themselves, and Fessenden and the *Farmer's Museum* had no connection with them, though Dennie courted their assistance, both in the *Museum* and the *Port Folio.* The same confusion appears in Mr. E. L. Bradsher's *Mathew Carey, Editor, Author, and Publisher*, p. 65.

of the country, and the number of young lawyers, doctors, scientists, and divines who varied their professional activities with literary efforts was considerably larger there than at Boston or New York. Hartford likewise was surpassed, though probably no Philadelphian except Brown equalled in the next decade the national reputation of Barlow, Trumbull, and Dwight; and twenty years later a group comprising Percival, Hillhouse, Pierpont, Lydia Sigourney, and Goodrich was to bring Connecticut again into the forefront of national popularity. Among the lawyers of Philadelphia who sought recognition as writers between 1780 and 1810 were the Hopkinsons—Francis, who wrote the *Battle of the Kegs*, and his son Joseph, author of *Hail Columbia;* the Ingersolls, Charles Jared, and Edward, sons of Jared Ingersoll, a Connecticut man; the Peterses, Judge Richard and his son of the same name; William Meredith and his kinsman Gouverneur Morris, of New York; General Thomas Cadwalader; Horace Binney; Richard Rush; Robert Walsh; and the Biddles, Ewings, Sergeants, and Halls. The literary physicians included Benjamin Rush, the hero of the plague of 1793, and Doctors Caspar Wistar, Benjamin Smith Barton, Philip Syng Physick, Thomas Chalkley James, Charles Caldwell and Nathaniel Chapman. Among the preachers who contributed to the literary fame of Philadelphia were William White, Bishop of the Protestant Episcopal Church, James Abercrombie, John Blair Linn, Samuel B. Wylie and "Parson" Weems. The scientists and teachers included within their ranks William Smith, D.D., Provost of the University; Robert Proud, schoolmaster and historian; Alexander Wilson, the ornithologist; George Ord, the naturalist; John Sanderson, teacher and biographer, and many others. The work of three Englishmen, a part of whose lives and activities were spent in the vicinty of Philadelphia, namely Thomas Paine, William Cobbett, and Joseph Priestley, has already been referred to, as have the two Irishmen, Matthew Carey[1] and William Duane, the former important as magazine editor, political essayist, and a political antagonist of Cobbett.

1. Mathew Carey (1760-1839), was long the head of the most flourishing publishing house in America. An excellent sketch of his work and significance, and of the general state of publishing in this country from 1784 to 1839 is given in Bradsher's *Mathew Carey, Editor, Author, and Publisher*.

In addition to these, a small group of writers deserve particular mention. Elizabeth Graeme Ferguson (1739-1801), after a romantic career, one incident of which was a Petrarchan courtship with Nathaniel Evans, the most noteworthy Philadelphia poet of the middle of the eighteenth century, settled down to translating from the French, paraphrasing the Scriptures, and writing excellent letters and journals; and entertained at her father's home at Greene Park the most gifted personages in the country. Alexander Graydon (1752-1818) published in 1811 a delightful account of his career as law student, soldier, and man of leisure, entitled *Memoirs of a Life Chiefly Passed in Philadelphia within the Last Sixty Years.* William Cliffton (1772-1799), the son of a Quaker blacksmith, with political and literary tenets singularly like Dennie's, during his short, consumptive life wrote some lyric verse of unusual promise, as well as vicious political satire in *The Group,* 1793. Dennie would have subscribed heartily to his lines about America:[1]

> "In these cold shades, beneath these shifting skies,
> Where Fancy sickens and where Genius dies—
> Where few and feeble are the Muse's strains,
> And no fine frenzy riots in the veins—
> There still are found a few to whom belong
> The fire of Virtue and the soul of Song,
> Whose kindling ardor still can wake the strings
> When Learning triumps and when Gifford sings."

Another Quaker, Charles Brockden Brown (1771-1810), whose novels were all five written at New York between 1798 and 1801, was nevertheless a native of Philadelphia and too well known to need discussion here.[2] In 1799 and 1800 he conducted at New York a magazine, the *Monthly Magazine and American Review,* which compared favorably with its American predecessors. He later returned to his native city and conducted two good periodicals, the *Literary Magazine and American Register,* 1803-1808, and the *American Register,* 1806-1810. Philip Freneau (1752-1832), was not a Philadelphian, but was at different

1. In the *Epistle to Gifford.*
2. At New York he was a member of the Friendly Club, and intimately associated with Dr. Elihu H. Smith, a friend and correspondent of Dennie's.

times connected with the city; in 1779, when he helped his classmate, H. H. Brackenridge, conduct the *United States Magazine* there; in 1781-1784, when he edited the *Freeman's Journal;* and again in 1791, when in the *National Gazette*, the organ of the Jeffersonian party, he endeavored to rival the virulence of the Federalist satirists.

Men like these had enlivened the pages of several magazines in Philadelphia during the decades from 1780 to 1800, and to them Dennie made his appeal for support in an elaborate and lengthy Prospectus, issued sometime in December, 1800. This Prospectus contained five pages of printed matter, and the sixth was left vacant for subscribers' names. It was "submitted to men of a uence, men of liberality, and men of letters," approximating, as nearly as might be, John Adams' "the rich, the well-born, and the able." The beginning of Dennie's introduction of himself and his paper may well be quoted:

"A young man, once known among village-readers,[1] as the humble historian of the hour, the conductor of a *Farmer's* Museum and a *Lay Preacher's* Gazette, again offers himself to the public as a volunteer-editor. Having, as he conceives, a right to vary, at pleasure, his *fictitious* name, he now, for higher reasons, than any fickle humour might dictate, assumes the appellation of OLDSCHOOL.[2] Fond of this title, indicative of his moral, political, and literary creed, he proposes publishing every Saturday, on super-royal quarto sheets,

A new weekly paper,
to be called,
THE PORT FOLIO[3]
By Oliver Oldschool, Esq.

"Warned by 'the waywardness of the time,'[4] and the admonitions of every honest printer, the Editor begins his work on a Lilliputian page, and, like a saving grocer, gives of his goods only a small sample, but subscribers, if peradventure[5] the Editor should have any, *must not 'despise the day of small things.'* It is proposed always to give plenty of letter-press, in propor-

1, 2, 3, 4, 5, 6, and 7. The figures inserted correspond to very copious footnotes, occupying nearly half the sheet, replete with references and extracts from Cowper, Vergil, Bolingbroke, Steele, Bunyan, Lyttleton, and Milton, to mention only the notes on the passage quoted above.

tion to the public demand, and, as the exigency of the season, or copiousness of materials may require, to double, treble, and even quadruple the pages in the PORT FOLIO. Hereafter, more may be done, if more be wanted, and if more be fostered. At present, with the prudent policy of wary beginners, it is judged expedient to risk but little. No sonorous promises are made, and no magnificence of style attempted. The paper is to be neither *wire-woven*, nor *hot-pressed*, and it certainly, in more senses than one, shall not be cream-coloured; but in a plain dress of Quaker simplicity, may, perhaps, offer something tolerable on political, literary, and transient topics, and something, auxiliary to sound principles, which *after church*, 'retired leisure'[6] may read on Sunday.[7]

"Empirical vaunting is always nauseous and arrogant; and the plausibility of mighty promise has generally a pitiful conclusion. The Editor, with honest diffidence, declines making specious engagements; timid, lest time or chance, lest laziness, sickness, or stupidity, should step between stipulation and fulfilment, he applies to himself one of the didactics of Solomon; and 'boasts not himself of to-morrow, for he knows not what a day may bring forth.' "

He would, however, undertake to *avoid* certain things, such as publishing an *impartial* paper, aspersing the government, church, or literature of England, attempting, like the Jacobins, to subvert government and morals, or indulge in ill-mannered controversy. The things he *would* attempt to accomplish, are summed up in a sentence. "To relieve the dryness of news, and the severity of political argument, with wholesome morals and gay miscellany—to insert interesting articles of biography, criticism, poetry, and merriment, and 'bind the rod of the moralist with the roses of the Muse.' " "It must be apparent to the most heedless observers, that it is the object of this undertaking, to combine literature with politics," he went on, "and attempt something of a more honorable destiny, than a meagre journal. To accomplish this purpose, the co-operation of many minds is requisite." The fate of many American gazettes, without the assistance of talent, is thus described:

"An obscure and illiterate individual, of mere mechanical skill in the art of printing, contracts debts for his press and paper, and issues proposals for a Gazette. As education or habit, as chance or interest may determine, he professes himself a republican, or a federalist, or, what is more common, a man of no party; willing to publish trash for all, and pretending to be unbiased by any. *Fervet opus.* The press groans, the work begins, and *with* the paltry aid of *two* or *three hundred* subscribers, and *without* assistance, either literary or political, he, of necessity, prints from week to week a *thing*—'without a name,' without correctness, without consistency; in narration, turbid, or false, in comment clumsy, in its original departments crude and juvenile, in its selections uncouth, vicious in the humblest combinations of grammar, and a trespasser on all the limits of language. A puny bantling from the press, 'so faint, so spiritless, so dull, so dead in look,' quickly 'goeth to its long home' its *inky* 'mourners go about the street' and its numerous sponsors and friends strongly wonder at its dissolution.''

Accordingly Dennie called for aid from men of letters, the clergy, the gentlemen of the bar, the liberal merchants and the country gentlemen, ''the tranquil sect of Quakers,'' and, by no means least, the ladies. A long list of specific contributions desired, next follows, succeeded by the Conditions:

''I. The Port Folio will be published every Saturday morning, and will always contain at least eight pages of letter press. The Prospectus is a specimen of the size[1] and quality of the paper, and of the typographical execution.

''II. It will be published by the EDITOR, and ASBURY DICKINS, sole Proprietors of the work.

''III. The price will be five dollars annually, and it is requested of subscribers that the money be paid in advance.

''IV. No advertisements to be inserted in the body of the work; but as they principally contribute both to the profit and the circulation of every *city* paper, the Editor hopes that Merchants and Booksellers will not forget this circumstance. Their advertisements shall be conspicuously printed on a separate sheet, which will serve as an useful *envelope* to the Port Folio.''

The Prospectus closes with a brief notice of the editor's past labors and his hopes. He says:

1. Fourteen by twelve inches. This size was maintained throughout the first five volumes.

"At an early season of life, he voluntarily forsook the path of ordinary business, for a lowly seat in the Muses' bower. Though his choice has not enriched, or advanced him, yet of its propriety he has never doubted. . . . But though the gains of Authorship have been trivial, yet once they secured him a portion of *rural* comfort, and, perhaps, they will enable him to flourish in a city. . . . With a spirit lofty, yet not insolent, with a voice timid, yet not servile, he calls on his countrymen to inspect and value his labours; and with a *moderate* estimate, he will persevere and be cheerful."

The first number of the *Port Folio,* which appeared 3 January, 1801, was almost wholly the work of two men, Dennie and John Quincy Adams. The latter contributed a verse translation of the thirteenth satire of Juvenal, which, with the Latin text subjoined, took up the last three pages. It began with the promising couplets,

"From Virtue's paths, when hapless men depart,
The first avenger is the culprit's heart;
There, sits a judge, from whose severe decree
No strength can rescue, and no speed can flee."

The rest of the poem is not equally good, though nothing Adams ever did was lacking in a certain formal excellence. This is true as well of the first letter of a *Journal of a Tour through Silesia,* which formed the opening piece of the *Port Folio.* These letters were written by J. Q. Adams to his brother, Thomas Boylston Adams, at Philadelphia, who turned them over to his friend Dennie, it is said, without his brother's knowledge.[1] The series ran in the *Port Folio,* always occupying the front page, until 7 November of that year. In 1804 they reappeared, in London, in book form, and were later translated into French and German. The letters were always interesting, full of shrewd observations on the government and the characteristics of the regions traversed.

Besides a poem called *The Misanthrope* (probably Dennie's) the editor contributed *An Author's Evenings* and Literary Intelligence. The scheme of the former series is compared to the *Noctes Atticae* of Aulus Gellius. "A plenty of curious or

1. The story of the transaction is told by C. F. Adams in the *Memoirs of John Quincy Adams*, Vol. I, pp. 240-241.

valuable extracts will be given from the works of others, and these will be followed up by incidental remarks, or easy and obvious criticism." Variety is their chief merit. Contrary to the statements usually made,[1] these were almost wholly from Dennie's pen, not Tyler's, though they still purported to come from the "Shop of Messrs. Colon and Spondee." The contents of the column of Literary Intelligence are very interesting. The two projected works, the *Lay Preacher* and the *Farrago* are discussed, their character is outlined and their appearance prophesied, though with the admission that "the author is prepared for the mortification of witnessing a narrow subscription, and is slow to anticipate, either the honorable premium for his literary labour, or even a full requital for his bookseller's cares." More interesting is the plan of a new series to appear in the *Port Folio,* called the *Wandering Jew,* based upon an incident in M. G. Lewis' *Monk,* which had appeared in 1795. Referring to the achievement of the authors of the *Mirror,* 1779-1780, and the *Lounger,* 1785-1787, he said, "If the Lay Preacher, a young man, valetudinary, without fortune, without a patron, without an auxiliary, without popular encouragement, should accomplish *three* works of this class, it will be something novel in the history of literary adventure." The *Wandering Jew,* however, remained always a visionary project, the *Lay Preacher* and *Farrago* went unpublished, and eventually, one by one, most of the old essays appeared again in the columns of the *Port Folio.*

Another attraction of the first number of the magazine was several letters, hitherto unpublished, written to Smollett by John Armstrong, William Pitt, Richardson, Hume, and Boswell. They were found in Smollett's trunk at Leghorn, where he died in 1771, thence transmitted to America, and communicated to Dennie by "a learned friend, whose good taste selects, and whose care preserves, many a literary gem, and many a valuable fragment."[1] The second number, 10 January, 1801, included two letters from Boswell to the Reverend James Abercrombie, of Philadelphia; and other unpublished letters appeared at intervals during the year, under the heading Epistolary, besides

1. Several of the summaries of Tyler's work give him the credit for *all* the *Author's Evenings* in the *Port Folio.* Several times in the *Port Folio,* Vol. I, Dennie laments the absence of his partner, *Spondee.*
2. Perhaps James White, bookseller, of Boston.

some, from Burke and others, which had appeared in English publications but not yet in America. Contributions like these to the lore of British literary history soon established the *Port Folio* on an eminent plane in American literary circles.

The departments in the *Tablet* and the *Farmer's Museum* were continued and elaborated in the *Port Folio.* These included the Drama, criticism of plays presented on the local stage; Literary Intelligence, a useful commentary on contemporary American publications and on the activities of British authors; Law Intelligence, accounts of trials before British courts; Biography, generally copied from British periodicals or reprinted, in a few cases, from the *Tablet;* Morals, staid homiletic essays; Political Synopses, including Foreign Occurrences and Domestic Occurrences; various departments of amusement entitled Levity, Humorous, Anecdotes, or Amusement; Original and Selected Poetry; and late in the year Musical Intelligence, the Fine Arts, and the Festoon of Fashion. Under the heading Miscellany were reprinted from time to time *Lay Preacher* or *Farrago* essays, *An Author's Evenings,* and occasional essays by other writers. Translations and criticisms of Foreign Literature also appeared, from Schiller, Gessner, and Florian.

The department of Politics was well patronized, with anti-Democratic essays by good Federalists using such names as *The Looker-on, Common Sense, Falkland,* etc.; addresses by General Hamilton; letters on politics from "an American gentleman in —— to a friend in Philadelphia"; and tirades against Jacobin influence, by Dennie. A series of articles from 28 March on, purporting to be Criticism, shows the pettiness which characterized many of the attacks upon Jefferson before and after his election to the presidency. The *Declaration of Independence,* doubtless written hastily and in a burst of enthusiasm, is taken up phrase by phrase, and strictures are made upon the grammar, use of words, etc., of the document, rather than its sense or spirit. In one communication[1] it is styled "that false, and flatulent and foolish paper, denominated the Declaration of Independence." Dennie heartily agreed with these attacks and called for more, whereupon others followed, dealing with the Inaugural Address

1. *Port Folio,* 11 April, 1801.

and other utterances of Jefferson. The return of Thomas Paine, author of the *Rights of Man*, to America at the invitation of Jefferson, aroused the bitterest opposition on the part of the Federalists. The mere rumor of his coming produced the following indignant outburst by Dennie:[1]

"If, during the present season of national abasement, infatuation, folly, and vice, any portent could surprise, sober men would be utterly confounded by an article, current in all our papers, that the loathsome Thomas Paine, a drunken atheist, and the scavenger of faction, is invited to return in a national ship, to America, by the first magistrate of a free people! A measure so enormously preposterous, we cannot believe has yet been adopted, and it would demand firmer nerves, than those, possessed by Mr. Jefferson, to hazard such an insult to the moral sense of the nation. If that rebel rascal should come to preach from HIS bible to the populace, and if the hair-brain'd Fayette should vex us with HIS diplomacy, it would be time for every honest and insulted man of dignity to flee to some *Zoar*, as from another *Sodom*, to 'shake off the very dust of his feet,' and abandon America."

The notes To Readers and Correspondents make an interesting series in themselves, and furnish many of the hints upon which identification of the contributors is based. The following extracts will show the reception awarded to lucky and luckless correspondents:

"Political writers are requested again, to communicate freely. 'Come over to Macedonia and help us.' "

"Floricourt is a coxcomb writer, and his essay is overwhelmed with cant expressions."

"A 'Pathetic Tale' merits the study of the philosophic, and will elicit a sigh from the tender."

"We are doomed, of late, to read much miserable poetry, the feeble offspring of unfledged boys and crude girls. These communications pass in a direct line from our letter-box to the fire."

" 'Lines on a Lady Bathing' are inadmissible. The subject is dangerous and indelicate, and it is prudent to suffer this

1. 18 July, 1801.

'Lady' to remain in that *flannel,* with which the bard has invested her."

"'Bibo' has the frolic of a Bacchante, and the wit of Mercury. We shall be glad to hear from him again."

During the summer months, when correspondence flagged, the notes To Readers and Correspondents became more numerous, sprightly, and pungent, as did also the synopses of Foreign and Domestic Occurrences. The following account of a letter of the Secretary of the Treasury illustrates Dennie's idea of a news item:[1]

"Gallatin, whose English is almost as correct as the language of Dr. Caius, in the *Merry Wives of Windsor,* has addressed a circular letter to the collectors of the customs. This *maiden* official, from the desk of the Genevese, might sound very well in the canton of Berne, but it will hardly escape the animadversion of the most careless critic here. It is not English, it is not French. Like chaos, in Genesis, it is '*without form and void.*' It is a most coarse, untunable and misshapen thing. It is as limping and weak, as the sophistry of its author; the pen, the tongue, and the politics of this foreigner are all 'of hobbling kind.' The diction of this refugee is described by BUTLER.

'It is a party colour'd dress
Of patched and pye-ball'd languages.
It has an odd promiscuous tone,
As if he talk'd three parts in one,' etc."

The Original Poetry of the first volume of the *Port Folio* was varied and not uninteresting. Translations from Horace and other Classic poets, and from the French, Spanish, German, and Gaelic, love lyrics, narrative poems, ballads of the supernatural, epigrams, reflective verse, idylls, parodies and other humorous pieces, all are represented. Fragments of *Ossian* were translated by Jonathan Sewall and others. Doctor Thomas C. James, over the initials "P. D.," sent in some attractive translations from the German of Gessner, and from other languages. Doctor John Shaw of Annapolis contributed poems written on his voyage abroad. George L. Gray of Baltimore was another poetical correspondent from Maryland. The English writer,

1. *Port Folio,* 8 Aug., 1801.

John Davis, republished some of his nature poems in the *Port Folio.* Perhaps the most constant writer was Samuel Ewing, a young lawyer, author of a poetical series called *Reflections in Solitude.* Charles Jared Ingersoll, a youth of nineteen years, contributed to the *Port Folio* for 24 October a poem called *Chiomara,* the story of a Gaulish princess, more resembling Brunhild than Lucrece, who killed the Roman that sought to ravish her, and cast his head at her husband's feet. The narrative, despite youthful flaws and stiffness, is skillfully and effectively told. Mony other offerings, by "Q. V.," "O.," and others, cannot be readily identified. The last-named correspondent wrote for the last number of the year a long ballad, *Edric and Sir Albert the Brave,* in imitation of the then popular *Tales of Terror* (1799), and *Tales of Wonder* (1801), of "Monk" Lewis. Two stanzas taken at random will illustrate adequately the poem and the type.

"Midst the shades, where the taper its feeble light cast,
Strange phantoms, half viewless were seen:
For its rays soon were lost in a cavern so vast,
And the flame palely quivered beneath the cold blast,
That roar'd mid the hollows within.

"Not long he gaz'd round him, when lo! mid the shade,
Cloath'd in darkness, an arm met his view;
A scroll of large size in its grasp was convey'd;
And as its contents to his sight were display'd,
Sir Edric the covenant knew."

The Selected Poetry is commonly chosen from reputable English books or periodicals. The *Lyrical Ballads* were better received in America than in England, and Dennie, contrary to the statements of Professor Smyth,[1] and others, was among the earliest to welcome them. In the *Farmer's Museum* and the *Gazette of the U. S.* some of the ballads had been reprinted and praised. In the *Port Folio,* 17 January, appeared *Simon Lee,* "extracted from *Lyrical Ballads,* a collection remarkable for originality, simplicity, and nature." On 21 March *The Thorn* was printed without comment. On 13 June the favorable review of the second edition of the *Ballads,* from the *British Critic,*

1. *Philadelphia Magazines,* etc., page 109.

was copied and in the notices To Readers and Correspondents, Dennie said, "We have had frequent occasion in the course of our literary selections, to express the warmest admiration of the genius, spirit, and simplicity of 'Lyrical Ballads,' a volume, which contains more genuine poetry, than is to be found, except in the volumes of *Shakespeare* and *Chatterton.*" He added that he had ordered the second volume from England, in order to "adorn his pages with *gems* of a soft and permanent lustre." There followed the *Anecdote for Fathers* and *The Mad Mother,* 18 July, *Strange Fits of Passion Have I Known,* 12 December, and *The Waterfall* and *The Eglantine, Lucy Gray,* and *Andrew Jones,* 19 December. These last three were prefaced by the remark, "The following delightful fable, and the subsequent poems, are from the magical pen of *William Wordsworth,* 'a genuine poet, who judiciously employs the language of simplicity and *nature* to express the tones of passion; and who has forsaken the necromantic realms of German extravagance, and the torrid zone of Della Cruscan ardour, and has recalled erring readers 'from sounds to things, from fancy to the heart,' " These facts and citations are enough to prove that he *did* appreciate the excellences of Wordsworth and the romantic poets. Dennie was by temperament a sentimentalist, who dared to nickname Dr. Johnson "Goliath."[1] He was often enough wrongheaded in his critical estimates, but never more sound in judgment than when he said, speaking of the *absurdities* of Wordsworth's verse, in the *Port Folio,* March, 1809, "William Wordsworth stands among the foremost of those English bards, who have mistaken silliness for simplicity; and with a false and affected taste, filled their pages with the language of children and clowns."[2]

The prose essays in the first volume of the *Port Folio,* besides the *Lay Preacher, Farrago,* and political papers already mentioned, included two numbers of the *Rural Wanderer,*[3] by James Elliot, who seems to have intended continuing his series from the *Farmer's Museum;* a few essays entitled *Philology,* perhaps contributed by J. S. J. Gardiner; a series of seven articles of

1. *Port Folio,* 12 July, 1806.
2. *Port Folio,* (2nd) New Series, Vol. I, 1809), page 256. This is the extract quoted by Smyth.
3. No. XVII, 14 Feb., contains some interesting biographical details.

criticism on the plays of Shakespeare, ascribed by Smyth to Joseph Hopkinson; and numerous works unsigned, or by unknown authors. The first number of a new series, *The Barber Shop,* probably by Dennie, was not followed by any second. During July and August the paper, except for the editor's own work, was duller than usual; the summaries of news were expanded, long sermons and items from British critical magazines were printed, and selected poetry largely replaced original. This decline during the hot summer months, due to relaxed support and the lassitude of the editor, was to become an annual feature of the magazine, which always got upon its feet again, however, with the return of fall.

The success of the *Port Folio* was striking. Dickins, Dennie found, was "an associate, who, to the spirit of enterprize, adds an adherence to principle and a taste for letters; a *liberal* bookseller, who is unaccustomed to measure talents with a *two foot rule.*"[1] On 25 April the two proprietors announced to the public that,

"One thousand copies, constituting the first edition of the Prospectus of the Port Folio, having been distributed, a *second edition* of a like number has been printed, and is nearly exhausted. At the commencement of this work, the Editor, dubious of success, wished to restrain his partner and printer to the number of one thousand copies of the *Port Folio.* . . . His partner adventurously extended the number to fifteen hundred, and the partiality of the public has justified the enterprize of a young and sanguine friend. This edition being nearly sold, the Editor, animated by success, and justly confident of an increasing demand, both at home and *abroad,* for this miscellany, has directed a *second* edition of the initial numbers, and now regularly causes to be printed *two thousand* copies of this paper."

He had, moreover, succeeded in winning the patronage of the literary classes throughout the country, and in arousing the efforts of many able pens in behalf of his undertaking. At last he seemed to be on the highroad to the recognition he so eagerly desired.

No one, probably, was more surprised by his success than

1. *Port Folio,* 17 January, 1801.

Dennie himself. The whole tone of the Prospectus—ambitious as was its outlook,—the course there outlined, the size of the sheet, all indicate that he anticipated publishing little more than an improvement upon the *Farmer's Museum* and the *Gazette of the U. S.* The *Port Folio* was still to be a newspaper and a political gazette, in appearance and in aim, varied and enlivened by literature. It turned out to be a literary magazine, eclipsing in its range and excellence anything on the continent before it. Yet Fortune, in awarding Dennie this success, was capricious. In the successful and busy editor the author was lost. The subscribers who packed the lists for the *Port Folio* had neglected his books, and the *Lay Preacher* remained unpublished. Had the reverse been true, Dennie, spurred on by success to new efforts of composition, might have outgrown the absurdities of his style and made a permanent name for himself as an American man of letters. His influence upon the literature of his country, however, would probably not have been greater.

In 1801 there was issued from Carlisle's press at Walpole a volume called:

"THE SPIRIT OF THE FARMER'S MUSEUM AND LAY PREACHER'S GAZETTE

"Being a judicious selection of the fugitive and valuable productions, which have occasionally appeared in that paper, since the commencement of its establishment. Consisting of a part of the essays of the Lay Preacher, Colon and Spondee, American biography, the choicest efforts of the American muse, pieces of chaste humour, the easy essays of the Hermit, the most valuable part of the weekly summaries, nuts, epigrams, and epitaphs, sonnets, criticism, etc., etc." Of this volume of selections, of a type common and popular at that time, Dennie is said to have been editor. It cannot have added much to his reputation. It contained six of his *Lay Preacher* essays, two of his *Hermit* papers, and many extracts from *Colon and Spondee* and the weekly summaries, besides examples of the work of Tyler, Thomas, Fessenden, and the other *Museum* worthies, except Story, whose effusions had already been published. The copy owned by the Boston Public Library bears this entry on the fly-leaf, "This volume was presented to James Abercrombie, Decr. 26th, 1801, By His learned and facetious Friend, Joseph Dennie, Esq." Scattered annotations throughout the volume, in Dennie's handwriting, have aided greatly in identifying the contributors to the *Museum*.

In 1801, the year of the publication of the *Spirit of the Farmer's Museum* and the establishment of the *Port Folio*, there appeared in England, Cobbett's *Works of Peter Porcupine*, Hogg's *Scottish Pastorals*, Charles Lamb's tragedy, *John Woodvil*,[1] Lewis' *Tales of Wonder*, Thomas Moore's *Poems of Thomas Little*, Scott's *Wild Huntsman*—his first serious attempt at verse—, and Southey's *Thalaba*. The second edition of Wordsworth and Coleridge's *Lyrical Ballads* had appeared the year before. In the United States in the same year, besides Adams' *Tour through Silesia*, there were published three novels of Charles Brockden Brown, *Edgar Huntly, Clara Howard*, and *Jane Talbot*, Dickinson's *Political Writings*, Linn's *Powers of Genius*, Ramsay's *Life of Washington*, Rush's *Introductory Lectures*, and the *Miscellaneous Poems* of Jonathan M. Sewall. Irving was a youth of eighteen years, Cooper a boy of twelve, and Bryant a child of seven.

An adverse, but not unreasonable, estimate of the most prominent American writers of 1801 is that of Mr. Lucas George, described in Davis's *Travels in the United States*, 1798-1802:[2]

"Mr. *George* had a supreme contempt for *American* genius and *American* literature. In a sportive mood, he would ask me whether I did not think that it was some physical cause in the air, which denied existence to a poet on *American* ground. No snake, said he, exists in *Ireland*, and no poet can be found in *America*.

"You are too severe, said I, in your strictures. This country, as a native author observes, can furnish her quota of poets.

"Name, will you, one?

"Is not *Dwight* a candidate for the epic crown? Is he, Sir, not a poet?

"I think not. He wants imagination, and he also wants judgment; Sir, he makes the shield of *Joshua* to mock the rising sun!

1. See Talfourd's *Life and Letters of Charles Lamb*.
2. Pages 137-139.

"Is not *Barlow* a poet? Is not his *Vision of Columbus* a fine poem?

"The opening is elevated; the rest is read without emotion.

"What think you of *Freneau?*

"*Freneau* has one good ode: *Happy the Man Who Safe on Shore!* But he is voluminous; and this ode may be likened to *the grain in a bushel of chaff.*

"What is your opinion of *Trumbull?*

"He can only claim the merit of being a skilful imitator.

"Well, what do you think of *Humphreys?*

"Sir, his mind is neither ductile to sentiment, nor is his ear susceptible of harmony.

"What opinion do you entertain of *Honeywood?*

"I have read some of his wretched rhymes. The bees, as it is fabled of *Pindar*, never sucked honey from his lips.

"Of the existence of an *American* poet, I perceive, Sir, your mind is rather sceptical. But, I hope, you will allow that *America* abounds with good prose.

"Yes, Sir; but, then, mind me, it is imported from the shores of *Great Britain.*

"Oh! monstrous! Is not *Dennie* a good prose-writer?

"Sir, the pleasure that otherwise I should find in *Dennie*, is soon accompanied with satiety by his unexampled *quaintness.*

"Of *Brown,* Sir, what is your opinion?

"The style of *Brown,* Sir, is chastised, and he is scrupulously pure. But nature has utterly disqualified him for subjects of humour. Whenever he endeavours to bring forth humour, the offspring of his throes are weakness and deformity. Whenever he attempts humour, he inspires the benevolent with pity, and fills the morose with indignation.

"What think you of the style of *Johnson,* the Reviewer?[1]

"It is not *English* that he writes, Sir; it is *American.* His periods are accompanied by a yell, that is scarcely less dismal than the warwhoop of a Mohawk."

---

1. Samuel Johnson, Jr., lexicographer and reviewer for the New York magazines. Davis had a not ungrounded aversion for Johnson, who had severely censured his *Farmer of New Jersey.*

CHAPTER IX

PHILADELPHIA, 1801-1808—OLIVER OLDSCHOOL AND HIS FRIENDS

Dennie's correspondence with his parents after his removal to Philadelphia was very scanty. Only four letters, of the years 1800, 1802, 1803, and 1809, are to be found among those carefully preserved by his mother. His justification for this neglect is found in a passage from one of these letters, dated 15 June, 1803:

"Why should I, for many years of a life, singularly ill-fated, have harassed you with the gloomy details of my adversity? They would have made you more unhappy, and they would not have relieved me. You receive my works regularly, and in them find or make my letters. The *Port Folio* will inform you that I am not yet deaf to the calls of *Fame*, and my private letters, if you received them hourly, would not edify you with a brilliant history of my Fortune."

In an earlier letter, 10 January, 1802, he wrote, "The simple truth is, I am a man of a weak habit of body, with a mind volatile and chagrined, obliged to drudge in literature for a mere subsistence in this miserable Country." His chagrin was doubtless caused by his failure to publish his books the preceding year, though he still hoped to publish "some book" during 1802, and had not relinquished his dream of winning literary reputation in Great Britain. He was occupying, he said, creditable lodgings on Walnut Street, with an elderly lady, a clergyman's widow, Mrs. Roberts by name. His manservant he had, however, relinquished. With regard to his parents, he wrote, with his old pride about appearances:

"*If it be possible* for me to visit you, *with any eclat,* I will go to Lexington this year, if not I must *painfully* postpone my very earnest desire to converse with you, until 'a more *convenient season,*' as the good apostle saith.

"I am glad to hear that my father is tranquil. I fervently hope that the evening of his life will be long, bright and serene. I most earnestly desire that, if he think me worthy, he will send me his blessing."

Though not opulent in purse, Dennie enjoyed the society of the most intelligent and highly esteemed persons in Philadelphia. Among his intimates were for a time Edward Thornton, secretary of the British legation, later a noted diplomat; and a young English nobleman, Henry Stuart, a younger son of the Marquis of Bute.[1] John Davis, the English traveller referred to previously, who passed through Philadelphia in June or July, 1801, on his way to Washington, in search of a political office, said of Dennie's associates:[2]

"At *Philadelphia,* I found Mr. *Brown,* who felt no remission of his literary diligence, by a change of abode. . . . Mr. *Brown* introduced me to Mr. *Dickins,* and Mr. *Dickins* to Mr. *Dennie;* Mr. *Dennie* presented me to Mr. *Wilkins,*[3] and Mr. *Wilkins* to the Rev. Mr. *Abercrombie,* a constellation of *American* genius, in whose blaze I was almost consumed.

"Mr. *Dennie* passed his mornings in the shop of Mr. *Dickins,* which I found the rendezvous of the *Philadelphia* sons of literature . . . *Blair,*[4] author of a poem called the *Powers of Genius; Ingersoll,* known by a tragedy, of which I forget the title; *Stock,* celebrated for his dramatic criticisms; together with several Reviewers . . . assembled with punctuality in *North Second Street,* to the great annoyance of Mr. *Dickins,* who could scarcely find room to sell his wares."

Davis, a native of Salisbury, England, born about 1775, had already made several voyages to the East and served in the navy against the French before embarking from Bristol, for the United States, 7 January, 1798, equipped with an ardent enthusiasm for literature and a considerable knowledge of the classics, industriously picked up at odd moments. From New York, where he met Aaron Burr and translated *Bonaparte's Campaign in Italy,* he began a pedestrian tour to fever-stricken Philadelphia and the Southern States, supporting himself by

1. Among various other papers Dennie sent from Philadelphia to his mother are the cards of these two gentlemen, with invitations to walk with them. On Henry Stuart's card he wrote proudly, "With this young nobleman I was very intimate." This may be the same Henry Stuart concerned in a romantic episode told in Simpson's *Eminent Philadelphians,* pp. 555-560.

2. *Travels in the U. S. A.,* pp. 203-205.

3. Possibly the Wilkins who published an *Essay on Animal Motion,* Philadelphia, 1792. He was a graduate of the University of Pennsylvania Medical College.

4. John Blair Linn, author of the *Powers of Genius.*

teaching occasionally. Some of his poems in the *South Carolina Gazette* during his stay in the South attracted the favorable comment of Dennie in the *Farmer's Museum*. Back at New York, he met Brockden Brown and published in 1800 a narrative, *The Farmer of New Jersey*, which was so severely criticized that he wrote a continuation, the *Wanderings of William*,[1] published at Philadelphia in 1801. He attended Jefferson's inauguration, published at New York another small volume, *Poems, Chiefly Written in South Carolina*, and was pleasantly entertained by Burr, then Vice-President, but was disappointed in his hopes for an office. After another year, spent chiefly in Virginia, he embarked for home from Baltimore, 3 August, 1802. The narrative of his story in America appeared in his *Travels of Four Years and a Half in the United States of America*, published in London in 1803, and dedicated to Jefferson. This work, though marred by a conceit far exceeding Dennie's, is interesting and on the whole a more healthy view of America and Americans than that of almost any other European observer. In England he published an American tale, *Walter Kennedy*, a *Life of Chatterton*, and a novel, *The Wooden Walls Well Manned*. In 1804 he returned to America, and soon set up as a juvenile bookseller in Philadelphia. His *First Settlers of Virginia*, New York, 1806, is an enlargement of his *Pokahontas, an Indian Tale*. He returned, after a few years, to England, where several works of his were published, including *The American Mariners* (Salisbury, 1822), with a vindication of the American character and an impartial view of the War of 1812. At that time he was a stationer in Winchester.

Further references to Dennie and his literary confreres occur in the satirical *Philadelphia Pursuits of Literature*,[2] which appeared in two parts in 1805. This has been generally ascribed to Davis, though he may have been telling the truth in saying it was the work of "a Scholar, a Poet and a Gentleman . . . on the banks of the Raritan." The poem was written as a retort

1. One reason for the harsh reception of this work may be guessed from its dedication to *Flavia*. "Take it, read it, there is nothing to fear, your governess is gone out, and the family are not yet risen. Do you hesitate? *Werter* has been under your pillow, and the *Monk* has lain on your toilet."

2. Imitating the *Pursuits of Literature*, a satrical work by Thomas James Mathias, sixteen editions, London, 1794-1812.

to a parody, in the *Port Folio*, 16 February, 1805, on an *Ode to the River Raritan*, sent in by Davis shortly before. In the *Philadelphia Pursuits*, after a brief introduction in which he stated his purpose to depict "the Philadelphia lounging, scribbling crew," the satirist, writing "From my Farm house on the Raritan," thus characterizes Dennie:

"Columbia's genius! Dennie! deathless name!
Bless'd with a full satiety of fame!
Thee to peruse was once my humble lot,
When not another book was to be got.
What though thy name has never reach'd the shore,
That claims the birth of loose, lascivious Moore;
What though thy works did never make a show,
With other drugs in Pater-Noster Row;
Yet to the Yankee thou canst light impart,
Improve the mind, and rectify the heart.
Jemima oft had read thy sermons droll,
Where Merrimac and Androscoggin roll;
And there's no clown from Walpole to Hell Gate,
But ribaldry from thee has learn'd to prate."

After a gibe at the ill success of Dennie and the Federalists, the poet delivers a home-thrust in these lines:

"Such is our Dennie, high exalted name,
Eager alike for dollars and for fame,
Procrastination's son! he trumps up lies
Of works to come that in the project dies;
And loud delights to sound the praise of Moore,
Who, God be prais'd, has left Columbia's shore.
O prodigal of commas to thy lines,
Whose borrow'd wit through all thy periods shines;
O Superficial, formal, pert, and quaint,
Thy style is like a harlot daub'd with paint."

In the profuse prose "Notes" at the end of the poem, the commentator adds, "In his style Mr. Dennie is scarcely to be exceeded. It is true that he is prodigal of his inverted commas, and that the business of the reader in perusing his works is generally to recollect the authors from whom he borrows his thoughts; but then, he discovers reading, and it may be said of this attic, sprightly pungent writer, that though he seldom has any money in his purse, he will always borrow thousands." Dennie's associates are thus described in a passage itself palpably imitative of Pope:

"Gods! how the city does with rhymes abound,
Without his song no fop is to be found!
Is there a Parson fond of anecdote,
A man who has his Boswell all by rote;
A clerk foredoomed his father's soul to cross,
Who translates Voltaire when he should engross;
Each flies to Eighth-street and at thirty-two
Finds the man-midwife to the scribbling crew."[1]

The part played by literary clubs in the history of American literature would make an interesting and valuable study. It was frequently the case, during the century from 1750 to 1850, that a small group of literary friends, banded together for social and literary ends, combined their efforts in the production and support of a magazine or other periodical, which was to be the organ of the society. In this way the Friendly Club at Hartford, including Trumbull, the Dwights, Barlow, Elihu H. Smith, Richard Alsop, and others, contributed to the *Anarchiad* and the *Echo* between 1785 and 1807. So Dennie's Literary Club at Walpole supported the *Farmer's Museum* from 1796 to 1799. So Elihu Smith's offshoot, the Friendly Society, of New York, of which Brockden Brown and William Dunlap[2] were members, supported Smith's *Medical Repository*, 1794-1798, and later Brown's *Monthly Magazine and American Review*. So the *Anthology Club*, of Boston, supported the *Monthly Anthology and Boston Review*, 1803-1811. So also the Club of the Transcendentalists enriched the *Dial*, 1840-1844, with the writings of

1. A more dispassionate estimate of Dennie's defects and excellences is contained in the comparison of his style with Brown's, in Book II of the *Pursuits*. An extract follows:

"As a writer, Mr. Dennie possesses great acuteness of mind and although he may be given to procrastination, his genius seldom slumbers. He has an exuberance of wit; an exuberance so great that it o'er-informs its tenement. Hence his tone is seldom or never grave, dispassionate, or dignified; but he is ever ambitious to surprise by remote and unexperienced allusions. For humour he is less eminent; he knows not the art to make others laugh without laughing himself."

2. William Dunlap (1766-1829), the most important early American playwright, and author of the *History of the American Theatre*, 1832, and the *Life of Charles Brockden Brown*, 1815.

Emerson, Thoreau, Margaret Fuller, Bronson Alcott, and many more. Other prominent literary clubs, all more or less intimately connected with magazines, were the Delphian Club of Baltimore, which included John Neal, Jared Sparks, F. S. Key, Paul Allen, Samuel Woodsworth, and several others less distinguished;[1] Cooper's Bread and Cheese Lunch and Irving's Sketch Club, both of New York; and the famous Saturday Club, at Boston, of which Lowell, Longfellow, Emerson, Hawthorne, Holmes, and the other notable New England writers were members.

Such a combination of social and convivial gatherings with literary discussion and production appealed strongly to Dennie's taste. He was already acquainted, from his experience at Walpole, with the pleasures and advantages to be derived from clubs of this sort, and before long a similar organization, probably due largely to his efforts, came into existence at Philadelphia. This society, known as the Tuesday Club, was composed chiefly of young men of the legal profession, and held its meetings at various places, particularly at the homes of Joseph Hopkinson and William Meredith, and a Dickins's bookstore at 25 North Second Street, opposite to Christ Church. Most of them were graduates of the University of Pennsylvania or other colleges, most of them were Federalist in politics, and all were imbued with a love of literature, and ambitious of gaining literary fame. All were likewise fond of good dinners and exchange of wit, and their meetings overflowed with eloquent conversation and rollicking fun.

Besides Brown, Linn, Ingersoll, and Stock, named by Davis, the Tuesday Club is said to have included Horace Binney, Nathaniel Chapman, Samuel Ewing, Joseph Hopkinson, William Meredith, Richard Rush, Thomas Cadwalader, Thomas I. Wharton, Richard Peters, Philip Hamilton, and at a later date, Nicholas Biddle, Robert Walsh, Alexander Wilson, and William B. Wood.[2] Other Philadelphians who were contributors to the *Port Folio* and may have been connected with the club were James Abercrombie, Thomas Chalkley James, Alexander Gray-

1. These men contributed to the *Portico*, 1816-1818.
2. Oberholtzer. *Literary History of Philadelphia*, pp. 176-177. See also Smyth, *op. cit.* p. 116.

don, John Sanderson, Charles Caldwell, Francis Cope, John E. Hall and his brothers, and Thomas Sergeant. In comparatively few cases can the individual productions of these men in the *Port Folio* be determined, owing to the almost invariable use of initials or pseudonyms, several of which might be employed by one writer. A series of brief sketches of the members of the Tuesday Club and their associates will give an idea of the literary conditions during the early years of the magazine.[1]

Charles Brockden Brown (1771-1810), by far the most important of Dennie's coadjutors, was during most of the time engaged in waiting for periodicals of his own; but prior to the establishment of his *Literary Magazine and American Register*, in 1803, he doubtless contributed occasionally to the *Port Folio*. After that date they were to some extent rivals until Brown's early death. The latter possessed analytic and critical qualities of mind which Dennie lacked, and the numerous reviews in his magazines are perhaps their best feature. Brown's six novels, *Wieland*, 1798, *Ormond*, 1799, *Arthur Mervyn*, 1799-1800, *Edgar Huntley*, 1801, *Clara Howard*, 1801, and *Jane Talbot*, 1801, were praised by Dennie, and his ill-health was deplored. These two writers share the honor of being the first Americans to adopt literature as a profession; the question of priority would be difficult to determine. The credit is generally given to Brown, who was certainly the greater genius, and whose literary reputation has long since outstripped Dennie's; but in their own day the latter was probably the better known and more admired of the two. Dennie was fluent and trifling; Brown was turgid and absurdly solemn, but he had more to say.[2]

The Reverend John Blair Linn (1777-1804), Columbia 1795, whose sister Brown married, was a pastor of the First Presbyterian Church, at Philadelphia.[3] His works were *Bourville Castle*, a drama; a poem on the Death of Washington;

---

1. The general sources of these sketches are Smyth's *Philadelphia Magazines and their Contributors*, Oberholtzer's *Literary History of Philadelphia*, and Scharf and Westcott's *History of Philadelphia*, Vol. II, Chapter XXXV.

2. Lives of Brown were written by Dunlap (Philadelphia, 1815, 2 vols.), and by Prescott (Sparks's *American Biography*, 1834).

3. A Memoir of Linn, by Brown, may be found in the *Port Folio*, 1809, for January, February, and March.

the *Powers of Genius*, 1801, a poetic work highly praised in America and republished in England; and an unfinished narrative poem, *Valerian*, dealing with the early Christian Church. At the end of his short life he was engaged in a controversy with Priestley, then living at Northumberland, Pennsylvania, on the nature, divine or human, of Christ.

Charles Jared Ingersoll (1782-1862), the name of whose tragedy, *Edwy and Elgiva* (1801), Davis could not remember, later became a celebrated lawyer, and served four terms in Congress. His poem, *Chiomara*, in the *Port Folio* 24 October, 1801, has already been noticed. He was a Democrat in politics and resented Dennie's complacent attitude toward the sneers of foreign critics and the impositions of the British government, in *The Rights and Wrongs, Power and Policy, of the United States*, 1808, and the better known *Inchiquin the Jesuit's Letters*, 1810. The latter work occasioned a reviewers' war, in which Timothy Dwight and James K. Paulding upheld the American side. In mature years he wrote another tragedy, *Julian*, in 1838, and a *History of the War of 1812-1815*, in four volumes, 1845-1852.[1]

John Edmonds Stock, M. D., an Englishman, graduated from the Medical School of the University of Pennsylvania in 1797, the title of his essay being *The Effects of Cold.* He probably wrote the theatrical criticisms under the heading *Drama* in the *Port Folio* in 1801-1803. Before 1805 he had removed to Bristol, England, whence he transmitted some poetry for the magazine. He published later *Medical Collections on the Effect of Cold as a Remedy*, London, 1806, and *Memoir of Thomas Beddoes*, Bristol, 1811.[2]

Horace Binney (1780-1875), Harvard 1797, was a prominent Philadelphia lawyer, noted for his eulogies upon his contemporaries, nearly all of whom he outlived. He is said by Symth to have contributed clear and careful sketches of classical literature, "as well as the shrewdest of political satires to be found in the early volumes of the *Port Folio.*"[3]

Doctor Nathaniel Chapman (1780-1853) was a Virginian, who

1. His younger brother, Edward, was in later years a contributor to the *Port Folio*, using the signature *Horace in Philadelphia.* Ingersoll's *Life*, by Wm. N. Meigs, was published at Philadelphia in 1897.
2. See Allibone's *Dictionary of Authors.*
3. Smyth, *op. cit.* p. 128.

studied medicine at Philadelphia and Edinburgh, and was from 1813 to 1850 a medical professor in the University of Pennsylvania. He was President of the American Philosophical Society and founder and first editor of the *Philadelphia Journal of the Medical and Physical Sciences,* since the *American Journal of the Medical Science.* He contributed to the *Port Folio* in 1801, 1804, 1807, and later, political, medical, and literary articles, using the pen name *Falkland.*

One of the most constant correspondents of the *Port Folio* was Samuel Ewing (1776-1825), a young lawyer and son of the literary Provost of the University, John Ewing (1732-1802). Young Ewing used the pseudonym *Jacques,* but by no means exclusively, as stated by Smyth.[1]

He also used, as is proved by Hall's *Philadelphia Souvenir,* the names *Celebs, Touchstone, Timon Sensitive,* and probably others. Several specimens of his graceful verses and essays, with a brief biography, are printed in the miscellany mentioned above, by his nephew, John E. Hall. His most important contribution was a series of poetic *Reflections in Solitude,* in 1801 and 1802. The author of the *Philadelphia Pursuits of Literature* awards him two lines:

> "Of melancholy Jacques what shall I say?
> That son of blank song heavier than clay,"

and the note,

"Jacques, another *Port Folio* poet, whose lines breathe all the melancholy madness of poetry without the inspiration." He was one of the founders of the Philadelphia *Athenaeum.* From 1809 to 1812 he edited the *Select Reviews and the Spirit of the Magazines.* This became the *Analectic Magazine* in 1813, and Washington Irving succeeded him as editor.

Joseph Hopkinson (1770-1842), likewise the son of a more famous father, Francis Hopkinson (1737-1791), had a distinguished career as Congressman, Judge, Vice-President of the American Philosophical Society, and President of the Academy of Fine Arts. He is best known as author of the song *Hail Columbia,* written in 1798. Several of his articles on the plays of Shakespeare appeared in the *Port Folio* from 1801 to 1806. He frequently entertained the members of the Tuesday Club at his house at the corner of Fourth and Chestnut streets.

1. *Op. cit.* page 136.

A sketch of William Meredith has already been given.[1] The nature of his contributions is not known. Four other lawyers who were occasional correspondents were Rush, Cadwalader, Wharton, and Peters. Richard Rush (1780-1859), Princeton 1797, son of the famous Doctor Benjamin Rush (1745-1813) libeled by Cobbett, was successively Attorney General of the United States, 1814-1817; Temporary Secretary of State, 1817; Minister to England 1817-1825; Secretary of the Treasury, 1825-1828; candidate for the Vice-Presidency with Adams, 1828; and Minister to France, 1847-1851. He wrote various legal and historical works, and is said to have sent in official and personal anecdotes for the *Port Folio.* Thomas Cadwalader (1779-1814), lawyer and student of military science, contributed translations of Horace. Thomas Isaac Wharton (1791-1856), U. of P. 1807, author of various legal works and editor for a time of the *Analectic Magazine,* was also a correspondent. Judge Richard Peters (1744-1828), U. of P. 1761, the wealthy and learned farmer-lawyer of Belmont, is said by Smyth to be the author of many choice bits of political and personal history drawn from his experience as a traveller abroad and a participant in stirring events in American history. His son, Richard, Jr., however, was probably the member of the Tuesday Club.[2] The son was also a lawyer and a writer on legal subjects. Philip Hamilton (1782-1801), Columbia 1800, is said to have written for the *Port Folio* during its first years. He was killed in a duel, 24 November, 1801, at Weehawken, New Jersey, on the same field where his father, Alexander Hamilton, was to fall three years later.

The Reverend James Abercrombie (1758-1841), U. of P. 1776, Assistant Minister of Christ Church and St. Peter's from 1794 to 1832, was one of Dennie's closest friends. He was also Head Master of the Philadelphia Academy, 1803-1817, an exact scholar, an ardent lover of England, and, it is said, an eloquent preacher. He was the "Parson" of the *Philadelphia Pursuits,* "who has his Boswell all by rote," and issued proposals in 1811 for an American edition of Johnson's works. He published many texts, addresses, sermons, and religious works. Several

1. Chapter VIII, pages 113-114.
2. See Oberholtzer, *op. cit.* p. 177.

of his addresses before the Philadelphia Academy appeared in the *Port Folio,* and some of the letters condemning American innovations were probably his.[1]

One of the most enthusiastic early contributors was Thomas Chalkley James (1766-1835), a physician educated at Pennsylvania and in London and Edinburgh. He was Professor of Obstetrics at Pennsylvania, 1811-1834, and for eleven years an associate editor of the *Eclectic Review.* In 1801 he contributed to the *Port Folio* several excellent verse translations from the *Idylls* of Gessner, over the initials *P. D.* His production seems to have ended with that year.

Alexander Graydon (1752-1818), author of the interesting *Memoirs of a Life Chiefly Passed in Pennsylvania within the Last Sixty Years,* was a friend of Dennie and his associates and a later contributor to the *Port Folio.* John Sanderson (1783-1844), a schoolmaster and a native of Carlisle, best known for his *Lives of the Signers of the Declaration of Independence,* wrote for the *Aurora* and for the *Port Folio,* especially during the editorship of John E. Hall. Francis Cope contributed verse in 1806 and essays in later years, using the initials *C. F.* Thomas Sergeant (1782-1860), Princeton 1798, a grandson of Jonathan Dickinson, while beginning a long and successful law practice, wrote prose and poetry for the magazine, using the signature *Imlay* and others.

Doctor Charles Caldwell (1772-1853) was a North Carolinian who went to Philadelphia in 1792 to study and practise medicine. His contributions to the *Port Folio* during Dennie's editorship were probably not extensive, but after the latter's death Caldwell became editor, engaging to furnish ninety-eight pages for each number. In 1819 he established a medical school at the University of Transylvania, at Lexington, Kentucky, where he spent the remainder of his life. His published works, including works translated and edited, pamphlets and essays, between 1794 and 1851, number over two hundred.[2]

John Ewing Hall (1783-1829), a Princeton man and another subsequent editor of the *Port Folio,* contributed extensively

1. A sketch of his life is given in Sprague's *Annals of the American Pulpit.*
2. He also wrote an *Autobiography,* the most complete source of information about him.

from 1804 on, adopting the name of *Sedley*. In 1804 and 1805 he was studying law in the office of Joseph Hopkinson, and afterward practised and conducted the *American Law Journal* at Baltimore. At the suggestion of Thomas Moore, translator of the *Odes of Anacreon,* he undertook a series of papers, the *Memoirs of Anacreon,* constituting a fictitious biography of the Greek poet, supposed to have been written by Cneius Crito, a Samian, and translated by *Sedley*. Moore's translations of the *Odes* were woven at intervals into the tissue of the story. The plan, modeled upon the *Athenian Letters* of Philip Yorke, Earl of Hardwicke, was pursued irregularly and finally abandoned until 1820, when it was resumed. The essays of *Sedley* were in general serious and well written criticisms of life and manners.

Hall was a nephew of Samuel Ewing, his mother being Sarah (Ewing) Hall (1761-1830), a daughter of Provost Ewing. This excellent and gifted lady, using the pen names *Constantia* and *H.,* contributed to the magazine throughout its long life. One of her best productions was an allegory, *The Garden of Wedlock.*[1] Her book, *Conversations on the Bible,* was once widely read and admired. A selection from her writings, with a memoir of her life, was published by her son, John E. Hall, in 1833. It was printed by a second son, Harrison Hall. A third, James Hall, went west to Illinois, and later Ohio, where he became a prominent lawyer, editor and author. A fourth, Doctor Thomas Mifflin Hall, like his brothers a contributor to the *Port Folio* in the 1810's, went to South America and was not heard from again.

Two other female contributors were Harriet Fenno and Gertrude Gouverneur (Ogden) Meredith. The former was a daughter of John Fenno, founder of the *Gazette of the United States* and sister of John Ward Fenno, its continuer. Her few poems bore the signature *Violetta.* Mrs. Meredith is described by Robert Walsh, in his *Didactics* (Philadelphia, 1836), as "a writer, who displayed a masculine vigor of thought and expression, and literary powers and acquisitions of uncommon value and variety; who wielded her pen without the least ambition or pride of authorship, yet with the utmost intentness,

1. Number LVII of the *American Lounger* essays, in the *Port Folio,* 2 April, 1803.

and any sacrifice of self when instruction or comfort could be conveyed, however privately or remotely." She may have been the sprightly essayist *Beatrice,* thus introduced in the *Philadelphia Pursuits of Literature:*

"See sweet Beatrice, writing by the light
Of tapers, at the witching hour of night.
See how the topaz glitters in her ears,
See how her eyes are both brimful of tears."

Others, probably Philadelphians, who appeared under assumed names, were *Harley,* "an English gentleman," author of many sensible essays; *Mercutio,* a member of the Club (possibly Horace Binney), who wrote jovial songs, clever parodies, and witty but scurrilous verse satires on Jefferson and his followers: *Lysander,* whose *Rural Sketches* in verse were printed in the *Port Folio* in 1803 and 1808; and *Florian,* a satiric essayist whose darts were levelled at feminine follies during 1803 and 1804. Still others, from other places, were *Lodinus* of New York, who wrote amatory poems of considerable warmth; *Dactyl and Comma,* and *Verbal and Trochee,* two "shops" which competed with *Colon and Spondee; E. W.,* a woman in New York State who corresponded regularly, furnishing a series of *Cursory Sketches* of a tour through Virginia and Pennsylvania in 1807-1808; *Carlos,* a student at Yale; *B.,* a regular correspondent from Baltimore; *F. C. C.* of Carlisle; *N. N.,* a Canadian poet, and many more.

The list just given will show how extensive were the support and circulation of the *Port Folio* during its palmiest days. It had contributors and subscribers from Maine and the shores of Lake Ontario to Kentucky and South Carolina, and in England and Scotland. A complete list of authors who furnished material for its columns would probably contain the names of a majority of the writers of any prominence in the country The former Walpole wits drifted in at infrequent intervals. *The Rural Wanderer* (Elliot) appeared twice in Volume I and *Beri Hesdin* somewhat later. Tyler's support was desultory, though he probably contributed to *An Author's Evenings. Simon Spunkey,* now *Doctor Caustic,* published a few poems in the *Port Folio* after his return from England. J. S. J. Gardiner was probably a more frequent supporter, with articles of literary criticism and comment. Besides this group, however, there were several others who deserve mention.

The *Tour through Silesia* and *Thirteenth Satire of Juvenal* of John Quincy Adams (1767-1848), in the first volume of the *Port Folio* have already been mentioned. Adams, who would have liked to be remembered as a writer, had the busy cares of political life allowed, was author of several works, the *Letters from Silesia* (London and Philadelphia), 1804; *Lectures on Rhetoric and Oratory,* written while he was Boylston Professor of Rhetoric at Harvard, in 1810; *Dermot Mac Murrough,* a verse romance, in 1832; *Poems of Religion and Society,* 1848,. and his *Memoirs,* edited by Charles Francis Adams and published in 1874-1877. His plan to translate all of Juvenal's *Satires* was arrested by the announcement of Gifford's forthcoming translation in England, but Adams published a version of the *Seventh Satire* in the *Port Folio* 18 May, 1805, because of its particular application, he said, to American society. Hall states[1] that he also supplied "several beautiful versions from the German."

Another New England contributor was Adams's cousin and Dennie's classmate, Josiah Quincy (1772-1864), Representative to Congress from Massachusetts, 1808-1813; U. S. Senator, 1813-1820; Mayor of Boston, 1823-1828; and President of Harvard College, 1829-1845. He also found time to publish such valuable histories or biographies as those of his father, Josiah Quincy, Jr.; of Harvard University; John Quincy Adams and others; the Boston Athenaeum; and the Municipality of Boston.[2] In 1804 and at intervals later he contributed to the *Port Folio* a series of political articles called *Climenole*.[3] This professed to be a review, political and literary, of *Memorabilia Democratica, or the History of Democracy,* by Slaveslap Kidnap, Esq., and satirized vigorously the Democratic administration.

Another classmate who may have written for the magazine was Thomas Boylston Adams, a brother of John Quincy Adams. A letter from Dennie to his mother, 15 June, 1803, says:

"I now live with Mr. T. B. Adams, the second son of the

1. J. E. Hall. *Philadelphia Souvenir*, p. 9. Adams's *Thirteenth Satire* is there reprinted.
2. See his *Life*, by his son, Edmund Quincy.
2. The name of the flappers used to arouse the inhabitants of Laputa, in *Gulliver's Travels*.

former President. Mr. A. was my classmate, and is my constant friend. He is a respectable lawyer here, and we reside in a Quaker family of repute."

Jonathan Mitchell Sewall (1748-1808), a lawyer-poet of Portsmouth, New Hampshire, who versified Washington's *Farewell Address* and paraphrased parts of the Bible and of Ossian, contributed to the *Port Folio* in 1801 a few short versions of Ossian. His *Eulogy on Washington* and *Poems* were published in 1801. Charles Stewart Davies (1788-1865), Bowdoin 1807, of Portland, was probably the author of several poems which appeared in the magazine in 1806 over the signature *H. L.*

Robert H. Rose, M. D., of Susquehanna County, Pennsylvania, was for several years perhaps the most prolific correspondent of the *Port Folio.* His commonest pen-name was *Asmodeo,* with its variants *A., O., A. O., A——o,* and *A——O,* but he also used *Robert Shallow, Troilus, Phosphor,* and *Il Retirato,* and probably others. It was his *Ode to a Market Street Gutter,* parodying the *Ode to the River Raritan,* which caused the writing of the *Philadelphia Pursuits of Literature.* The author of this work called *Asmodeo*

"To sense and judgment each a mortal foe,"

and added, in a note about the *Ode to a Market Street Gutter:*

"This little poem of A. O. is remarkably simple, voluble, and sweet. It is an address to the *Genius Loci* of his birth, and awakens the most agreeable associations."

Rose submitted to the *Port Folio* several attractive verse translations from Persian and Arabic poets, sensuous lyrics, and clever but coarse satires on Jefferson. A volume of his *Sketches in Verse,* edited by Dennie, was published in 1810. Not much seems to be known of his life.

John Leeds Bozman (1757-1823), U. of P. 1777, a Maryland lawyer and writer, contributed prose and verse to the *Port Folio.* He was author of the *History of Maryland,* and other works. George L. Gray, of Baltimore, editor in 1802 and 1803 of a paper bearing the misnomer, *The Republican, or Anti-Democrat,* was the author of several versions of *Ossian,* and other poems in the *Port Folio,* 1801-1803. He died at St. Helena, 24 March, 1808. Another Marylander was Doctor John

Shaw (1778-1809), of Annapolis. He studied medicine at Pennsylvania and made a trip to Algiers as ship surgeon in 1798. His poems, with a memoir and correspondence, were published in 1810. Some of them appeared in the *Port Folio* in 1801, 1804, and 1805. The best, a song which is included in Stedman's *American Anthology,* may be quoted as an example of the better poetry of the magazine:

SONG.

"Who has robbed the ocean cave,
To tinge thy lips with coral hue?
Who from India's distant wave
For thee those pearly treasures drew?
Who, from yonder orient sky,
Stole the morning of thine eye?

"Thousand charms, thy form to deck,
From sea, and earth, and air, are torn;
Roses bloom upon thy cheek,
On thy breath their fragrance borne.
Guard thy bosom from the day,
Lest thy snows should melt away.

"But one charm remains behind,
Which mute earth can ne'er impart;
Nor in ocean wilt thou find,
Nor in circling air, a heart.
Fairest, wouldst thou perfect be,
Take, oh take, that heart from me."

John A. Collier (1787-—), while a law student at Troy, New York, contributed a few poems to the *Port Folio.* He was later a prominent lawyer in that state, residing at Binghamton. Gouverneur Morris (1752-1815), King's College (Columbia) 1768, led a life of distinguished public service, at home and abroad. He served in various Congresses and on important embasses to France and England. He was a one-legged man, who is said to have jested when his servant was carrying away his amputated limb. Near the end of his life he contributed satires in verse to various periodicals, including the *Port Folio.*

John Davis sent to Dennie several of his *Odes* and a few essays, both before his return to England in 1802 and after his second coming to America. His works received in the *Port Folio* the praise and dispraise which they deserved. He is described in the *Philadelphia Pursuits of Literature*—which fact does not preclude the possibility of his authorship—as "an itinerant bard, who has been all his life travelling from Dan to Beersheba, and scribbling on the road." He was a prolific writer of odes, on all the manifestations of nature, and reproached Dennie and Brown for neglecting natural beauties in their works. Lucas George, a young Irishman of talents and tastes similar to Davis's, and an intimate friend in their wanderings, also contributed a few poems to the *Port Folio* in 1807.

Davis and George were not the only minor British writers whose productions graced the *Port Folio*. Anne Bannerman, a little-known Scotch poetess, who died in 1829, was another. She published at Edinburgh a volume of *Poems* in 1800, *Tales of Superstition and Chivalry* in 1802, and a second *Poems*, including the contents of the two former volumes, in 1807. A literary friend secured for Dennie in 1803 some of her unpublished manuscript poems, which appeared in the *Port Folio* in the early part of 1804. George Brewer (1766-——), sailor, editor, lawyer, playwright, essayist, and writer of tales, published certainly some eleven works between 1791 and 1808, besides others doubtfully attributed to him. He contributed to the *European Magazine* a series of essays in imitation of Goldsmith, which were published separately with the title of *Hours of Idleness*, in 1806. These he forwarded to Dennie, who reprinted them in 1807. Robert Semple (1766-1816), born in Boston of British parents, traveled extensively in the course of a mercantile life, recording his impressions and experiences in several volumes of clear, interesting narrative. Dennie states in the *Port Folio*, 2 May, 1807, that Semple was "formerly a frequent writer in the *Port Folio*." While acting as Governor of the Hudson Bay Factories in 1816, he was killed in an altercation with agents of the Northwest Company. Edward Thornton (1766-1852), while Acting Charge d'Affaires of the British Legation from 1800 to 1804, may have contributed the *Harley* essays mentioned above.

In his notices To Readers and Correspondents, 1 January, 1803, Dennie made the following statement:

"An American gentleman, resident of Edinburgh, has favored the Editor with several *original* poems, from the pen of the celebrated T. Campbell. . . . Few things are more grateful to the Editor, than to maintain this literary intercourse with the learned and polished capital of a shrewd and sensible nation, whose *liberally instructed* metropolis has long been justly called the seat of science, the *hot bed of genius*, and the darling of literature."

In the same number appeared a poem entitled *Patience*, "For the *Port Folio*, by Thomas Campbell, Esq." Campbell was then still a young poet, whose *Pleasures of Hope*, 1799, had nevertheless gained him considerable fame, and whose *Poems* were to be published later in 1803. None of his poems in the *Port Folio* possesses any great merit.

Later in the same year, 28 May, 1803, Dennie wrote a long essay in praise of Leigh Hunt, the boy of nineteen whose *Juvenilia* was just reaching its third edition in London. Hunt's mother, it should be remembered, was a native of Philadelphia, and his father, Isaac Hunt, an Englishman from Barbadoes, was educated in the law at Philadelphia and practised there until the troubles preceding the Revolution, when, after being carted through the streets for Tory utterances, he left the city. The number for 11 June printed several poems from the *Juvenilia*, and announced:

"An original manuscript from *Mr. Hunt*, the juvenile poet of so much renown, shall be inserted with alacrity. It affords the Editor the purest pleasure to have it in his power to advance the claims of a *Child of Genius*, a nephew of Sir Benjamin West,[1] an honour to that country from which he descended, and to that, which *protects him*." The original poem, sent in by J. E. H., appeared in the *Port Folio*, 18 June, 1803. It comprised two ten-line stanzas on *Melancholy*.[2]

A greater poet than Leigh Hunt, and one better known than

1. Isaac Hunt and Benjamin West, the famous painter, married sisters, daughters of a Philadelphia merchant, Stephen Shewell.

2. A poem *Pleasure and Desire*, "from an unpublished manuscript of M. G. Lewis, Esq.," author of *The Monk*, appeared in the *Port Folio*, 16 July, 1803.

Thomas Campbell, was Thomas Moore, who came to Philadelphia in the summer of 1804 on his overland trip from Norfolk, Virginia, to New York and thence through Canada by way of Niagara. Moore, who was then twenty-five years old and had just completed a sojurn of four months at Bermuda in his official capacity of Register of the Court of Vice Admiralty there, had already acquired a national reputation by his *Odes of Anacreon* published in 1800, and the *Poetical Works of Thomas Little,* 1801, though sober minded readers like Jeffrey, in America and England, condemned his verses as extravagantly amatory if not actually salacious. Several of his poems had been copied and highly praised in the *Port Folio* in 1803, while Brown's *Literary Magazine and American Register* said of him, "I never heard of any merit he possessed beyond that of a writer of drinking songs and love ditties."[1] Many extracts from Moore's *Odes of Anacreon* appeared in Dennie's magazine during the spring and summer of 1804.[2] Moore's attitude toward America was in general that of most European travellers at that uncouth period of our national development—sneering and contemptuous. This attitude is reflected in his *Poems Relating to America,* as in the first stanza of *To Thomas Hume, Esq.*, which is in the same spirit as the rest of the poem:

" 'Tis evening now; beneath the western star
Soft sighs the lover through his sweet cigar,
And fills the ears of some consenting she
With puffs and vows, with smoke and constancy.
The patriot, fresh from Freedom's councils come,
Now pleased retires to lash his slaves at home;
Or woo, perhaps, some black Aspasia's charms,
And dream of freedom in his bondmaid's arms."

A footnote appended by Moore precluded any mistaking, on the part of the reader, of this allusion to the President of the United States. His correspondence and later accounts of his tour continue his abuse of Americans in general.

That there was one striking exception, however, to Moore's

1. Quoted in Oberholtzer's *Literary History of Philadelphia*, p. 180.
2. Dennie seems not to have known the authorship of *Little's Poems*, and his confusion was ridiculed in three satiric poems called *Criticism*, Nos. I, II, and III, in Duane's *Aurora*, in October, 1804.

unpleasant impressions, is evident from the following oft-quoted stanza from the epistle *To the Honorable W. R. Spencer:*

"Yet, yet forgive me, oh ye sacred few,
Whom late by Delaware's green banks I knew;
Whom known and loved through many a social eve,
'Twas bliss to live with, and 'twas pain to leave.
Not with more joy the lonely exile scanned
The writing traced upon the desert's sand,
Where his lone heart but little hoped to find
One trace of life, one stamp of human kind,
Than did I hail the pure, the enlightened zeal,
The strength to reason and the warmth to feel
The manly polish, and the illumined taste,
Which,—mid the melancholy, heartless waste
My foot has traversed—oh ye sacred few!
I found by Delaware's green banks with you."

Moore's footnote to this poem says:—

"In the society of Mr. Dennie and his friends, at Philadelphia, I passed the few agreeable moments which my tour through the states afforded me. Mr. Dennie has succeeded in diffusing through his cultivated little circle that love of good literature and sound politics which he feels so zealously himself, and which is so rarely the characteristic of his countrymen. They will not, I trust, accuse me of illiberality for the picture which I have given of the ignorance and corruption which surround them. If I did not hate, as I ought, the rabble to which they are opposed, I could not value, as I do, the spirit with which they defy it, and in learning from them what Americans *can be,* I but see with the more indignation what Americans *are.*"

The coming of a real, live British man of letters did, in fact, create a considerable flutter in the little circle of literary ladies and gentlemen at Philadelphia, who lionized him to his heart's content. True admirers of England, they were willing to accept whatever mud might fall upon them in the general bespattering, in the confident assurance that it was intended for their Jacobinical and Democratic fellow-countrymen.[1] He was

1. Moore did not visit Federalist New England, but his reception at Puritan Boston would probably not have decreased his dislike for Americans in general.

the guest of Dennie on several evenings with the Tuesday Club, evenings which he thus described:[1]

"Though few the days, the happy evenings few,
So warm their heart, so rich with mind they flew.
That my charmed soul forgot to wish to roam,
And rested there, as in a dream of home.

"Yes,--we had nights of that communion free,
That flow of heart, which I have known with thee
So oft, so warmly; nights of mirth and mind,
Of whims that taught, and follies that refined."

Besides Dennie, Moore's chief friends at Philadelphia were Ewing, Rose, J. E. Hall, and the Hopkinsons. Mrs. Hopkinson is said to have wept on hearing him sing one of his songs, a compliment which Moore repaid, as was his wont with sentimental ladies, in some amatory stanzas, rather more mild than usual.[2] Complimentary poems addressed to Moore, who was in Philadelphia in June,[3] appeared in the *Port Folio,* 22 and 29 September, 1804, by *Mercutio*, Ewing, and Hopkinson. Several of Moore's poems were first printed in the *Port Folio,* including *The Wedding Ring,* "Printed from the author's manuscript," 14 June, 1804. The well-known *Lines Written on Leaving Philadelphia,* beginning,

"Alone by the Schuylkill a wanderer roved,"

were sent to Dennie for publication in the *Port Folio* soon after Moore left Philadelphia,[4] but for some reason were not printed there until 31 August, 1805, after they had appeared elsewhere. Two letters from Moore to Dennie have been preserved, one from New York, 2 July, 1804, and one from Halifax, 29 September of the same year.[5] The gifted young Irishman's visit was not soon

1. *Epistle to the Honorable W. R. Spencer.*
2. Stanzas 4-6, in *Lines Written on Leaving Philadelphia.*
3. This fact is shown by the dates of his letters from America in the *Memoirs,* Vol. I, pp. 137-177.
4. See Dennie's prefatory note to the poem. Dennie's memory was at fault in assigning this meeting to the *autumn* of 1804. Smyth, *op. cit.*, p. 114, accepts this error.
5. Printed in the *Critic,* New York, 2 June, 1888. Two letters from Moore to J. E. Hall in 1816 and 1818 may be found in the *Collector,* New York, Vol. IX, 1895-96, pp. 65-67. These contain references to Dennie and his friends. A paragraph of a third letter, 23 April, 1807, was printed in the *Port Folio,* 22 August, 1807.

forgotton in Philadelphia, and its echoes lasted in the pages of the Port Folio[1] long after his departure.

A group truly representative of American and English literature in the first decade of the century, were these friends of *Oliver Oldschool.* On this side of the Atlantic he gathered around him the literary lawyers, doctors, divines, and teachers of the national metropolis, keeping in touch with the declining wits of Hartford and the rising geniuses of New York, Baltimore, and Boston. Abroad, his friends included Moore, Gifford, Campbell, and Leigh Hunt, men who, though not as great, were nearly as prominent as were Wordsworth, Coleridge, and Scott. Amid all these planets, of greater or lesser magnitude, Dennie, affable, enthusiastic, talented, was easily the center of the Philadelphia constellation at the time of its greatest brilliance.

1. Although Dennie felt called upon, 12 January, 1805, to defend their morals against the censures of "faded gossips and bridling prudes."

CHAPTER X

PHILADELPHIA, 1802-1808—THE PORT FOLIO

The years from 1802 to 1805 witnessed perhaps the high tide of the popularity of the *Port Folio.* Its subscription list was larger than that of any earlier American magazine. Its ablest American contributors were then writing actively for it, and occasional productions of Moore, Hunt, Campbell, Lewis, and other English authors were appearing in its columns. It was soon recognized in America as far superior to its predecessors in this country, and praise of it was general. Cobbett, in a letter from London, 4 September, 1801, uttered guarded commendation for the magazine, "to resemble which there is nothing in this country." Another letter, from Doctor Robert Anderson, of Edinburgh, the biographer of Smollett, commended Dennie for publishing the Smollett letters, and praised the *Port Folio,* which he said exhibited genius, but not novelty.

In the editor, however, Dennie lost the author. Instead of continuing his old series of essays or starting a new series, he devoted his attention to the contributions of others, utilizing extracts from English magazines, reviews, or newspapers to fill the remaining space in the *Port Folio.* His own output was confined to the summaries of domestic and foreign news, to prefatory comments, often of considerable length, on the articles submitted, to the departments of Literary Intelligence and To Readers and Correspondents, and to occasional political articles, sporadic essays, and letters for the *American Lounger.* Hall, Smyth, and other biographers of Dennie have stated that he wrote a new series of *Lay Preacher* and *Farrago* essays for the *Port Folio.* As a matter of fact, all but one of the seventeen *Farrago* essays in the magazine and all the *Lay Preachers* except a new introductory sermon, 17 January, 1801, and a short series of ten numbers in 1807 and 1808, had been published before, in the *Eagle,* the *Tablet* or the *Farmer's Museum.*[1]

1. Some of the essays had been printed several times. Thus the *Farrago* essay, *My Aunt Peg,* appeared in the *Eagle,* 3 March, 1794; in the *Tablet,* 1795; in the *Farmer's Museum,* 4 March, 1794; and in the *Port Folio,* 1801.

The odd *Farrago* had been written at Walpole, as was perhaps the case with the *Lay Preachers* also. Hall says[1] that Dennie's head was turned by his success and that he relaxed his efforts as an author when it was no longer necessary for him to rely upon his own labors for the support of his paper. Certain it is that, in the society of his friends in the Tuesday Club, he gave himself up again to the old careless, easy-going life he had led at Walpole.

An anecdote concerning him, told in the *Curiosities of Literature* of D'Israeli and Griswold, illustrates both Dennie's wit and the opinion of serious-minded people regarding him.[2] Dennie once had occasion to put up for the night at a New Jersey inn of limited accommodations, and found that nearly all the rooms had already two occupants, except that engaged by Timothy Dwight, President of Yale, and author of the *Conquest of Canaan*. Dennie asked to be admitted to Dwight's presence, saying, "Although I am a stranger to the reverend doctor, perhaps I can bargain with him for my lodgings." Dwight courteously received his anonymous guest, who soon engaged him in a discussion of the merits of Washington, Franklin, Rittenhouse, and other statesmen and authors. Eventually Dwight said:

" 'Dennie, the editor of the *Port Folio*, is the Addison of the United States, the father of American Belles-Lettres. But, sir, is it not astonishing, that a man of such genius, fancy and feeling, should abandon himself to the inebriating bowl, and to Bacchanalian revels?'

" 'Sir,' said Dennie, 'you are mistaken; I have been intimately acquainted with Dennie for several years, and I never knew or saw him intoxicated.'

" 'Sir," says the Doctor, 'you err; I have had the information from a particular friend. I am confident that I am right and that you are wrong.' "

Dennie did not argue the matter further, but changed the conversation to the subject of preachers, and after praising Abercrombie and Mason, added:

---

1. *Philadelphia Souvenir.*
2. New York edition, by Griswold, 1848. *Curiosities of American Literature*, pp. 51-52.

" 'Doctor Dwight is the most learned theologian, the first logician, and the greatest poet that America has ever produced. But, sir, there are traits in his character unworthy so great and wise a man—of the most detestable description—he is the greatest *bigot* and *dogmatist* of the age.'

" 'Sir,' said the Doctor, 'you are grossly mistaken. I am intimately acquainted with Doctor Dwight, and I know to the contrary.'

" 'Sir,' says Dennie, 'you are mistaken. I have it from an intimate acquaintance of his, who I am confident, would not tell an untruth.'

" 'No more slander,' says the Doctor, 'I am Doctor Dwight, of whom you speak.'

" 'And I too,' exclaimed Dennie, merrily, 'I am Mr. Dennie, of whom you spoke.'

"They mutually shook hands, and were extremely happy in each other's company."[1]

In the first number of Volume II of the *Port Folio*, 16 January, 1802, appeared the first of a long series of essays called *The American Lounger*, of which the author of the *Philadelphia Pursuits of Literature* said, "I look upon the *Port Folio Lounger* as the very worst periodical work ever published." This was a rash statement, though the essays would seem to bear out his declaration that "Its personages have no likeness to anything in heaven above, or in the earth beneath, or in the waters under the earth." Whether it was under the direction of Dennie or of someone else, as the first essay would seem to indicate, it was the work of many hands, some of which were inexperienced in writing. Of the 184 numbers which appeared from 1802 to 1807, Dennie's work is evident in less than forty. Rose, Mrs. Sarah Hall, John E. Hall, Ewing, and John Davis were among the other contributors; but the most important writers, *Harley*, *Florian*, *Beatrice*, *Agricola*, and *Staterus*, have not been identified. The series was made up chiefly of literary criticisms, moral essays, and satires on manners. Most of the contributions were in the form of letters to

1. *The House of Sloth*, an original poem by Doctor Dwight, appeared in the *Port Folio*, 13 Oct., 1804.

2. Thirty-eight numbers appeared in 1802; 40 in 1803; 25 in 1804; 44 in 1805; 32 in 1806.

Mr. Samuel Saunter, who was supposed to preside over the department. Six of the first twenty-two essays deal with the Tuesday Club. A favorite subject of satire in the earlier numbers, especially in those contributed by Dennie, was the current vogue in woman's attire, which, according to the fashion plates of the time, allowed a considerable display of bare arms and bosoms.[1] Dennie was as intolerant of this as of other French innovations, and many were the letters inveighing, in every degree of banter, scorn, and seriousness, against the "naked beauties" of the day. Americanisms of various sorts, and Yankee ignorance and indifference to literature came in for their share of ridicule. Some cleverly-drawn characters appear in the scribbling wife of *Timothy Plainsense; Lucy Artless's* uncle, the projector; and *Sam Scapegrace*, the unsuccessful lawyer.[2] Two good allegories were Mrs. Hall's *Garden of Wedlock* and Rose's *Temple of Fashion.*[3] Rose also contributed, in several numbers, translations from Hafiz and other oriental poets. In Number XXVI, 10 July, 1802, Dennie suggested that the Philadelphia Public Library be opened in the forenoon, as well as later, for the benefit of persons of "literary leisure." Three series of critical articles, by *Florian* on Miss Williams' *Edwin and Eltruda*, by *Agricola* on the *Iliad*, and by *Staterus*, defending the poetry of Gray, appeared in May-June, 1804, October-November, 1805, and March-June, 1806, respectively. Perhaps Dennie's best contribution was two mock-criticisms on *A Virginia Advertisement* for a horse, "lost, strayed, or stolen," 28 December, 1805, and 11 January, 1806. The cleverest thing in the entire series was the mock criticism of *Jack and Jill*, 14 and 28 July, 1804.[4] A parody on the style of Wordsworth's ballads, by Rose, 18 August of the same year, is also good in spots, as the following stanzas will show:

---

1. See, for instance, two plates, "Early Philadelphia Costumes," and "Philadelphia Costumes and Headdresses," in Scharf and Westcott's *History of Philadelphia*, Vol. II, pp. 890 and 916.
2. 5 March, 1803, 12 March, 1803, and 26 May, 1805, respectively.
3. 7 May, 1803, and 2 April, 1803.
4. Usually ascribed to Dennie, and reprinted as a specimen of his work in *The Philadelphia Book*, and elsewhere. It was, however, signed *N.*, and is credited in Hall's *Philadelphia Souvenir* to *N. B.* The author was probably Nicholas Biddle.

"My walking stick was in my hand,
And by my hand I held it fast,
I took it in my own right hand,
And so right on I past.

"It is a right down honest stick,
In truth I've had the stick so long,
And 'tis so old, 'tis hard to say
If ever it was young.

"So on I went, foot after foot,
Not thinking, onward did I go;
For animals, that think, we're told,
Move always rather slow."

During 1801 the *Port Folio* had been published by "The Editor and Asbury Dickins, sole proprietors of the work," at 25 North Second Street, Hugh Maxwell, printer. The issue of 16 January, 1802 announced that the sole management had now devolved upon Dennie, and that in consequence of complaints about irregular and tardy delivery to city patrons, the *Port Folio* in the future would be published *for the city*, by William Fry, bookseller, at 36 Chestnut Street. The name of Elizabeth Dickins also replaced that of Asbury Dickins in the signature at the end of each number. After 11 September, 1802, Fry seems to have succeeded the Dickinses at 25 North Second Street; from that date until 24 September, 1803, the paper was "published for the Editor, by William Fry," and the last number of Volume II, 15 January, 1803, gave notice that "The Copartnership, in the *Port Folio* establishment, which has hitherto subsisted, between the Editor, Asbury Dickins, and Elizabeth Dickins, is this day dissolved, 31st of December, 1802." From 1 October, 1803, until the end of 1805, the magazine was published for the editor by Hugh Maxwell, who had been the printer from the start, at 25 North Second Street.

Several reasons may perhaps be assigned for these changes, most important of which was the uncertainty and delinquency of subscription payments.[1] In reviewing his first two years, Dennie

1. Another source of annoyance was the habit booksellers had, of expecting notices of books, pamphlets, etc., in the *Port Folio*, for no compensation, such a notice being "notoriously a source of emolument to publishers." On 19 May, 1804, the rule was made that the price of subscription must be sent with every such request.

announced that "the public encouragement of this Journal is so moderate, that the Editor, far from receiving the *labourer's hire,* has *gained* nothing, but the kindness of a few of the most partial of his friends."[1] On 21 May, 1803, he remarked, "On the subscription list of the *Port Folio* we enumerate many who, from want of opportunity, want of attention, or culpable negligence, postpone their payment for this paper"—a paper, he adds, "which neither derives, nor can derive, any support from the lucrative aid of advertisements; which *never has been, nor never shall be* a source of emolument to its proprietor in consequence of *its servility to any party;* and, lastly, which, though composed of more copious materials, conducted with more labour, and published at a greater expense than any other periodical miscellany, either at home or abroad, is sold for a very moderate consideration." At Philadelphia as at Walpole, Dennie found, it was difficult for a paper depending for its support solely upon the patrons of literature, to keep its head above water.[2] Duane, who had troubles of his own,[3] wrote to a friend, 30 September, 1801, that Dennie had come thither "expecting to find the city inhabited by such men as Mecaenas [sic] and Cosmo de Medici. He has been disappointed in everything . . . even the *Port Folio* is now tumbling under its own weight . . . and cannot outlive the year"[4]—a prophecy which, in spite of financial discouragements, frequent illness, and insufficient patronage, was not to be fulfilled.

Meanwhile the newspaper war went merrily on. Duane had promptly nicknamed the new magazine the *Portable Foolery,* and described its editor as having been "employed by Pickering as a kind of literary Jackall at a salary paid out of the public Treasury,"[5] and Dennie did not long refrain from answering with equal virulence. A series of political essays called *The Examiner,* in the *Port Folio,*[6] attacking Thomas Paine and bearing the motto:

---

1. *Port Folio,* 15 Jan., 1803.
2. The price of the *Port Folio* was increased from five to six dollars, January, 1804.
3. In the *Aurora,* 3 November, 1803, he stated that, while the paper had the largest circulation in the Union, $22,000 was due to him for subscriptions.
4. Letter to Joseph Nancrede. See *Mass. Hist. Soc. Proceedings,* 2nd Series, Vol. XX, May, 1906.
5. *Aurora,* 3 August, 1801.
6. *Port Folio,* November, 1802.

"A hoary drunkard, with each vice imbued,
Malignant without wit, and without passion lewd,"

was answered in the *Boston Chronicle* by a series of the same name and using for its motto an utterance of Dennie's, "A democracy is scarcely tolerable at any period of national history," etc. This series was copied in the *Aurora*. The *Chronicle* Dennie termed "a dull democratic gazette, intolerably tedious, egregiously stupid, audaciously false, and unspeakably absurd;"[1] and the best name he had for Duane's paper was "the strumpet Aurora."[2] Five columns of the *Aurora*, on Monday, 20 June, 1803, were devoted to an attack upon "a New England lad of the name of Joe Denny, who from various causes and visible connexions, as well as from the character and cast of his paper we must consider as in the pay of some hostile government." There follows an amusing parody on *An Author's Evenings*, entitled "*An Author's Moonlight Nights.* For the *Portable Foolery,* From the Garret of Messrs. Lunatic and Lumbago." Dennie's grandiose and alliterative style is well hit off in passages like the following:

"Here doomed to dwindle in the dreary darkness of dull and dizzy democracy, let me cheer my spirit eager to flit to regions where order is distinguished by gradations where each grade gradually grows greater from the lowest degradation to the greatest grandeur."

Stung by the cleverness of this staire, Dennie retorted in the *Port Folio* the following Saturday with an attack upon the Democratic Ward Meetings as unlawful assemblies. Duane had condemned John Fenno and Dennie for conducting Federalist papers while enjoying respectively positions as printer to the Senate and the Treasury Department, and a federal clerkship. Now Dennie accused Duane, as Stationer General, of buying the paper for his press so cheaply that he could distribute the *Aurora* among the rabble for almost nothing. Two weeks later,[3] in *Advice to the Editor of the Aurora*, Dennie addressed himself directly to his enemy, proffering some needed instruction on points of orthography, grammar, rhetoric, ethics, and other

1. *Port Folio*, 13 November, 1802.
2. *Port Folio*, 28 May, 1803.
3. *Port Folio*, 9 July, 1803.

such little matters. For several years skirmishing of this sort kept on, with lessening acrimony after 1803.

Duane, however, was small game for the *Port Folio* satirists, who generally aimed their darts at the head of the administration. Dennie's own *forte* was satire, rather than argument, and he once declared:[1]

"Nothing wounds a malignant Democrat more than the keen javelin of wit. The popular ballad is an admirable vehicle for satirizing knaves and fools. Horace well describes the . . . tota cantabitur urbe . . . and we exhort each trembling caitiff of the democrats to remember,

> Whoe'er offends at some unlucky time
> Slides into verse or hitches into rhyme,
> Sacred to ridicule the whole year long,
> And the sad burden of a merry song."

In 1802 the notorious Callender, a professional liar and libeller, who had assailed Washington as an "old British Tory," and Adams as a "hoary headed traitor," turned upon Jefferson, who had refused his request for office, the full current of his organ of slander, the *Richmond Recorder*. The scandal he collected and issued, based upon distorted facts and his own unclean invention, was accepted by the Federalists as justifying their long-standing opinion of Jefferson, and was published broadcast by the press of the North. This gave rise, in the *Port Folio*, as elsewhere, to many indecent satires in verse and prose, on Jefferson's supposed amours with a slave named Sally. The President was also attacked for inviting Paine to visit America. A third occasion for satire was the presentation to Jefferson, in 1801, by the inhabitants of Cheshire, Massachusetts, of what was known as the Mammoth Cheese. Many derisive ballads celebrated this unprecedented honor, such as the *Reflection of Mr. Jefferson,* of which some stanzas follow:[2]

> "Ye men of Cheshire, little did you know,
> When urg'd by love, this ponderous gift you sent,
> That on this heart you struck a sick'ning blow,
> And gave a thousand damning feelings vent.

1. *Port Folio*, 19 Aug., 1804.
2. *Port Folio*, 27 March, 1802.

"In this great cheese I see myself portray'd,
My life and fortune in this useless mass,
I curse the hands, by which the thing was made,
To them a cheese, to me a looking-glass."

"Once I was pure . . . Alas! that happy hour,
E'en as the milk, from which this monster came,
Till turn'd, by philosophic rennet, sour,
I barter'd virtue for an empty name.

* * * * * *

"Delusive view! where light is cast aside,
And principles surrender for *mere words*,
Ah me! how lost to just and noble pride,
I am become indeed a man of curds."

Fully as witty was the supposed fragment of a journal picked up on the banks of the Potomac, from which the following extracts are taken:[1]

"Monday 8 o'clock, 20th February, 1804

"Left Sally—damn's bore, to rise early—but must seem industrious, though nothing to do. Met Madison at breakfast—don't much like him—talked of virtue and conscience—thought he looked hard at me—Gallatin's the man—never hear such stuff from him—no danger, too, of his pushing me out—good fellow, pay him well and he'll do anything—'point d'argent, point de Suisse.'

"*10 o'clock.* Wrote half a page of my dissertation on cock-roaches—servant came in to say people below wanted to see me on public business—cursed their impertinence—sent word I was out. Why don't they go to Gallatin or Madison?—office of President must be a sinecure—trouble enough to sign bills and messages—returned to my cock-roaches in a fret, and couldn't write. Received note from Gallatin, including bill I told him to read yesterday—says it's all right—signed it and sent it to the Senate. Mem. to ask Gallatin, what's its purport.

"*12 o'clock.* Randolph[2] came in—looked rather queer—found he'd been trying to answer that damn'd fellow, Griswold[3]—

1. *Port Folio,* 18 Aug., 1804.
2. John Randolph of Virginia.
3. Roger Griswold of Connecticut.

desperate case—made many bold assertions, but was detected in all—got into a cursed scrape, and was obliged to sit down—damn'd provoking, can't find any one to cope with Griswold—Jack's flippant enough, but quite on the surface, better than any of our side, though—tried Giles,[1] found he wouldn't do—been looking out someone to buy over a Fed of talents—can't meet with one who'd take a bribe—very strange, that.

"Ordered my horse—never ride with a servant—looks proud—mob wouldn't like it—must gull the boobies. Adams wouldn't bend so—had rather lose his place—knew nothing of the world. Pass'd Merry[2] and his wife—saw her whisper and smile—look'd foolish—thought she was laughing at me—Why do women of fashion come to this country?—wish she had staid in England—heard her jest once about my dirty stockings—must cringe to 'em now, though—hope he hasn't written home about my reception of them—only did so to please our party, and to show the world, that republicans affect not to conduct themselves by the rules of gallantry and politeness."

But there were limits of endurance, even to the "leathern ears" of Jacobinical Americans, long inured to abuse. In the *Port Folio*, 23 April, 1803, Dennie "wrote and caused to be printed and published" the following paragraph:

"A democracy is scarcely tolerable at any period of national history. Its omens are always sinister, and its powers are unpropitious. With all the lights of experience blazing before our eyes, it is impossible not to discern the futility of this form of government. It was weak and wicked in Athens. It was bad in Sparta and worse in Rome. It has been tried in France, and has terminated in despotism. It was tried in England, and rejected with the utmost loathing and abhorrence. It is on its trial here, and the issue will be civil war, desolation, and anarchy. No wise man but discerns its imperfections, no good man but shudders at its miseries, no honest man but proclaims its fraud, and no brave man but draws his sword against its force. The institution of a scheme of polity, so radically contemptible and vicious, is a memorable example of what the villainy of some men

1. William B. Giles of New York. The discussion was probably about Louisiana, the purchase of which was deplored by the *Port Folio*.

2. Anthony Merry, the British ambassador. There was a difference of long standing between Jefferson and the Merrys.

can devise, the folly of others receive, and both establish, in despite of reason, reflection and sensation."

This utterance was speedily copied in a number of the Federalist papers, which, as Dennie said, indicated that certain editors considered its doctrine just, if not popular. It was also noticed in the *Aurora*[1] and other Democratic papers, and the editor was denounced as a traitor and libeller, who should be chastised by the courts. On the Fourth of July a presentment of the paragraph was made to the Grand Jury, and an indictment for inflammatory and seditious libel was issued the same day. Dennie selected his legal advisers wisely[2] and awaited the trial, but action was postponed during 1803 and 1804, until near the end of 1805. Meanwhile the violence of *Port Folio* politics, though by no means abandoned, was abated sufficiently for the *Boston Democrat* to remark complacently, in May, 1804, "We have silenced Mr. Denny, on his slanders on Democracies, and must silence Mr. *Novanglus;*[3] the effort will not be troublesome, as his ability is weaker, and his offence is of a deeper hue." At length, on Friday, 28 November, 1805, the trial began. It lasted until Monday, 2 December, when, after an able defence by Jared Ingersoll and Joseph Hopkinson, Dennie was awarded a unanimous verdict of not guilty. The *Port Folio* for the following Saturday[4] briefly summarized the case, thanked the court, the attorney general, and the jurors, promised a more copious account in the next issue, and delivered this final exultant blast:

"Thus far the editor has been triumphant in his warfare with Democracy, a fiend more terrible than any that the imagination of the classical poets ever conjured up from the 'vasty deep' of their Pagan hell."

Anything more characteristic than Dennie's treatment of his "more copious account" could hardly be imagined. It did not appear, as was promised, in the next issue, or in the next. It was begun in the last number of the year, 28 December, 1805. The first two documents in the case, the Presentment and the Indictment, consuming, with all the tedium of legal verbiage, repetition, and parenthesis, the space of six columns, were

1. See the *Aurora*, 7 May and 20 June, 1803.
2. Jared Ingersoll, Joseph Hopkinson, William Meredith, and William Lewis. Only Ingersoll and Hopkinson spoke at the trial.
3. In the *Boston Centinel.*
4. 7 December, 1805.

printed entire. At that point Dennie became weary of his task and abandoned it forever, with this naive valediction:—

"The Editor inscribes *vici*, upon the white shield of his innocence, but is wholly incapable of vaunting at the victory."

Dennie's condemnation, however, was not confined to politics. Pretty nearly everything distinctively American came in for its share of sharp censure or mocking gibe. The typical Yankee farmer or trader, the *Jonathan* of Tyler's *Contrast*, shrewd and honest, but often unlettered and uncouth, whom, as Uncle Sam or Brother Jonathan, we have adopted as our national prototype, represented to Dennie nearly all the evils of American life which he desired to eradicate. The efforts of certain well-meaning Connecticut gentlemen[1] to establish an American standard of English was combated fiercely in the columns of the *Port Folio* by Dennie and his friends of similar views. The *Restorator* articles on Americanisms in the *New England Palladium* by J. S. J. Gardiner were copied and subscribed to. In these papers Noah Webster, whom the Democratic Duane hailed as "that walking monument of human folly, tergiversation, and literary quackery,"[2] was urged to give to his American Dictionary, "the projected volume of *foul* and *unclean* things," his own name, and call it "Noah's Ark."[3]

Dennie himself, in *An Author's Evenings,* made the following sugestions:[4]

"The papers have announced that a certain critic of Mr. Gibbon, and a grammarian who had the hardihood to oppose Bishop Lowth,[5] and fairly kick the *subjunctive mood* down stairs, is about to publish a Dictionary of the *American vulgar* tongue. We deem it, therefore, our duty as good patriots, and as fond lovers of provincial idioms, and colloquial meanness, and, in short, of every thing, hostile to English sense, and English stile, to furnish this great lexicographer with all the barbarous words and phrases which we can procure. We hope in process of time, to add to our collection, and everyone who is laudably anxious to debase his diction; to degrade the language of literature, to the low level of vulgar life; and to deride the study and imitation of the ancients, will do well to profit by our labours.

---

1. The Rev. John Elliot, Noah Webster, and Samuel Johnson, Jr.
2. *Aurora*, 22 June, 1803.
3. *Port Folio*, 21 Nov., 1801; copied from the *New England Palladium.*
4. *Port Folio*, 28 August, 1802.
5. Author of *Lowth's Grammar.*

Evincial	Boston Newspaper.
Lengthy	True American.
Spry	Provincial.
If I Was He	Provincial.
Carniverosity	Boston Newspaper.
I most guess	Provincial.
Hellniferous	Officers of the Federal Army.
Happify	Presbyterian clergy.
He laughed and gurned[1]	Provincial.
Rowen	Provincial.
On the Side Hill	Provincial.
My dafter	Provincial.
Truck trade	Provincial.
Stilish	Boston advertisement.
A likely pair of oxen	New Hampshire idiom.
Of and about[2]	Boston Newspaper.
Caucus	Boston Newspaper.
A little bit ago	Philadelphia idiom.

His worst offense, however, was probably the republication of a series of "*Interesting Travels in America,* translated from the German of Bülow"[3]—a "fatal work of mingled spleen and rage,"[4] characterized by a misrepresentation of American life and character seldom equalled by even European malice and German credulity. Dennie admitted in introducing it that it was "a frightful caricature," "amounting to nearly a libel upon the country,"[5] yet he published it, with perverted zeal, in order that "some wholesome, though perhaps unpalatable truth" might be conveyed to the readers; and as a result he is said to have lost a hundred subscribers.[6] Dennie's attitude did

1. Grinned, an English dialect survival.
2. Of or about. Some of the words in this abbreviated list were in good use then; some have won sanction since.
3. In the *Port Folio*, 8 May, 1802, to 29 January, 1803.
4. *Philadelphia Pursuits of Literature.*
5. *Port Folio*, 8 May, 1802.
6. *Philadelphia Pursuits of Literature.* The following libel upon the German Baptists will sufficiently illustrate the truthfulness of Bülow's *Travels.* "Young, grown-up anabaptist girls, some of whom are very pretty, are baptized near Philadelphia, in the Schuylkill. They undress themselves; the priest takes them before him, and throws them down backward into the river. . . . I have often met them upon their return from this baptismal bath, to the city: they are always remarkably frolicsome."

not, of course, escape hostile comment. The *Aurora* called his productions, "a mongrel species of criticism, a kind of apery, of what is called the *modern English* style—an insipid and inflated coxcombery in writing, bearing about the mark of erudition, without anything solid or real behind it."[1]

For the publication of another series, *The British Spy in Boston,* which gave offense to John Quincy Adams, Dennie apologized, saying that he had been able to read only the first number of the series, being at the time "occupied with the care of an edition of Shakespeare, and of Sir W. Jones."[2] Smyth stated[3] that Dennie was the first American editor of Shakespeare, but this honor cannot be claimed for him. Miss Jane Sherzer, in her study of the *American Editions of Shakespeare,*[4] seems to have demonstrated that the first Shakespeare plays were published in Boston in 1794, and that two sets of the complete dramatic works, at Philadelphia (1795-1796) and at Boston (1802-1804), both apparently *edited* to some extent, preceded the Philadelphia edition of 1805-1809,[5] with which Dennie was concerned. Moreover, Dennie's connection with this edition was very much slighter than even Miss Sherzer has believed, as the following facts will show.

The *Port Folio,* 11 February, 1804, contained the prospectus of the "first complete edition in America" of the works of Shakespeare, from the text of the 1803 London edition of Isaac Reed. It was then proposed to publish the first volume in April, and one of the ensuing fifteen volumes every month thereafter, at a price to subscribers of $1.50 a volume. It was to be "printed under the immediate direction and superintendence of an Editor [unnamed], assisted by several men of letters." A month later, the following request appeared in the column To Readers and Correspondents:

---

1. *Aurora,* 16 June, 1803.
2. *Adams Papers*, Mass. Hist. Soc. Library, Boston. Letter to J. Q. Adams. Sir William Jones (1746-1794), made many translations from Oriental literature.
3. *Op. cit.,* p. 108.
4. *Publications of the Mod. Lang. Assoc. of Am.,* Vol. XXII, pp. 639-648.
5. According to Miss Sherzer, Volumes 2-6 appeared in 1805; 7-8 in 1806; 9-10 in 1807; 11 in 1808; 1 and 12-17 in 1809.

"The Editor having, at the request of his publisher,[1] undertaken to superintend a new edition of the plays of *Shakespeare*, is particularly desirous of inspecting the *first* folio edition. This is probably very scarce, and may be found only in the cabinet of some *distant virtuoso.* But the owner of this rare book will be very gratefully thanked, if the Editor can have permission to consult it, for a short season."

In the issues for 14 and 21 April, Dennie called for a long list of works on Shakespeare, which, during the researches of several weeks, he had been unable to find. The expectations of the publishers to issue a volume in April were fruitless. Not until 1 Septembr, 1804, did the following notice in the *Port Folio* appear:

"The first volume of the new American edition of Shakspeare is now in the press of *Mr. Manning,* one of the proprietors, and the work is advancing with as much speed as the difficult nature of the task will justify. In reprinting an edition, from the text of *Steevens* and *Reed,* the pages, mottled with many varieties of typographical character, and abounding in quotations from authors, whose style is obsolete, or uncouth, demand a revision at once scrupulous and *slow.* To *drive* such a work, with celerity, through the press, would be disgraceful to the Editor, detrimental to the Printer, and a disappointment to the Public."

The tone of this announcement would seem to indicate a retort, on the part of an editor both meticulous and dilatory, to the urging of the publishers and subscribers, for haste in issuing the work. Whatever the reason, however, Dennie's connection with it terminated abruptly. An advertisement of a new edition at Boston, by Lemuel Blake, was warmly greeted in the *Port Folio,* 21 November, 1807, and introduced by the following remarks:

"Sometime since, a Printer in this city undertook the publication of Shakspeare's Plays according to the text of Johnson, Steevens, and Isaac Reed, with voluminous notes. The Editor of this Journal wrote the prospectus, and anticipated the success of the work. But the execution of the initial volume did not equal his wishes, nor the public expectation. The Pro-

---

1. Hugh Maxwell. His partner was Thomas S. Manning.

prietor, perhaps wisely, determined to make it a commodious and cheap edition, and the Editor withdrew himself from the task. Partial to the fame of this immortal writer, and solicitous that his works may be generally perused, it is pleasing to him that this edition sells, though he has no interest in the work, nor is responsible for its execution. Though the Editor was not treated with much frankness, or liberality on this occasion, yet he will not suffer resentment to prejudice the interest of the Proprietor, and is perfectly willing to allow, in a spirit of candour, that, if it is not a very elegant, it is a very useful edition, and ought to be purchased by those whose limited resources forbid them to indulge in expensive literature.''

I have not found the ''useful notes in the 1807 edition, signed 'J. D.,' '' which Smyth mentions,[1] and it is difficult to see what was meant by the ''1807 edition.'' Presumably the first volume issued—the only one Dennie supervised—was Vol. II, containing *Richard III, Two Gentlemen of Verona,* and *A Midsummer Night's Dream.* The last two plays have no notes in addition to those of Reed and his predecessors; the few in *Richard III* are signed *Am. Ed.*, uniformly with those in the other volumes. His chief attention was evidently given to typographical matters and verbal criticism. Who edited the remaining plays is not known, but judging from Dennie's own testimony his part in the undertaking must have been slight.[2]

The pages of the *Port Folio* for the years 1802-1808 contain notices and encomiums of the most prominent English and American authors and poets then writing. The praise of Wordsworth's and Coleridge's ballads has been cited. Southey's poetry was alternately praised or condemned, according to its varying orthodoxy.[3] Moore's was reprinted copiously, and his strictures were accepted with humility. When Crabbe, in 1807, broke his twenty years of silence, his return was hailed with

1. Smyth, *op. cit.*, p. 108.
2. Miss Sherzer's remark, "we have no doubt it was Mr. Dennie, for what other scholar handled the pen in Addisonian style in Philadelphia, or in any other city of the U. S. from 1805-1809?", appears not very astute. As much Addisonian style as can be discerned in the handful of notes in the entire seventeen volumes could probably have been produced by at least a dozen Philadelphians in 1805.
3. See the *Port Folio*, 2 July, 1803, and 5 and 12 Apr., 1806.

gladness.[1] Gifford, with whom Dennie carried on correspondence, was praised chiefly for his translations and imitations from the Classics.[2] Anne Radcliffe was blamed for her subjects and praised for her treatment of nature.[3] Scott's *Minstrelsy of the Scottish Border* received favorable comment, and several of his poems were reprinted.[4] Charlotte Smith, the Della Cruscan poetess and novelist, frequently the butt of *Colon and Spondee's* fun, was nevertheless sometimes quoted with commendation.[5] Another poet who was praised was the Rev. W. L. Bowles, "author of a series of sonnets, incomparably the best in the English tongue, and, neither in tenderness nor sweetness inferior to those of Petrarch."[6] Among foreign writers, translations from Schiller, Gessner, Chateaubriand, and others appeared; Kotzebue was travestied;[7] Goethe was somewhat neglected.

On the American side, Trumbull, Fessenden, Robert Treat Paine, and Dunlap, among many others, received their share of encouragement.[8] The precocious John Howard Payne, later a noted poet and playwright, and composer of the song *Home, Sweet Home,* was highly commended in the *Port Folio,* in a letter from New York, 22 February, 1806. He was then fourteen years old and already editor of the *Thespian Mirror,* a paper devoted chiefly to the theatre. His *Epitaph on Dermody* appeared in the *Port Folio,* 23 May, 1807. Barlow's *Columbiad* received some "faint praise" on its appearance in 1807.[9] By far the best American poet then known was Philip Freneau (1752-1832), to whom a series of critical essays was devoted in the *Port Folio* from 17 October to 28 November, 1807. In publishing these remarks Dennie says:

"For the *politicks* of the authour it is pretty well known that we have no peculiar partiality, but of the *poetry* of this versatile

1. See the *Port Folio*, 28 Oct., 1808.
2. See the *Port Folio*, 12 June and 18 Sept., 1802.
3. See the *Lay Preacher* essays in the *Port Folio*, 9 July, 1803, and following.
4. See the *Port Folio*, 21 May, 1803, 29 Aug., 1807.
5. See the *Port Folio*, 21 Feb., 1807.
6. See the *Port Folio*, 15 July, 1803.
7. See the *Port Folio*, 24 Aug., 1805.
8. See the *Port Folio* for 12 Aug., 1804; 12 Oct., 1805; 27 March, 1806; and 7 Nov., 1807, respectively.
9. See the *Port Folio*, 31 Oct., 1807.

bard we must say that, by the impartial, it will be, at length, considered as entitled to no ordinary place in a judicious estimate of American genius.''[1]

Freneau wrote, together with some excellent poems, a considerable amount of trash. The critic, in this case, took cognizance of the fact in his concluding sentence: ''Should another edition of these poems be published, we recommend that the 455 closely printed pages of the present one be diminished to less than half that number, by the omission of a large part of its contents.'' A well-selected list of the poems most worthy of republication was appended.[2]

Among American periodicals, Brown's *American Register*, of Philadelphia, and the *Monthly Anthology* (1803-1811) of Boston, were praised and quoted.[3] When Irving and Paulding's *Salmagundi* appeared at New York in 1807, the young authors, who, though concealed from the public, ''are not unknown to us,''[4] were hailed as jovial fellow-satirists of Columbian and Jacobinical shortcomings. The writer of the *Mustapha* letters[5] especially, was called ''a well-principled Federalist, a wit, and a cavalier.'' The *Salmagundi* wits were then engaged in a merry war with *Doctor Costive*[6] (Thomas G. Fessenden), who, in his newly-established *Weekly Inspector*, had ridiculed their paper. *The Stranger in Pennsylvania* and several others of their productions reappeared in the *Port Folio* in the spring of 1807.[7]

The other departments continued in about the same fashion. To Readers and Correspondents is fully as interesting as any other part of the paper. Many of the notes are doubtless pure

1. Freneau was a Democrat, and had conducted, in the Jeffersonian interests, the *National Gazette* at Philadelphia, 1791-1793, opposing Fenno's *Gazette of the U. S.*
2. See the *Port Folio*, 31 Oct., 1807.
3. See, for instance, the *Port Folio* for 31 Oct., 1807, and 12 March, 1808.
4. *Port Folio*, 16 May, 1807.
5. Irving was author of the letter in No. VIII, which was the one referred to.
6. A parody on Fessenden's assumed name, *Dr. Caustic.*
7. Many of these notices by authors were contained in the department of Literary Intelligence, which was designed to keep readers informed concerning the activities of British and American men of letters. Literary Intelligence for 29 Sept., 1804, for instance, contains notices of Campbell, Southey, Scott, Bowles, Gifford, Mitford, and Dr. Jortin.

fiction, belaboring imaginary Jacobin contributors for the amusement of the readers. Such are these:

"As we look upon him to be defunct, and as his muse is as dead as he, to the consideration of his executors, we recommend Potter's field, rather than the *Port Folio*, as the repository for Damon and his ditties."[1]

"'The Ode to the Moon' surpasses in stupidity whatever of crude or imperfect we have ever had the misfortune to read."[2]

"'Sidney' is rejected. We dislike his *name*."[3]

"During the lassitude of the summer, and the terrors of the sickly season," Dennie wrote, "the Editor receives but little aid from his correspondents." At such times he was fain to fill an occasional column with notes which merely served to introduce a well-turned or obscure verse, as in this case:[5]

"The character and writings of C. may be described in a couplet which Pope applies to the most brilliant nobleman of his time,

> "Correct with spirit, eloquent with ease,
> Intent to reason, or polite to please."

The Biographies, generally from the *Edinburgh Review* or other British periodicals, occupied a considerable space. Anderson and Aiken were the authors of most of the articles quoted. The list of lives for 1803 included those of Florian, Fenelon, Henry MacKenzie, Lindley Murray, Talleyrand, Gray, Cowper, Richard Glover, John Scott, Camoens (author of the *Lusiad*), Bennet Langton, William Wilkie, and William Mitford. The Epistolary department included original letters from various sources, including a long series by Cowper in 1805, and others by Franklin, Johnson, and other worthies. *An Author's Evenings* continued with considerable regularity. The range of Dennie's reading and literary interest may be judged from the *Evening* of 29 October, 1803, which contains notices of Thomas Warton, Thomas Moore, Cowper, Doctor Bentley, Robert Floud, Gilbert Wakefield, Lord Strangfield, Hayley, and Soame Jenyns. The Original Poetry was of varying quality and quantity. At

1. 10 July, 1802.
2. 15 October, 1808.
3. 17 July, 1802. The allusion is to Algernon Sidney, author of the *Discourse concerning Government*.
4. 15 August, 1807.

the beginning of the volume for 1804 it was announced that henceforth only *original* poetry should grace the last page of the *Port Folio,* but even with Dennie's liberal treatment of the word "original," the project had to be given up. Occasionally for two or three weeks at a time the magazine was destitute of poetry, original or selected. Much of the native verse was very juvenile and the "exotic" poems were not always well chosen. Monk's *Tales of Terror* and *Tales of Wonder* had an extensive vogue in the magazines, and many were the "hobgoblin ballads" which in spite of Dennie's professed aversion, found their way into the *Port Folio,* though he eased his conscience by admitting frequent parodies of that style of writing. The influence of Moore tended to encourage for a year or so a tendency toward rather salacious amatory verse-writing, which was the occasion for a "Dissertation on the Lasciviousness of the Port Folio Poets" in the *Philadelphia Pursuits of Literature.*

The first number for 1806 began a New Series, with a considerable alteration in the form of the magazine. Hitherto it had comprised eight pages of a large newspaper-like sheet. Now it was reduced to the usual magazine size, 5 by 8 1-2 inches, with sixteen pages of print to each issue. Otherwise it was not greatly changed.[1] A rather unsatisfactory periodical essay, *The Day,* ran through most of 1806. The *American Lounger* ceased with that year, and a perhaps more chaotic series, *The Planets,* took its place for a while. A new series of *Lay Preacher* essays, or more probably a number of old sermons which had been kept back in anticipation of the long-looked-for volume, appeared consecutively from 12 December, 1807, to 13 February, 1808. These include sermons for Christmas and New Year's, and the stories of Samuel, Saint Paul—who seems to have represented Dennie's ideal of a man—, Job, Esther, and Adonijah. The two others deal with reading and a retired life. They are in general a little soberer, and keep more closely to Scripture story than do the other sermons.

During 1807 and 1808, in spite of strenuous efforts, the *Port Folio* became duller and less interesting. Several of the

1. During 1806 the *Port Folio* was printed by John Watts, 42 Walnut Street (After June 28, "N. E. corner of Second in Dock Street"); in 1807, printed, and in 1808 printed and published, for the editors, by Smith and Maxwell, 28 North Second Street.

livelier correspondents of the earlier volumes dropped off, long controversial and critical articles were admitted, and the poetry in especial became scantier and less attractive. Much of this state of affairs was due to increasing ill-health on Dennie's part, which kept him from pursuing his affairs vigorously. As long before this as 15 June, 1803, he had written to his mother, sending a picture "of a countenance haggard, severe, and melancholy"; and with increasing frequency his addresses to his readers complained of bodily ills which retarded his energies in carrying on the *Port Folio*. On 31 October, 1807, after indignantly denying a rumor which had gone about to the effect that the magazine had been sold, he stated:

"He [the editor] is the sole proprietor of this paper, of which, for years, he has had the absolute direction, and, if any emoluments arise from the subscription, the property is exclusively his."

A year later, 8 October, 1808, he announced that "for some time past ill-health and the effects of the Embargo, have compelled him to give to the pages of the *Port Folio* nothing but an interrupted and desultory attention." Owing to the crippled state of commerce in the country, he said, he was a claimant upon his subscribers for ten thousand dollars, which he could not collect.

In ill-health, and deprived of the support of many of his best contributors, Dennie had recourse more and more to the British press for borrowed material. The British reviewers, Aiken, Anderson and MacKenzie, were pressed frequently into service, and some of the poorer numbers, such as that for 24 January, 1807, are made up almost wholly of extracts and abstracts. The range and nature of the publications thus used is illustrated by a list in the *Port Folio*, 20 April, 1805, of those which were regularly received then. The list follows:

"From Paris.

Le Decade Philosophique, Litteraire et Politique.
Le Gazette Nationale, ou le Moniteur Universel.
Echo du Commerce From Bourdeaux
The Edinburgh Review From Edinburgh

From London

The Annual Review	*The Monthly Magazine*
The Anti-Jacobin Review	*The Encyclopedian Magazine*
The Monthly Review	*The Poetical Magazine*
The Critical Review	*The Universal Magazine*
The Imperial Review	*The Sporting Magazine*
The British Critic	*Tilloch's Philosophical Magazine*
The Old Annual Register	*The Orthodox Churchman's Magazine*
The New Annual Register	
The Literary Journal	*Lady's Magazine*
The Gentleman's Magazine	*Lady's Museum*
The Asiatic Annual Register	*The Monthly Mirror*
The European Magazine	*The Monthly Epitome*

The Monthly Fashions of London and Paris.
Annals of Philosophy (Cadell and Davis)

British Public Characters	*The Court Calendar*
Spirit of the Public Journals	*The Morning Post*
The Repertory of the Arts	*The Morning Chronicle*
Naval Chronicle	*The Oracle*
Steel's Monthly Army and Navy List	*The Morning Herald*
	Lloyd's Evening Post
St. James' Chronicle	*London Packet*
Cobbett's Weekly Register	*Public Ledger*
The London Chronicle	*The Times*
Whitehall Evening Post	*The Courier*
The Sun	*The Traveller*
The Star	*The Evening Mail*

The Oxford, Bristol, Birmingham, Liverpool and York papers."

From England Dennie still hoped eventually to win recognition, and to England he still looked for standards of politics, manners and language. His ill-health and repeated ill success in his literary projects doubtless intensified the obstinacy with which he refused to see any good in many American institutions, and the churlishness with which he attacked any innovation not in keeping with British conventions, and as a result led him into frequent absurdities. Thus in adopting the British standard in the case of words ending in "-or, -our," he went so far as to write "authour," "professour," and other words not sanctioned by Johnson. For this he was censured, and he replied vigorously. Americanisms of every sort were held up to ridicule in the *Port Folio.* In an inclusive satire in the *American Lounger,* 25 January, 1806, the American language, Webster's dictionary, American educational institutions, sermons, speeches, and government, and the naked bosoms and painted cheeks of Philadelphia belles, are attacked through the medium of an account of the visit of twenty Indian chiefs to Washington. Some of the contributions which he published naturally aroused strenuous protests. Thus *Caradoc's* "Picture of Boston," in the *Port Folio,* 2 May, 1808, brought an immediate reply in the *Monthly Anthology,* in which the liberality of the Boston merchants was vindicated from *Caradoc's* charges.[1] The *Anthology* had earlier praised Dennie "for his perseverence in the ungrateful task of disciplining a money-getting age."[2] An account of "bundling," in the magazine, 8 February, 1806, occasioned a letter of reproof from Dennie's old superior, Pickering, in which the prevalence of the practice was indignantly denied.[3] In the vexatious matter of the impressment of American seamen, Dennie at first did not take sides, but admitted arguments impartially into the *Port Folio;* but on 5 September, 1807, he announced definitely:

"The editor of this paper will combat without ceasing all war measures against England. . . . We are totally unprepared for warfare. We are cursed with a pusillanimous government, a divided people, and a defenceless frontier."

He could, on occasion, defend himself with a dignity and sincerity which compels one to recognize how much of justice was on his side. In replying to an angry correspondent who had rebuked him for unceasing condemnation of his countrymen, he wrote:[4]

"The conductor of this Journal is in possession of no graduated scale, by which he can ascertain with mathematical preciseness the exact difference between the patriotism of one American and another; for, like our correspondent, the Editor is an American; he *educated himself* in America; he lives in

1. *Monthly Anthology,* Vol. IV, pp. 289-295.
2. *Monthly Anthology,* Vol. II, p. 176.
3. *Pickering Papers,* Mass. Hist. Soc. Collections, Vol. XIV, p. 144.
4. *Port Folio,* 24 Jan., 1807.

America; and as he does not contemplate a change in his situation, the probability is that he will die in America. He has some stake in the country. His family friends, literary friends, social friends and party friends, are American. To America alone he looks for that ordinary measure of encouragement due to pretensions humble like his own; and for a magnanimous America, a *well-governed* America, a noble, loyal, generous, gallant, high-spirited America, he feels an affection more intensely warm than all the *flickering* flames of the patriotism either in Junius Brutus, or John Hampden, or John *Pym* or Algernon Sidney."

In March, 1807, Washington Irving, then twenty-three years old, visited Philadelphia and met Dennie. The character of *Launcelot Langstaff*, a creature of irritable nerves and whim-whams, which he contributed to *Salmagundi* on his return was, it is said, recognized by Dennie as a faithful sketch of himself. The most notable passage follows:[1]

"Langstaff inherited from his father a love of literature, a disposition for castle-building, a mortal enmity to noise, a sovereign antipathy to cold weather and brooms, and a plentiful stock of whim-whams. From the delicacy of his nerves, he is peculiarly sensible to discordant sounds; the rattling of a wheelbarrow is 'horrible'; the noise of children 'drives him distracted'; and he once left excellent lodgings merely because the lady of the house wore high-heeled shoes, in which she clattered up and down stairs, till, to use his own emphatic expression, 'they made life loathsome' to him. He suffers annual martyrdom from the razor-edged zephyrs of our 'balmy spring,' and solemnly declares that the boasted month of May has become a perfect 'vagabond.' As some people have a great antipathy to cats, and can tell when one is locked up in a closet, so Launcelot declares his feelings always announce to him the neighborhood of a broom; a household implement which he abominates above all others. Nor is there any living animal in the world that he holds in more utter abhorrence than what is usually termed a notable housewife; a pestilent being, who, he protests,

1. *Salmagundi.* No. VIII. For Pierre Irving's remarks, see the *Life and Letters of Washington Irving*, of which there are various editions fully indexed.

is the bane of good-fellowship, and has a heavy charge to answer for the many offences committed against ease, comfort, and social enjoyments of sovereign man. He told me not long ago 'that he had rather see one of the weird sisters flourish through his key-hole on a broomstick than one of the servant maids enter the door with a besom.'

"My friend Launcelot is ardent and sincere in his attachments, which are confined to a chosen few, in whose society he loves to give free scope to his whimsical imagination; he mingles freely with the world, however, though more as a spectator than an actor; and without any anxiety, or hardly a care to please, is generally received with welcome, and listened to with complacency. When he extends his hand it is a free, open, liberal style; and when you shake it you feel his honest heart throb in its pulsations. Though rather fond of gay exhibitions, he does not appear so frequently at balls and assemblies since the introduction of the drum, trumpet, and tambarine; all of which he abhors on account of the rude attacks they make on his organs of hearing: in short, such is his antipathy to noise, that, though exceedingly patriotic, yet he retreats every fourth of July to Cockloft-hall, in order to get out of the way of the hubbub and confusion which makes so considerable a part of the pleasure of that splendid anniversary.

"I intend this article as a mere sketch of Langstaff's multifarious character; his innumerable whim-whams will be exhibited by himself, in the course of this work, in all their strange varieties; and the machinery of his mind, more intricate than in the most subtle piece of clock-work, be fully explained. And trust me, gentlefolks, his are the whim-whams of a courteous gentleman, full of most excellent qualities; honourable in his disposition, independent in his sentiments, and of unbounded good-nature, as may be seen through all his works."

CHAPTER XI

PHILADELPHIA, 1809-1812—"THE PORT FOLIO"—LAST YEARS AND DEATH

The only extant letter from Dennie to his parents after 1803 is one dated 15 July, 1809, and written in the hall of the Philosophical Society of Philadelphia, of which, he said, he was an honorary member. The letter was occasioned by a visit of James White, the family friend, to Philadelphia. Dennie seized this opportunity to calm his mother's anxiety about his health and money affairs "by the general and just assurance, that, by the present arrangement of my humble property and pretensions, I am in a better situation than formerly. I am neither rich, nor independent, nor anything like it, but I am not dishonoured, nor a beggar." The details of his life, for which we should be grateful, he unfortunately left for Mr. White to describe. He could not afford the long and expensive trip home, he said, and besides, "I am in favour with the Public and must not lose it by neglect."

"My health," he went on, "is not worse than usual. My spirits are sometimes gay, but oftener depressed . . . In the midst of perils, I have found friends to the *stranger*, and while so many millions of my fellow creatures are suffering all the varieties of pain, when I reflect upon my own *comparatively tolerable* fortune, I am, in the language of the best of all books, not a little comforted. . . . I cannot without the tears running down my cheeks, reflect upon the deplorable condition of my revered and unhappy father. That such a noble mind as his should thus be buried in ruins is a most mournful spectacle. His disorder has taken exactly the turn of that of the poet Cowper, and while my venerable friend *fancies* that he is exposed to the malignance of malevolent beings, nothing but the grace of God, of which I fervently hope he may yet feel the benignity, can ever relieve him."

The resigned spirit and modest tone of this letter are very different from the ardor and egotism of the earlier ones, filled with "my assiduous literary labours, and the dictates of my high and impetuous spirit."[1] Yet hope and vanity were not quite dead. He writes in a postscript:

"I understand from authentic sources, that my efforts as a man of letters are very candidly appreciated at London, Edinburgh, and Paris. In the last edition of his Biography of Smollett, Doctor Robert Anderson has taken occasion to speak of me and my works with great complaceny. Indeed, he is too partial. The favourable opinion of my judges will not, I hope, create a foolish pride, but act as an incentive to generous exertion. You may be assured I have many good friends and liberal critics on the other side of the Atlantic. The circulation of the *Port Folio* augments, and the Literary Club, who assist me, includes some of the most distinguished characters in the Country. . . . The *pictures* please the ladies, and now and then a page is *tolerated* by the philosophers."

Dennie's position was, as a matter of fact, in some respects worse, and in others better, than it had been. His health became steadily poorer, especially in the sickly summer seasons, during most, if not all, of which he had remained at his post in the city. Hall, who was somewhat given to moralizing, and who was not intimately associated with Dennie during this part of his life, would lead one to believe, in his *Philadelphia Souvenir,* that Dennie made excessive use of stimulants to overcome his weariness and low spirits. While he was always convivial in his tastes, and fond of good living, the testimony of closer friends, like the Merediths and Abercrombie, indicates that he did not indulge in wines to the extent of intoxication. His mind never wholly lost its buoyancy, or his wit its sparkle, in all his sickness and adversity. A letter from Meredith to Vose, 16 January, 1816,[2] speaking of this period, mentions the "warmth of heart & playfulness of disposition, & the same fits of gloom and depression, which continued to endear him and occasion anxiety to his friends.

"I remark in his earliest letter to you," he goes on, "an expression of sentiment which he often expressed after he came to this city, that his life would be short. He often fixed upon 40 years as the utmost probable limit and in fact after that

1. Letter to his mother, 15 June, 1803.
2. Vose Letters. William Meredith to Roger Vose, 16 Jan., 1816.

time his existence did not seem to afford much gratification to himself and his literary labours were in a great degree suspended.''

In his years of decline Dennie was attended by as faithful a group of loving friends—including the Merediths, the Reverend James Abercrombie, Doctor Chapman, Nicholas Biddle, and others—as has ever followed the varying fortunes of an author. When health permitted, too, he was an admired figure at such of the prominent social gatherings in Philadelphia as he graced by his presence. D. P. Brown, in his *Forum*,[1] speaks of him in the following terms:

''At the time to which I refer, say 1810, Joseph Dennie, Esq., well known for his literary attainments, and holding a high social position, was the editor of the *Port Folio* and an author of great merit and celebrity. He was upon the most intimate terms with John Quincy Adams, the elder Meredith, Hopkinson, and most of the master spirits of the time.''

A certain Jewish lawyer named Levy, Brown says, ''was invited upon one occasion to dine with a distinguished member of the bar, where it was expected Mr. Dennie would be present. As was not unusual with that gentleman, he did not make his appearance; he was a man subject to all the skiey influences, and was regulated more by the weather than by his engagements.'' The aspiring Hebrew was greatly disconcerted at this circumstance, and complained to the guests present that he had spent all the morning reading Plutarch's *Lives*, that he might be able to contribute his share to the literary entertainment.

Financially, the *Port Folio* had not proved a success, and it went out of Dennie's hands, probably some time in 1808, leaving him considerably in debt. After January, 1809, the proprietors and publishers were Bradford and Inskeep at Philadelphia,[2] and Inskeep and Bradford, New York. Dennie remained the editor, probably at a fixed salary,[3] of the magazine

1. *The Forum, or Forty Years' Full Practice at the Philadelphia Bar.* Phila., 1856. Vol. I, pp. 548-549.

2. At No. 4 South Third Street. Smith and Maxwell remained the printers. The Bradfords were the Greens of Philadelphia. Up to 1818 Samuel T. Bradford was a rival of Mathew Carey.

3. The salary paid to his successor, Nicholas Biddle, was $2,500.

he had founded and fostered. Though for months at a time he was incapacitated by illness for the discharge of his duties, his management and literary prestige were too rich an asset to lose.

In accordance with a plan previously announced, the *Port Folio* appeared in a new guise at the beginning of 1809. A prospectus was accordingly issued, heralding "THE PORT FOLIO, *A Monthly Miscellany,* dedicated in chief, to original communications in the popular departments of science, combined with occasional criticism, classical disquisitions, miscellaneous essays, records of the progress of the fine and useful arts, with all the extensive and variegated departments of polite literature, merriment and wit. Conducted by *Oliver Oldschool, Esq.,* assisted by a Confederacy of Men of Letters." The prospectus itself, written by Dennie, praised Philadelphia as a center of culture; sketched the thorny past of the *Port Folio,* "commenced at a sinister epoch, exposed to the cavils of party, neglected in consequence of the bad health and misfortunes of the Editor, ill supported, and worse paid"; and outlined the scheme which it was hoped would be carried out for the future support of the magazine. The "squabbles of the State, and polemical brawls in the Church" were to be excluded, and no efforts would be spared to make the work both solidly and entertainingly useful. Since the magazine was to be non-partisan, the pseudonym *Oliver Oldschool* was soon abandoned, and in the first number for 1810, "Conducted by Joseph Dennie, Esq.," took its place on the first page.

The Confederacy of Letters which had banded together in support of the *Port Folio,* comprised men of various talents and professions, who were eager to keep alive in Philadelphia the best and most successful magazine the country had produced. It probably included several members of the Tuesday Club, as well as some older and more eminent men. In the letter quoted above,[1] Dennie wrote to his mother, "I am very powerfully supported. . . . We have Bishops and Lawyers in our Confederacy. The Chief Justice of the United States,[2] Judge Washington,[3] Judge Peters, and the Honourable Mr. Penn

1. Letter to his mother, 15 July, 1809.
2. John Marshall.
3. Bushrod Washington, nephew of the President, was a noted jurist.

are with us." Men like these probably aided the cause considerably more by their patronage than by their contributions. It was expected that each confederate should send in something to the magazine for each issue. Few, if any, lived up to their agreement in this respect, and after a few months the confederacy was dissolved.

Among the men not yet accounted for, upon whose shoulders fell the burden of support, were Robert Walsh, Condy Raguet, Alexander Wilson, and Nicholas Biddle. Walsh (1785-1858) was a Baltimorean, descended from Irish Catholic gentry, and educated at St. Mary's College, Baltimore, and at Georgetown. After travelling extensively abroad, he returned to America, studied law and was admitted to the bar at Philadelphia in 1808. A slight deafness, however, led him soon to give up this profession. He was editor in 1811-1812 of the *American Review of History and Politics*; in 1817-1818 of the *American Register*; and from 1820 to 1836 of the *National Gazette*; besides editing other works and writing political and historical pamphlets. About 1835 he removed to Paris, where he died in 1858. He was one of the most attractive figures in the literary group centered at Philadelphia. His contributions to the *Port Folio* antedated the appearance of his own quarterly, the *American Review.*

Condy Raguet (1784-1842), U. of P. 1805, at this time a merchant in Philadelphia, had a versatile career. He made two trips to the island of Hayti, where he witnessed the terrible scenes of the negro revolt and the subsequent massacres of the French population. These scenes he represented in his interesting *Memoirs of Hayti,* in the *Port Folio,* 1809-1812. He served in the War of 1812, with the rank of Colonel. At the age of thirty-six he was admitted to the bar. Later he was Consul at Rio de Janeiro, a member of the Pennsylvania legislature, author of treatises on commerce and banking, and editor of the *Free Trade Advocate,* 1829; *Examiner,* 1834-1835; and *Financial Register,* 1837-1839.

Alexander Wilson (1766-1813) is famous as a naturalist rather than a man of letters. A weaver at Paisley, Scotland, he first attempted, in his *Poems, Humorous, Satirical, and Serious,* to vie with his countryman, the peasant Burns. Failing in this, he came to America in 1794, and taught school near Philadelphia for some time, before giving up his life to the study of American birds. During the last ten years of his life he was almost constantly travelling throughout the country, collecting data and securing subscribers for his costly and valuable work, *American Ornithology,* of which seven volumes were published between 1808 and 1813. He died on one of his tours, at Great Egg Harbor, in 1813. Several of his poems and letters appeared in the *Port Folio* from 1809 on. In 1804 he made a trip to Niagara, of which a poetic journal, *The Foresters,* appeared in the *Port Folio* from June, 1809, to March, 1810. The following lines will perhaps show why he did not succeed in emulating Burns:[1]

> "Before us now the opening river pours,
> Through gradual windings and projecting shores;
> Smooth slopes the green where Newark's village lies,
> There, o'er their fort, the British ensign flies.
> '*From whence?*' they hail; we shout with trumpet's
> sound,
> '*From Fort Oswego, up to Queenstown bound.*'
> '*What news?*' '*the Speedy's pump on board we bear,*
> *The sole found fragment of that sad affair.*'
> Th' increasing distance drowns their faint reply,
> And up the adverse stream we foaming fly."

Some of Wilson's verse is better than this, but his dialect poem, *Watty and Meg,* in the *Port Folio,* October, 1810, is not of much greater excellence.

Among the other identifiable contributors to Dennie's periodical were Doctor David Hosack of Columbia College; Judge Thomas Cooper of Northumberland, Pennsylvania, and Dickinson College; the Reverend James Abercrombie; and Joseph Sansom, a merchant of New York. Most of these men transmitted letters or scientific items; Sansom was the author of several series of letters written on his travels in Europe. Some of the more prolific writers used initials, such as *W.*; *Q.*, author of a periodical essay, *My Pocket Book; E.*, a poetess from New York; *C.* (possibly Doctor Chapman), author of biographical and other sketches; *Proclus,* of Baltimore, author of a long

1. *Port Folio,* March, 1810.

disquisition on the *Genius and Polity of the Chinese.* Hall (J. E.), Ewing; and John Davis contributed occasionally. William B. Wood (1779-1861), actor and theatrical manager, of Annapolis, Baltimore, Philadelphia, and Washington, is also said to have contributed dramatic items to the *Port Folio.* Joel Barlow published in November, 1809, his controversial correspondence with Henri Gregoire, who had attacked Barlow's religious views in the *Columbiad.* Mrs. Sarah Morton's *Lamentation* for her only son, Charles, appeared in the number for March, 1809.

More closely associated with Dennie, however, than any of these was Nicholas Biddle (1786-1844). Biddle was a Philadelphian, who graduated from Pennsylvania at thirteen and at Princeton two years later, in 1801. He studied law and was admitted to the bar in 1804, but spent the next few years abroad as secretary to the United States minister to France, and to Monroe at London. In Europe he supplemented by travel a rich classical and literary education. He returned to America in 1807, and while practising law in Philadelphia, contributed to the *Port Folio* papers on the fine arts, biographical sketches—including one of his uncle, Commodore Nicholas Biddle—and critical articles. He was probably the *Bayard,* who wrote descriptions of the paintings of Benjamin West and others, and author of the *Artist* series. He succeeded Dennie as editor of the magazine from 1812 to 1814, but soon became engrossed in political activities, having entered the Pennsylvania legislature in 1811. In 1819 he became a director, and in 1823 president, of the United States Bank, which position he held until 1839. He was an accomplished scholar, a founder of Girard College, and an advocate of common schools in Pennsylvania. Biddle is said to have prepared the *Narrative of the Lewis and Clark Expedition,* but was obliged to give it over, in almost completed form, to Paul Allen, in whose name it was published.[1]

Allen, who lived from 1775 to 1826, was a Providence man, grandson of Nicholas Cooke, the war governor of Rhode Island, and graduated at Brown in the class of 1793. His successive movements and enterprises are difficult to trace. In 1801 he

1. See the *Autobiography of Charles Biddle,* edited by James S. Biddle, Appendix G, pp. 415-420, for a sketch of his life.

published at Salem a volume of *Original Poems*, considerably better than the average. Later he was at Philadelphia, where he contributed to the *Gazette of the U. S.* and the *Port Folio*, edited the *Journal of the Times*, and published in 1814 a two-volume *Narrative of the Lewis and Clark Expedition.* By 1816 he was established at Baltimore, where he edited the *Morning Chronicle*, 1816-1824, and the *Morning Post* and *Saturday Evening Herald*, 1824-1825. At Baltimore he was also a member of the Delphian Club and a contributor to the *Portico.* He is said to have been exceedingly indolent, and his *History of the American Revolution*, in two volumes, 1819, was nearly all written by his friends, John Neal and Watkins. He published also a *Life of Alexander I*, 1818, and a long poem called *Noah.*[1]

As a monthly miscellany, devoted chiefly to scientific and critical articles, the *Port Folio* naturally lost some of the sprightliness and interest of its palmier days. Each number contained about ninety pages of print, and one or more engraved plates. The plates represented American scenery, such as views along the Susquehanna, sketched by Rose, or drawings of Niagara; public buildings or monuments, such as the Pennsylvania Academy of Fine Arts, and the monument on Beacon Hill, Boston; portraits, such as those of William Penn, or of Dennie's friends, Bishop White and Abercrombie; drawings of new machines, such as McBride's spinning jenny; or reproductions of paintings, like West's *Death on the Pale Horse* and Raphael's *Holy Family.* The issue of June, 1809, contained two fashion plates.

The chief departments were biographical, critical, and scientific. The new series began with Brockden Brown's *Life of John Blair Linn*, which ran through the first three numbers. It was desired to obtain sketches of the chief American worthies, in accordance with which plan lives of Anthony Wayne, Horatio Gates, General Knox, Commodores Biddle, Preble, and Truxtun, Mrs. Ferguson, and William Penn, among others, appeared. The chief works of English or American authors were reviewed as they appeared. Most of the reviews were apparently original; a few were taken from the *Edinburgh Review* or other

---

1. This was originally composed in twenty-five cantos, but by Neal's advice was cut down to five.

publications. Among the productions thus passed upon were Byron's *Hours of Idleness* and *English Bards and Scotch Reviewers,* Barlow's *Columbiad,* Brown's novels, Wordsworth's poems, Scott's *Lady of the Lake* and *Don Roderic,* Campbell's *Gertrude of Wyoming,*[1] Southey's *Curse of Kehema,* Ingersoll's *Inchiquin the Jesuit's Letters,* Crabbe's *Borough,*[1] and Wieland's *Oberon.* The *Proposals* for Coleridge's periodical, *The Friend,* were reprinted in the *Port Folio* for August, 1809, "with the more alacrity because it is plainly perceived that Time, Experience and Observation, have totally changed the colour of this gentleman's mind, and that the reign of right principle is fully restored." An *Elegy to Brown* appeared in September, 1810, and some of Mrs. Ferguson's letters were printed in that year. The scientific articles included accounts of new inventions, disquisitions on rarified air and the manufacture of potassium,[2] mathematical problems, natural history data, and the like.

Travels, described in series of letters from the continent, formed another prominent department. Three rather trite sections, entitled respectively the "Laughing World," the "Classical World" and the "Sententious World," comprised humorous extracts, comments on Greek and Latin authors, and collections of proverbs. A few short and generally inferior periodical essays, *My Pocket Book, The Bee Hive, The Naturalist* (by Wilson), *The Scribbler, The Table d'Hote; The Artist;* and *Adversaria* (by Hall), ran through a few numbers each. *An Author's Evenings,* perhaps by another hand than Dennie's, reappeared at infrequent intervals. *The Fine Arts,* probably the contribution of Biddle, occupied an increasing space in 1811. Many anecdotes of American painters and a full catalogue of West's paintings appeared in this department. *Original Poetry* and *To Readers and Correspondents* became rather obscure divisions at the end of the magazine.

If the *Port Folio* was duller now than its contemporary, *The Monthly Anthology,* it had a national reputation which the latter did not enjoy. It was published in both New York and

---

1. From the *Edinburgh Review.*
2. By Thomas Cooper, of Northumberland. He was a scientist, who followed Priestley to America. Later he became Professor of Chemistry at Pennsylvania, and still later President of the University of South Carolina, which position he was obliged to relinquish, on account of his Unitarian belief.

Philadelphia, and had prominent contributors in all parts of the country—in Boston, Hartford, New York, Trenton, Baltimore, Washington, Richmond, and Charleston, as well as on the western frontier. It was pre-eminently the national magazine, and had already had in 1812 a longer and more successful existence than any of its American, or than most of its European, predecessors. In still another respect, too, it was becoming national. Dennie's statement that time, experience, and observation had changed the color of Coleridge's mind and restored the reign of right principle, could be applied almost equally to himself. As the final term of Jefferson's Democratic administration faded into the first term of Madison's without any resulting national paroxism; as the disgruntled Federalists found their way, one by one, into the new order of things; as the outrages of the British navy became more intolerable and the state of American learning and culture somewhat more tolerable, more independent and less provincial, Dennie, in his latest years, distressed as they were, seems to have come into a saner state of mind regarding his countrymen. Absurdities like "authour" and strictures on the American language and manners disappeared after 1808. How much of the change of sentiment expressed in the pages of the *Port Folio* from 1809 to 1812 is due to the suggestion of the proprietors and how much was uttered by those who assisted Dennie during his periods of illness is a matter of conjecture, but a real change, unaccompanied by any spirit of compromise, is certain. After defending the verse writers of America, "Continually reviled by foreign Criticism for a total want of poetical power and poetical thought," he could still justly assert, four pages later, "For more than fifteen years we have published, in periodical pages, our sentiments, in complete defiance of the choice or the dictation of the *many*."[1] That the many read and wrote for his pages—even if they did not pay for them—argues that his strictures, though often unmerciful, were not always unjust.

On 28 September, 1811, at Lexington, death mercifully re-

---

1. *Port Folio*, December, 1809, pages 579 and 583. He wittily compares an editor over-desirous of pleasing, to the father and son in the fable, who were censured alike whether either or both rode upon their donkey or whether they carried him.

leased Joseph Dennie, Senior, from his sufferings.[1] Nearly all that is known of him and his long life is what is written in his brief obituary in the *New England Palladium*[2] and other Eastern papers, "by a faithful friend of the family, and one of the most eloquent lawyers in New England."[3] Eight years afterward, 6 September, 1819, Mary Dennie was laid by the side of the husband she had cared for tenderly during many years of helplessness.[4]

The news of his father's decease came to Dennie when he was himself dangerously near to death. During the summer and autumn months of 1811 he was confined to his bed, and the fact that he was unable to be present at his father's death and burial affected him deeply. He appeared to recover, however, in spirits and health, with the advent of the winter season, during which he was usually strongest. In December he was able to supervise the January number of the *Port Folio*, which in his absence had been managed by Paul Allen. For this number he wrote a poem in honor of his father, of which the concluding stanzas follow:

"Teach me, thou venerable bower,
Cool Meditation's quiet seat,
The *generous scorn of mushroom power*,
The silent grandeur of retreat.

"When Pride by guilt to greatness climbs,
Or *raging factions* rush to war,
Here let me learn to shun the crimes
I can't prevent and *will not share.*

"But, lest I fall by subtler foes,
Bright Wisdom, teach me Mary's art,
My *swelling passions* to compose,
And quell the rebels of the *heart.*"

1. In the burial record at Boston his age is incorrectly given as 71. The cause of death was debility.
2. 4 Oct., 1811. See page 12 of this book.
3. *Port Folio,* Jan., 1812, p. 89.
4. Her burial is recorded as "from Brookline," where she lived after her husband's death. Records of the Registry Office, 100 Summer St., Boston.

As a result of this long sickness, the publishers, Bradford and Inskeep, had made a new arrangement, by which all the task of editing should not fall upon his shoulders, and an associate was provided for him. This plan, with a statement of Dennie's bereavement and illness and his hopes for the future, was set forth in his last address "To the Public," pathetically florid in its style and sanguine in its spirit.[1]

"The subscription list," he said, "has increased, is increasing, and *shall not be diminished.* The kindness, candour, liberality, and *long suffering* of the reading classes of the American people deserves, and *they shall receive* all the gratitude, which we can display. By that coy mistress, the Public, the Editor has always been treated as a sort of favoured lover; though, unquestionably, for this fond preference, he is indebted much more to *her* graciousness, than to *his* gallantry.

* * * * * * * *

"Fully to atone for the Editor's negligences, absences, and indispositions, a scheme equally specious and solid has been, at length, happily devised. Conscious that a lettered confederacy was exactly of that crumbling nature, as the allied army under the Duke of Brunswick; the Editor, for a very long season, has been anxious for a *colleague,* who should have *a direct interest* in the enterprize, who should be a confidential and favourite friend, and who should be capable of unlocking the stores of learning, and revealing the glories of Genius. This plan is of no hasty adoption. *Two years* ago, all the keenness of the Editor's inquisitive optics was intensely fixed upon a gentleman and a scholar,[2] who, from the liberal leisure, and still more liberal mind, was, of all men, *the* individual, whom the Editor would select, after the maturest deliberation. Fortunately for his gratification, the interest of the *Port Folio,* and the satisfaction of its subscribers, this beloved and accomplished associate is now in *full communion* with the Editor. With the joyful acquiescence of the Proprietor, they have formed a literary coparceny; they *have* embarked in a joint adventure to the regions of wit; the Editor contributing nothing to the com-

1. *Port Folio,* Jan., 1812, pp. 89-96.
2. Undoubtedly Nicholas Biddle.

mon stock, but the bankruptcy of his mind, while his opulent associate furnishes the amplest capital.

* * * * * * * *

"We now commence our career, and hope that, at least, we may *approach* the goal. We are governed by every noble power having a laudable influence over the mind of men: by the desire of glory, and the ignominy of defeat; by the goading of that blessed instinct, which will not suffer our faculties to rust with slothfulness or droop in lethargy; by all the documents of Reason and Experience which demonstrate that such exertions are salutary; by generous Emulation; by honest Pride, and by *a vivid sense of the power and resources of our country.* We call, and we hope, audibly, upon our contemporaries, for literary, for scientific, for *moral aid.* To such a call the most accomplished of the Americans cannot be inattentive. The Tutelary Genius of the country will then smile benignantly on our labours, and we shall be lightened to success, by a ray from heaven."

These roseate hopes were never to be realized by their author. Dennie's recovery of bodily strength and animation of mind was brief and deceptive. His disease suddenly returned, and on the seventh of January, 1812, surrounded by his closest friends, he died, like a brave gentleman and a Christian. The circumstances of his death are told in a letter from Mrs. Meredith to his mother:[1]

"His death was attended with no aggravating circumstances to himself. His disease was a violent cholera morbus, to which he has for many years been subject; but his attack was attended with very little pain, and his mind did not lose its elasticity, nor his language its brilliancy, until the last moment, when he sunk without a groan, and may truly be said to have died, firm, in the cheerful hope of a devout Christian. His faith had never been shaken, and his death was a glorious example of the excellency of our holy religion. But alas! it has left a void in our circle, which needs all its aid to enable us to support, and which never can be filled up, for we ne'er shall look upon his like again. . . . My husband attended his bed in his dying hour, and assures me he was placid, cheerful and easy, and

1. 9 Jan., 1812.

continued so, until his beatifick spirit sought its kindred skies. He spoke often of his beloved mother, and prayed fervently that God would not forsake her."[1]

Abercrombie, his pastor, Chapman, his physician, Biddle, his associate in the *Port Folio,* and Meredith, his closest friend, took charge of his funeral, which was largely and respectfully attended. He was buried in the churchyard of St. Peter's, in Philadelphia. Some years later a monument was erected over his grave, bearing an elaborate inscription, said to have been written by John Quincy Adams.[2] Hall, in his *Philadelphia Souvenir,* remarks that although enough was due Dennie to assure him a decent competency, he "owed to friendship the last repose of his mortal remains!" While he was probably never in actual want, he died owing considerable debts, for the partial payment of which his mother made provision in her will.[3] The following mortuary, by the Reverend Mr. Abercrombie, in the floridly eulogistic style of the day, appeared in the Philadelphia papers:[4]

"On Tuesday the 7th instant departed this life in the 45th year of his age, Joseph Dennie, Esq., a native of the state of Massachusetts, but for several years past a resident in this city. A liberal education engrafted upon a mind endowed with the most active and energetic powers, and an imagination fertilized by various and extensive reading, and glowing with all the fervor and brilliancy of genius, together with a heart overflowing with benevolence and ennobled by every private and social virtue, rendered him a distinguished ornament of general society, and

---

1. Mrs. Meredith and Parson Abercrombie kept up a correspondence, still preserved, with Mrs. Dennie for several years. A passage in one of Abercrombie's letters is significant:

"I have often heard you observe, and strongly fear, that he would inherit and suffer some of the melancholy maladies which his father so long lived under, and I must confess that I think it would have been realized if he had lived a few years longer."

2. See Appendix G.

3. Made 21 Sept., 1813; probated 5 Oct., 1819. Norfolk County Probate Records, Dedham. Mass. She left $2033.33 to Harriet Green, "and I earnestly recommend to her, that she cause the same or a like sum to be paid; after her decease, to the administrator [Richard Peters], of the estate of my late son, Joseph Dennie, of Philadelphia, toward the payment of the said Joseph's just debts."

4. Kindly copied for me from Poulson's *American Daily Advertiser.* 9 Jan., 1812, by Mr. Edward Biddle of Philadelphia.

the delight and solace of an extensive circle of friends and acquaintances.

Quis desiderio sit pudor aut modus
Tam cari capitis?
Cui Pudor et Justiciae soror,
Incorrupta Fides, nudaque Veritas,
Quando ullum invenient parem?
Multis ille bonis flebilis occidit.

His memory will be embalmed by his particular friends and most intimate associates, in a biographical and eulogistic memoir, in which his exalted character, and singularly superior talents, will be more copiously displayed, and more permanently recorded."

Doctor Chapman was the friend to whom was entrusted the editing of Dennie's works and the compilation of his biography. His efforts, however, were "tardy, and his disposition naturally indolent," as Mrs. Meredith wrote;[1] and the work went undone until 1816. It was then given over to John E. Hall, who issued a selected volume of the *Lay Preacher* and collected considerable biographical material, besides the papers and letters left by Dennie. He also communicated with Vose and Mrs. Dennie, but the only significant result was the brief sketch embodied in his *Philadelphia Souvenir,* in 1827; and a complete biography has never before been written. Two useful monographs have appeared in recent years, by William Warland Clapp[2] and Annie Russell Marble.[3] In 1818 an attempt was made to issue as a weekly pamphlet a series of unpublished *Lay Preacher* essays left by Dennie, but apparently only the initial number, the story of Michal, daughter of Saul, ever appeared. Later in the same year, in Buckingham's *New England Galaxy,* a series of *Postumi,* "anecdotes and remains of the late Joseph Dennie, Esq.," was printed. The paper for 10 July contained a *Lay Preacher* essay in defense of marriage for love, and that of 24 July, Tyler's description of Dennie's first trial. An account of the erection of Dennie's monument at Philadelphia appeared in the same paper, 19 November, 1819.

1. Letter to Mary Dennie, 13 June, 1814.
2. *Joseph Dennie*, Cambridge, 1880.
3. *Heralds of American Literature*, pp. 193-231.

The *Port Folio* for February, 1812, contained a well-written sketch of Dennie's character and literary abilities. His enthusiastic devotion to literature; his wide and varied reading, in many languages and fields of learning; his interest in the study of mankind; his classical taste, extraordinary memory, and vigorous imagination; and his felicity and gracefulness, were fully dwelt upon. His personal qualities also, his generosity, even in need; his lack of literary jealousy; his high standard of honor; his unwavering religious and political faith; his gentle and amiable manners; and his geniality in society, were also amply attested. A single sentence expresses admirably Dennie's constant aim in life:

"The great purpose of all his exertions, the uniform pursuit of his life, was to disseminate among his countrymen a taste for elegant literature, to give to education and to letters their proper elevation in the public esteem, and reclaiming the youth of America from the low career of sordid interests, to fix steadily their ambition on objects of a more exalted character."

The mortuary was followed by a *Monody on the Death of Joseph Dennie, Esq.*, occupying several pages, and signed *A*. It was probably penned by Paul Allen.

In this number the name of *Oliver Oldschool* reappeared on the first page. Nicholas Biddle immediately succeeded Dennie as editor of the *Port Folio,* and held his position until the early part of 1814.[1] Under his management it was not greatly changed from the last three years of Dennie's editorship. When he resigned his charge in 1814, owing to the pressure of political tasks, he was succeeded by Doctor Charles Caldwell. The latter was editor during the War of 1812, and the *Port Folio* under his administration contained full and accurate reports of the course of the war. He was ably assisted by Doctor Thomas Cooper, of Northumberland, an earlier contributor. In 1816 the magazine passed into the possession of the Hall family; Harrison Hall became the publisher and John Ewing Hall the editor. These positions they retained as long as the *Port Folio* continued. At the outset the new editor attempted to give the magazine the attractiveness that had characterized its earliest

1. The dates of Biddle's editorship have been kindly furnished me by Mr. Edward Biddle, from a memorandum left by his grandfather.

years. It was not a success, however; a large proportion of the subscribers never paid, and complaints for lack of patronage were unremitting. In 1820 it became a quarterly review, drawing upon British periodicals for most of its contents, but later it resumed a monthly appearance.[1] It was suspended during the first six months of 1826, was renewed for a short time by Hall, and finally abandoned in 1827, after an existence of twenty-six years, to that time a record unparalleled in America. It had outlived by fully ten years the literary preeminence of Philadelphia.

1. At the beginning of 1822. It was then called the *Port Folio and New York Monthly Magazine.*

CHAPTER XII

DENNIE'S LITERARY WORK AND SIGNIFICANCE

In passing judgment upon the literary output of Joseph Dennie, one is obliged to admit the justice of Hall's remark, that he was in his generation "an author of high reputation, who has left little to sustain that character."[1] Two series of essays, the *Farrago* and the *Lay Preacher*; part of a third, the *American Lounger*; a number of fugitive papers scattered through the pages of ten or a dozen periodicals and over a stretch of twenty years; the *Colon and Spondee* paragraphs, *An Author's Evenings,* and a mass of similar short pieces, political, critical, satirical, and editorial; a couple of political pamphlets; a few poems and epigrams; and perhaps eighty letters, constitute all his literary remains. The *Farrago* papers, light, racy satires on the follies of mankind, have never been collected and made accessible in a separate volume. The *American Loungers* have no coherent sequence, and in general little individual merit; and they are often assigned to Dennie on the uncertain basis of style and characteristic manner. The paragraph comments and political pamphlets are almost negligible as literature. Of the letters, always attractive and interesting, but often carelessly written, less than a dozen have been published. The few poems and epigrams which can safely be ascribed to him are fair eighteenth century verse, but show little poetical talent beyond a correct ear for meter, and familiarity with the language of the English poets.

Upon the *Lay Preacher,* his only extensive work, of which two volumes were published, in 1796 and 1816, respectively, his literary reputation must rest. Since these essays have not been dwelt upon above, and since they represent at once his most ambitious effort and his characteristic style, they may well be considered here. The series ran to 118 numbers, of which ninety appeared first in the *Farmer's Weekly Museum*, one in the *Eagle*, fourteen in the *Gazette of the United States*, eleven in the *Port*

1. J. E. Hall, in the *Philadelphia Souvenir.*

Folio, and two separately, after his death.[1] Seventy-seven of them may be found scattered through the volumes of the *Port Folio* from 1801 to 1808.[2] As has been said, the essays assumed the *form* of very short sermons. Each began with a motto, or text, and the preacher's style of direct address was frequently used. While the majority have a moral application, the wide range of subjects treated may be guessed from the following titles: No. 30, *Great Is Diana of the Ephesians* (an attack on Harvard); No. 25, *Character of a Good Wife;* No. 71, *The Power of Music;* No. 58, *Childishness of This Generation;* No. 45, *The Prosperity of America;* No. 50, *The Melancholy of Autumn.* Several of the "sermons" are political, like No. 8, *Against Democrats;* No. 48, *Sedition and Revolution,* and others. Some failings particularly characteristic of republics are satirized in No. 60, *Restlessness for Gold;* No. 53, *New Wine—Desire for Novelty;* No. 72, *Modern Philosophers;* and No. 87, *Gratitude.* A favorite method, the preacher's device of setting forth a number of types as examples to enforce some principle, is used often, as in No. 20, *Idols,* where the pictures of the coquette and her mirror, the drunkard and his glass, the sluggard and his bed, and others, are passed successively before the reader's vision. Characters appear in No. 11, *Dick Dronish;* No. 91, *The Versatile Man;* and No. 25, above. A number of essays deal with Old and New Testament personages, such as the stories of Rebecca in No. 36; Samson, No. 61; Ruth, No. 51; Hagar, No. 76; and Samuel, No. 107. Five numbers in succession, 78-82, are a criticism of Mrs. Radcliffe's *Mysteries of Udolpho,* in imitation of Addison's noted series on *Paradise Lost* in the *Spectator.* Special sermons are devoted to special occasions, like No. 7, *Thanksgiving;* No. 13, *New Year's;* and No. 83, *April Fool Pranks;* or to seasons, like No. 57, 4 April, 1797, appropriately named *It Is Foul Weather.* Next to Jacobinism, the vice most frequently satirized was scandal. Idle curiosity, fretting, instability of character, avarice, and sloth are also

1. See Appendix F. The numbers of the sermons named in this chapter are those given in the list there. The titles are mostly of my own invention.

2. Some of the *Lay Preachers* reprinted in the *Port Folio* were revised, but the alteration was generally only as much as was required to fit the latitude of Philadelphia.

attacked. The usual manner of the Preacher, however, where politics was not concerned, was genial and tolerant, and the popularity of the essays can easily be understood. Even today they may be read without effort, and frequently with delight.

Dennie was accused, by Davis and other unimaginative persons, of deriding the pulpit and the cause of religion by the levity of his Sermons. In the introduction to his 1796 volume, however, he had fully secured himself against such a charge, in a passage which may be quoted as an example of his style, as well as a statement of his design in the series:

"As the title of this work may appear ludicrous to some, and be obscure to others; as many start at the word *Preacher*, and may sneer at a *Lay* man, tampering with theology—it is proper to state that this is not a volume of sermons. It is a series of essays, modelled after the designs of Addison and the harmless and playful levity of Oliver Goldsmith. The mottos are copied from the oriental writings; but they are either a moral lesson, an economical precept, or a biographical picture. The topics to which they are prefixed, are didactic, descriptive, or airy, as the gravity or the humour of the hour prompted. On the fenced, and walled, and hallowed ground of religion, the author has never presumed to trench, nor carelessly nor wantonly approach the confines of the regular clergy. The doctrines and discipline of the church are sufficiently and gloriously illuminated from many a *golden candlestick;* and the citadel of christianity is well guarded by the lynx-eyed vigilance of Bishop Porteus, Watson, and Horseley. But a young man, sequestered and studious, imagined that the moral doctrines, and the literary beauties of the Bible might be familiarly illustrated in vehicles, cheap and popular. 'On this hint he spoke,' and volunteered in a village as a *Lay* Preacher, without even 'the laying on of the hands' of the presbytery. The author will soon respectfully appear at the bar of public opinion; and, in the impressive words of the ancient law, 'stand upon his deliverance;' nothing doubting of a fair trial from the discerning, and candid and catholic—and careless of the crude criticisms of the malignant vulgar."

One of the most prominent characteristics of Dennie's work is its humor—the playful satire noted by Irving in his sketch of *Launcelot Langstaff*. He was at his best when discussing with suppressed merriment, in the grave manner of a judge or parson, some subject offering in itself an opportunity for ridicule. This is what he did in many of his best pieces, as in the critique on the launching of the Frigate *President*,[1] in his *Virginia Advertisement*,[2] and in the mock criticism of *Jack and Jill*, if that be his work. The same thing appears often in the *Lay Preacher*, and in the ironical letters from imaginary correspondents in the *American Lounger*. In his bitter political satire he seems rather to have been emulating his British forerunners from Dryden down to the *Anti-Jacobin*, than following his natural bent.

A less fortunate, but equally noticeable trait of his work was his overwrought and florid style—a mode of expression often far above the nature of his subject. This tendency toward hyperbole and excessive ornament rendered his prose an unsuitable vehicle for sober thought, criticism, or argument. His use of balanced sentences, high-sounding terms, poetical phrases, and even alliteration, betrayed the showy superficiality which he confessed was one of his most prominent weaknesses.

Still more obvious was his habit of interlarding his work with passages, lines, or phrases, quoted from classic authors, a trait reminding one strongly of his contemporary, Hazlitt, and of surprising his readers with allusions to remote sources. Probably no one in America and few in England, especially of those with equal opportunities, had such a wide acquaintance with ancient and modern literature and history, and his essays, as well as his conversation, were redolent of his reading. While a law student at Charlestown, he wrote to his mother,[3] "If John Milton expresses an idea I wish to convey to you better than Jos. Dennie; or if in one word of my own, I more concisely proceed than by two of a lexicographer, these are reasons sufficient, both for quotation and for coining." When carried to an treme in practice, however, this process disfigured his pages with quotation marks and italics, and subjected him to ridicule as a mere repeater of other men's thoughts. His four months as lay reader at Claremont, and the diligent perusal of his

1. *Gazette of the U. S.*, 29 Apr., 1800. *Port Folio*, 17 Aug., 1805.
2. *Port Folio*, 28 Dec., 1805, and 11 Jan., 1806.
3. Letter to his mother, 6 Nov., 1791.

"little Scotch bible" at Charlestown, also stored his mind with expressive biblical phrases of which he made constant use afterward.

A further characteristic was the easy fluency with which he wrote. His was the rapid flow of ideas of an eloquent conversationalist, rather than the polished, orderly prose of a thoughtful and painstaking writer. His imagination was active, and his range of interest wide. A natural result is that frequently his essays are rambling and discursive, bringing in irrelevant ideas as they occurred to his vagrant fancy, and ending apparently at the bottom of the page, rather than at any logical conclusion.

Personally, in spite of his harmless foibles, his somewhat exalted self-esteem, and his ungentle reprobation of parties, creeds, and manners which he disliked, Dennie must have been a very attractive figure. His unvarying courtesy, his frankness and generosity, his loyalty to principle, his sincere love of literature, and the buoyancy of spirits which so frequently accompanies dilatoriness or failure in execution, endeared him to the circle of friends whom he charmed with his brilliant talents and sparkling conversation. He took his party, his church, and his literature very seriously, and was ever ready to give battle in their behalf at a moment's notice. All his editorial enterprises suffered as a result of this readiness to engage in controversy, political or otherwise, yet he retained his undisguised scorn for "the million," and the "malignant vulgar" to the end. He lived and died, as he aspired to do, a little Cavalier.

Dennie's significance in the literature of his time is much more considerable than is indicated by the bulk of his work, which was restricted by periodical illness and successive discouragements. As the conductor of the only literary magazine having a national circulation and patronage, he exerted his influence constantly, during a crude and often bombastic era, in the cause of correctness and classical literary ideals. That he misunderstood his countrymen, accepting as he did the only safe standards he knew, those of eighteenth century England; and that he sometimes followed these standards abjectly, is but natural. His excesses in this direction, however, were hardly more than a healthful reaction against the formlessness and "hyperbole of enthusiasm," then prevalent in the American press.[1] To what extent his efforts were responsible for a soberer and more classical tone in the literature of the decades succeeding his death, is not capable of demonstration, but the verdict of the *Port Folio* undoubtedly had great weight in forming the habits of the many fledgling authors who were then beginning to write.

Instances of Dennie's influence upon individual writers of prominence—he had, of course, many juvenile imitators—are not numerous. Washington Irving, who succeeded to his eminence as the foremost American wit and essayist, and who far excelled his efforts, was probably to some extent affected by him. *Jonathan Oldstyle,* the pseudonym over which Irving contributed his earliest essays to the *New York Morning Chronicle* in 1802, is not the only thing about them suggestive of the *Oliver Oldschool* of the *Port Folio.*[2] When he returned from Europe in

---

1. Henry Adams, *History of the U. S., 1801-1805,* Vol. I, pp. 172-173, admirably sets forth the conflict between American enthusiasm and European distrust in the following fashion:

"Look at my wealth," cried the American to his foreign visitor. "See these solid mountains of salt and iron, of lead, copper, silver, and gold! See these magnificent cities scattered broadcast to the Pacific! See my cornfields rustling and waving in the summer sun from ocean to ocean, so far that the sun itself is not high enough to mark where the distant mountains bound my golden seas! Look at this continent of mine, fairest of created worlds, as she lies turning up to the sun's never-failing caress her broad and exuberant breasts, overflowing with milk for her hundred million children! See how she glows with youth, health, and love!" Perhaps it was not altogether unnatural that the foreigner, on being asked to see what it needed centuries to produce, should have looked about him with bewilderment and indignation. "Gold! cities! cornfields! continents! Nothing of the sort! I see nothing but tremendous wastes, where sickly men and women are dying of homesickness or are scalped by savages! mountain ranges a thousand miles long, with no means of getting to them and nothing when you get there! swamps and forests choked with their own rotten ruins! nor hope of better for a thousand years! Your story is a fraud, and you are a liar and a swindler."

2. This title is, of course, too conventional to be regarded as proof of imitation. It is not impossible—there is no real evidence either way—that between 1801 and 1804 Irving may have contributed some of his youthful effusions to Dennie's paper, as some of his associates probably did.

1806, and when he began the publication of the *Salmagundi* papers in 1807, the *Port Folio* was still in its prime, and Dennie's fame as a writer of light, satirical essays was uncontested. It is not unreasonable to suppose that Irving and Paulding may have regarded him as a model worthy to be followed, with certain pretty obvious precautions, in the sort of thing which they were to do much better than he had done it.[1]

The almost total oblivion into which Dennie has fallen in the century since his death is due very largely, I believe, to his ill success in getting his works published, and to the negligence of his biographers, while the memory of contemporaries of less importance, like Paine and the minor Hartford writs, has been kept alive through no particular merit of theirs. Historically, he is entitled to rank with his contemporaries, Charles Brockden Brown and Philip Freneau. He was the first American essayist to achieve preeminence, as they were the first important American novelist and poet, respectively; but he was sooner eclipsed by Irving than they were by Cooper and Bryant. Brown, who had the greatest share of genius, is still sometimes read by the curious. Interest in Freneau, now known only by a few selections in the anthologies, will probably receive some slight impetus from the recent republication of his poems. Dennie seems quite forgotten. The world is, perhaps, not much poorer as a result; yet true lovers of American letters should remember at least that in the childhood of our Republic, and amid many discouragements,

HE DEVOTED HIS LIFE TO THE LITERATURE OF HIS COUNTRY.[2]

---

1. "Daniel Webster asserted that no one ever did him more good than Joe Dennie. Some of Webster's early productions were reviewed by Dennie in the *Farmer's Museum*. 'He declared them full of emptiness, and it did me good,' was Webster's frank admission." Bell's *Bench and Bar of New Hampshire*.

2. From the inscription on his tombstone. See Appendix F.

BIBLIOGRAPHY

PART I—WORKS WRITTEN, EDITED, OR CONTRIBUTED TO BY DENNIE.

A. Works by Joseph Dennie.

The Lay Preacher, or Short Sermons for Idle Readers. Walpole, N. H.: Carlisle, 1796. Pp. 132. 16 mo.

Desultory Reflections on the New Political Aspects of Public Affairs in the United States of America. New York: J. W. Fenno, 1800. Part I, 60 pp. Part II, 38 pp.

Spirit of the Farmer's Museum and Lay Preacher's Gazette. Walpole: Thomas & Thomas, 1801. Pp. 318. 12 mo.

The Lay Preacher. Collected and arranged by John E. Hall, Esq., counsellor at Law. Philadelphia: Harrison Hall, 1817. Pp. 168. 16 mo.

New and Original Essays by Joseph Dennie. (Only one issue known). Philadelphia, 1818.

B. Periodicals Edited or Contributed to by Joseph Dennie.

The Massachusetts Magazine. Boston, Thomas and Andrews, 1789-1895.

The Morning Ray: or the Impartial Oracle. Windsor, Vt.: Spooner and Hutchins, 1791-1792.

The Eagle: or Dartmouth Centinel. Hanover, N. H.: Josiah Dunham, 1793-1795.

The Federal Orrery. Boston: Thomas [Robert Treat] Paine, 1795.

The Tablet: A Miscellaneous Paper Devoted to the Belles Lettres (Edited by Dennie). Boston: Spotswood, May-August, 1795.

The New Hampshire Journal: or the Farmer's Weekly Museum. (Edited by Dennie, October, 1795-September, 1799. The title was several times altered.) Walpole: Thomas and Carlisle, 1793-1801.

The Gazette of the United States. (Edited by Dennie, June-December, 1800.) Philadelphia: J. W. Fenno and C. P. Wayne, 1799-1800.

The Port Folio. (Started and edited, 1801-1812, by Dennie; weekly 1801-1808; monthly 1809-1812; continued until 1827). Philadelphia: Various publishers, 1801-1812.

The New England Galaxy and Masonic Magazine. Boston: J. T. Buckingham, 1818.

C. Letters to and from Joseph Dennie.

The Dennie Papers. Forty-nine letters and numerous manuscripts by Joseph Dennie, and about ninety letters written by others to Dennie and his mother. In the Harvard University Library.

The Vose Correspondence. Twenty letters from Dennie to Roger Vose, 1788-1800, with replies by Vose, and letters to Vose from William Meredith and John E. Hall. In the possession of Miss Kate V. Marcy, Royalton, Vermont.

Letters from Dennie to John Quincy Adams. *Adams Papers: Massachusetts Historical Society Collections.*

Letters from Dennie to Timothy Pickering, and from Pickering to Dennie. *Pickering Papers: Massachusetts Historical Society Collections.*

Letters from Dennie to Jeremiah Mason. *Massachusetts Historical Society Proceedings,* March, 1880. Vol. XVII, pp. 362-365.

Letters from Dennie to Royall Tyler, in the unpublished MS *Memoir* of Tyler by his son, Thomas Pickering Tyler. In the possession of Miss Helen Tyler Brown, of Brattleboro, Vermont.

PART II—WORKS RELATING TO DENNIE AND HIS CIRCLE.

(The following list is intended to contain the titles most useful for a study of Dennie and his friends. The well-known biographical dictionaries, anthologies, and histories of literature are excluded, as are various works, incidental references to which are recorded in the footnotes. Asterisks are used to denote references of special importance.)

Adams, Henry. *History of the United States, 1801-1809.*
New York, 1889. 4 vols.
(Political and social background.)

Adams, John Quincy. *Memoirs.* Edited by Charles Francis Adams.
Philadelphia, 1877.

*Aldrich, George. *Walpole as It Was and as It Is.*
Claremont, N. H., 1880.

*Bell, Charles Henry. *The Bench and Bar of New Hampshire.*
Boston, 1894.

Benjamin, S. G. W. "Notable Editors between 1776 and 1800." *Magazine of American History.* February, 1887. (Portrait of Dennie.)

Bent, S. Arthur. "Damon and Pythias among Our Early Journalists." *New England Magazine,* August, 1896.

Boston, City of. *Reports of the Commissioners of Records.* 39 vols.

Buckingham, Joseph Tinker. *Personal Memoirs and Recollections of Editorial Life.*
Boston, 1852. 2 vols.

*Buckingham, Joseph Tinker. *Specimens of Newspaper Literature.*
Boston, 1850. 2 vols.

Burnham, Henry. *History of Brattleboro, Vermont.*
Brattleboro, 1880. (Account of Tyler, pp. 86-102.)

*Clapp, William W., Jr. *Joseph Dennie.*
Cambridge, 1880.

Clark, J. C. L. *Tom Moore in Bermuda.*
Boston, 1909. Second Edition.

The *Critic,* June, 1888.
(Two letters from Thomas Moore to Dennie).

*Davis, John. (?) *The Philadelphia Pursuits of Literature, a Satirical Poem,* by Juvenal Junius.
Philadelphia, 1805. Books I and II.

Davis, John. *Travels of Four Years and a Half in the United States of America, during the Years 1798, 1799, 1800, 1801, and 1802.*
London, 1803.

D'Israeli and Griswold. *Curiosities of Literature.*
American Edition. New York, 1848.

Goddard, Delano A. *Newspapers and Newspaper Writers in New England, 1787-1815.*
Boston, 1880.

Goodnight, Scott H. *German Literature in American Magazines prior to 1846.*
Madison, Wisconsin, 1907.

*Hall, John Ewing. *The Philadelphia Souvenir, a Collection of Fugitive Pieces from the Philadelphia Press.*
Philadelphia, 1827.

Hart, Charles Henry. "Tom Moore and America." In *The Collector.* New York, February, 1896. Vol. IX.
(Letters from Moore to J. E. Hall).

*Harvard University. Records of the College Faculty. Unpublished. In the Harvard University Library.

Harvard University. Records of the Quinquennial Office. Unpublished. At University Hall, Cambridge.

Historical Magazine, December, 1857, p. 389.
(Reference to Dennie's portrait.)

Hudson, Charles. *History of the Town of Lexington.*
Boston, 1868.

Hudson, Frederick. *A History of Journalism in the United States from 1690* to *1872.*
New York, 1873.

Irving, Pierre M. *Life and Letters of Washington Irving.* New York, 1862-1864. 4 vols.

*Irving, Washington. "Sketch of Launcelot Langstaff." *Salmagundi.* No. VIII, 1807.

Jackson, M. Katherine. *Outlines of the Literary History of Colonial Pennsylvania.*
New York, 1906.

Janson, Charles William. *The Stranger in America.*
London, 1807. Page 416.

*Marble, Annie Russell. *Heralds of American Literature.*
Chicago, 1707.
(Chapter on Dennie, pp. 193-231; and bibliography, pp. 343-346.)

Mason, Jeremiah. *Memoir and Correspondence,* Edited by George S. Hillard.
Cambridge, 1873.

Matthews, Albert. *Bibliographical Notes on Boston Newspapers, 1704-1780.*
Cambridge, 1907.

Matthews, Albert. *Lists of New England Magazines, 1743-1800. Publications of the Colonial Society of Massachusetts*, Vol. XIII.

Monthly Anthology, Boston, Vol. II, 1806, p. 176. Vol. IV, 1807, pp. 289-95.

Moore, John W. *Historical Notes on Printers and Printing.* Concord, N. H., 1886.

Moore, Thomas. *Memoirs, Journal, and Correspondence.* Edited by Lord John Russell.
London, 1856.

Moore, Thomas. *Poetical Works.*

**New England Galaxy.* Edited by Joseph T. Buckingham.
Boston, 10 July and 24 July, 1818.

North, S. N. D. *History and Present Condition of the Newspaper and Periodical Press of the United States.*
Washington, 1884.

*Oberholtzer, Ellis Paxson. *Literary History of Philadelphia.*
Philadelphia, 1806.

*Peabody, Andrew P. "The Farmer's Weekly Museum." In *The Report of the Council of the American Antiquarian Society,* 23 October, 1889.

Peck, Thomas Bellows. *The Bellows Genealogy.*
Keene, N. H., 1898.
(Accounts of Fessenden, Vose, etc., and pictures of Walpole).

Port Folio. May, 1816. Page 361.
(Silhouette of Dennie.)

Quincy, Edmund. *Life of Josiah Quincy.*
Boston, 1867.

*Scharf, J. T., and Westcott, T. *History of Philadelphia*, 1609-1884.
Philadelphia, 1884. 3 vols.
(Vol. II, Chap. XXXV, *Authors and Literature in Philadelphia.* Vol. III, Chap. XVLIII. *The Press of Philadelphia.*)

Sherzer, Jane. "American Editions of Shakespeare." *Publications of the Modern Language Association of America*, Vol. XXII, 1907, pp. 633-696.

Simpson, Henry. *Lives of Eminent Philadelphians.*
Philadelphia, 1859.

Smith, J. J., and Watson, J. F. *American Historical and Literary Curiosities*, Plate XLI.
New York, 1850.
(Facsimile of letter and poem sent to Dennie by Thomas Moore.)

*Smyth, Albert Henry. *Philadelphia Magazines and Their Contributors.*
Philadelphia, 1892.

*Thomas, Isaiah. *The History of Printing in America.*
Worcester, 1810. 2 vols.

Appendix A

THE FARRAGO, NO. I

Quicquid agunt homines, votum, timor, ira, voluptas,
Gaudia, discursus, nostri est *farrago* libelli.

Juvenal.

Imitated.

Manners and dress and newest fashions,
Books, characters, and human passions;
Men acting well, or who astray go
Ingredients form for the *Farrago.*

—*Anon.*

To a lover of abstruse science, desultory essays may appear a minor species of literature. Accustomed to the regularity of system, the sprightliness of an essay he may pronounce impertinence, and its brevity abruption. But the majority of mankind are not scholars, yet, though ignorant of science, they love instruction and seek it by the most obvious methods. Conscious that their taste is not sufficiently refined to relinquish the more exquisite viands, they content themselves with the simplest dishes of the literary banquet. Hence the currency of Essays. Of that host of readers, whose morals have been meliorated and whose intellects have been illumined by the efforts of genius, few have perused and still fewer have understood the abstract reasonings of Locke and Bacon. Nor is this assertion intended to depreciate the reputation of those valuable authors. Every votary of candor must allow that for the ingenuity and truth of their systems they deserve well of the literary republic. But, since their theories require the undissipated attention even of the professed man of letters, it is obvious to remark that to the busy, the indolent, and lower orders in the community, the labors of speculation can yield little emolument. Accordingly those who exclaim in the words of Armstrong,

Peace to each drowsy metaphysic sage
And ever may all heavy systems rest.

have been allured to the temples of wisdom and virtue by the suavity of Addison, the sprightliness of Steele and the sublime morality of Johnson and Hawkesworth.

Impatience of labor is the characteristic of the dissipated and the volatile. To them systems are useless, because they demand an intenseness of application, which indolence is unwilling to bestow. But to neglect the mental improvement of so numerous a class and suffer them to rove on through the mazes of vice and error without affording a clue to guide them through the labyrinth, were cruel and culpable negligence. Some work must therefore be projected to fix volatility and rouse indolence, neither too abstruse for the young, too prolix for the busy nor too grave for the fair. A performance, which should not resemble an austere monitor, who punishes while he chides, but a pleasant friend, whose conversation at once beguiles and improves the hour. The design was at length accomplished. Certain geniuses of the first magnitude arose, who, in the narrow compass of a sheet of paper, conveyed more useful knowledge to mankind than all the ponderous tomes of Aristotle. Of these ingenious writers Addison stands in the front rank. His Spectators contributed not a little to refine the taste and morals of his countrymen. Touched by the magic of his ridicule, the coxcomb grew ashamed of his frivolity and the libertine of his vices, the fair laid aside their paints and the hypocrite his mask. Even the Gamester, a character almost incorrigible, whom neither past losses nor future prospects can deter from dice and cards, was awed into honesty. The theist was laughed out of his irreligion and the sceptic resolved to doubt no more. The popularity of this novel species of literary entertainment was evinced by the reception it received. Thousands, who suffered dreary systems to moulder on the shelf, wore out the pages of the Spectator and the Guardian. All ranks experienced the sweetest satisfaction in dedicating their leisure moments to the speculations of Addison. From this variegated parterre they culled the fairest flowers; from this lowly station at the bottom of Parnassus they obtained many a glimpse of the higher region.

It is a common observation that mothers and authors are fond of their offspring. Although the Essayist is sensible that his partiality for that literary walk in which he himself proposes to ramble, may discover beauties in it, which appear dim to optics contemplating them through another medium, yet he cannot withhold that warmth of panegyric, which he thinks is due. This enthusiastic fondness the public will pardon, and will suffer the author to dwell a little longer upon the praises of the Essay, which merits further encomium for its consciseness, sprightliness and variety. From its size incapable of admitting widely expanded ideas, it exhibits in a page those useful truths for which the plodding students might toil through a volume. That condensation of thought, which Shenstone admired in Pope, and pronounced his chief beauty, in the succinct essay is everywhere prominent. Renouncing the sullen pomp of wisdom, it affects a vivacity, a gaiety, and an airiness peculiarly charming. This cheerful aspect may allure even the prodigal of moments; and though the essay may at first be read to waste time, it may at length contribute to its improvement. Every one from his own experience is sensible that even a hint may awaken the latent spark of wisdom and virtue. Hence, the random reader, who glances over the page for diversion may gain knowledge; as the ancient libertine, who went to deride the philosopher, was won by his persuasion and became a member of his sect.

Appendix B

THE FARRAGO. NO. III

———— "*Full Many a Prank*
He Played, and Tricks Most Fanciful and Strange.
—*Massinger.*

Men of tenacious memory, who retain information a week old, may recollect, in my last number, a portrait of Meander.

"A man so various, that he seemed to be
Not one, but all mankind's epitome;
Who, in the course of one revolving moon,
Was poet, painter, lover, and buffoon;
Then all for wenching, gambling, rhyming, drinking,
Besides ten thousand freaks, that dy'd in thinking."

Agreeably to a promissory note, given in a preceding essay, I now publish, from the diary of this fantastic wight, a selection, which, if judiciously improved, may sober giddy genius, may fix the volatile, and stimulate even loungers.

Meander's Journal.

April 8, Monday.—Having lately quaffed plenteous drafts of the stream of dissipation, I determine to bridle my fancy, to practice self-denial, to live soberly, and to study with ardour. That I may, with ease, discharge the various duties of the day, I propose, that "Strutting Chanticleer," and myself, should unroost at the same hour. With this resolve, I couple a determination, to study law with plodding diligence, and to make my profession, and a course of history, my capital objects.

Memorandum. Belles lettres must be considered a subaltern pursuit. If I rise at the dawn, and study jurisprudence till noon, I shall have the satisfaction to reflect, that I have discharged my *legal* duty for the day. This course, duly persisted in, will probably make me something more than a Tyro, in the language of the law. If I pore over my folios with the diligence I propose, I shall acquire, in Blackstone's phrase, such a legal apprehension, that the obscurities which at present confound me, will vanish, and my journey through the *wilderness* of law will, peradventure, become delectable.

Tuesday.—Overslept myself, did not rise till nine. Dressed, and went out, intending to go to the office; but, as the morning was uncommonly beautiful, I recollected an aphorism of Dr. Cheyne's, that exercise should form part of a student's religion. Accordingly, I rambled through the woods for two hours. The magic of rural scenes diverted Fancy, whom, on my return to the office, I wished to retire, that her elder sister, Judgment, might have an opportunity to hold a conference with the sage Blackstone: but, the sportive slut remained, dancing about, and I found my spirits so agitated, that, to calm them, I took up a volume of plays, and read two acts in Centlivre's *Busy Body.*

Afternoon, 2 o'clock.—Toook up a folio, and began to read a British statute; meanwhile, I received a billet, importing that a couple of my college cronies were at a neighboring inn, who wished me to make one of a select party. I complied. The sacrifices to Mercury and Bacchus wore away the night, and it was day before I retired to the land of drowsyhead, as Thomson quaintly expresses it.

Wednesday.—Rose at ten; sauntered to the office, and gaped over my book. Low spirits and a dull morning had raised such a fog around my brain, that I could hardly discern a sentiment. Opened a "dissertation on memory," read till my own failed. I then threw away my book, and threw myself on the bed; I can't tell how long I remained there, but, somebody shaking me by the shoulder, I opened my eyes and saw—the maid, who came to inform me that it was eight o'clock *in the evening,* and that coffee was ready.

Thursday.—Went out at seven, with a determination to attend to business; thought I might venture to call at a friend's house; on my entrance saw a brace of beauties, whose smiles were so animating that they detained me, "charmed by witchery of eyes," till noon. I returned to my lodgings, and finding my spirits too sublimated for serious study, I beguiled the remainder of the afternoon, by writing a sonnet to Laura.

Evening.—Lounged to my book-shelf, with an intent to open

Blackstone, but made a mistake, and took down a volume of Hume's History of England. Attention became quite engrossed by his narrative of the reign of Henry I. A versatile, brilliant genius, who blended in one bright assemblage ambition, prudence, eloquence and enterprize; who received and merited, what I think the most glorious of all titles, that of Beauclerc, or the polite scholar. The formidable folios, which stood before me, seemed frowingly to ask why I did not link to my ambition, that prudence which formed part of Henry's fame? The remorseful blush of a moment tinged my cheek, and I boldly grasped a *reporter;* but, straightway recollecting that I had recently supped, and that, after a full meal, application was pernicious to health, I adjourned the cause, Prudence versus Meander, till morning.

Friday.—Rose at the dawn, which is the first time I have complied with my resolution, of unroosting with the cock. "Projecting many things, but accomplishing none," is the motto to my coat of arms. Began my studies, noting with nice care the curious distinction in law, between general and special *Tail;* at length, I grew weary of my task, and thought, with Shakespeare's Horatio, that 'twere considering too curiously, to consider thus. Began to chat with my companions; we are, when indolent, ever advocates for relaxation; but, whether an attorney's office is the place where idling should be tolerated, is a question which I do not wish to determine in the negative. Finished my morning studies with "Hafen Slawkenbergius's tenth decade."

Afternoon.—Did *nothing* very busily till four. Seized with a lethargic yawn, which lasted till seven, when a dish of coffee restored animation, and on the entrance of a friend, fell into general conversation; made a transition to the scenes of our boyish days, and till midnight, employed memory conjuring up to view the shades of our departed joys.

Saturday.—Slept but little, last night. My imagination was so busy in castle-building, that she would not repose. Dreamed that Lord Coke threw his "Institute" at me. Rose at nine, looked abroad; and the atmosphere being dusky, and my spirits absent on furlough, felt unqualified for reading. For several days there has been a succession of gloomy skies. The best writers affirm such weather is unfriendly to mental labour. The poet says,

> "While these dull fogs invade the head,
> Memory minds not what is read."

Took up a magazine, which I carefully skimmed, but obtained no cream. Cracked, in the Dean of St. Patrick's phrase, a rotten nut, which cost me a tooth, and repaid me with nothing but a worm. Breakfasted; reflected on the occurrences of the week. In the drama of my life, Procrastination and Indolence are the principal actors. My resolutions flag, and my studies languish. I must strive to check the irregular sallies of fancy. I never shall be useful to others, till I have a better command of myself. Surely one, abiding in the bowers of ease, may improve, if industry be not wanting. Alfred could read and write eight hours every day, though he fought fifty-six pitched battles, and rescued a kingdom; and Chatterton, the ill-fated boyish bard, composed, though cramped by penury, poems of more invention than many a work which has been kept nine years, and published at a period of the ripest maturity. When I fly from business, let ambition, therefore, *think on, and practise these things.* I determine, *next week,* to effect an entire revolution in my conduct, to form a new plan of study, and to adhere to it with pertinacity. As this week is on the eve of expiration, it would be superfluous to sit down to serious business. I therefore amused myself, by dipping into Akenside's "Pleasures of Imagination"; read till five, visited a friend, and conversed with him, till midnight; conversation turned on *propriety of conduct,* for which I was a strenuous advocate. * * *

Here, the journal of Meander was abruptly closed. I was curious to learn, in what manner he employed his week of reformation. On the ensuing Monday, he grew weary of his books; instead of mounting Pegasus, he actually strode a hack-horse, of mere mortal mould, and, in quest of diversion, commenced a journey. He was accompanied, not by the muses, but by a party of jocund travellers; and, prior to my friend's departure, the last words he was heard to say, or rather *roar,* were the burden of a well known anacreontic, "*Dull thinking will make a man crazy.*"

The character and journal of Meander, scarcely need a commentary. There shall be none. I was not born in Holland, and only Dutchmen are qualified to write notes. But I will make an apostrophe.

Ye tribe of Mecurialists! in the name of prudence, avoid eccentricity; expand not your *fluttering* pinions; trudge the footway path of life; dethrone Fancy, and crown Common Sense. Let each one seek and fulfil his daily task; "one to his farm, and another to his merchandize."

Appendix C

(From the *Massachusetts Magazine*, February, 1789.)

PANEGYRICK ON THOMSON

Come, youthful muse, who, erst in cloister drear,
Didst chime, adventurous, thy poetick bells,
In jingling lays no longer vainly strive,
With brother bards, the laurel mead to gain.
Thine be the task, in rhyme-unfetter'd verse,
To hail the master of the rural song,
And sing the beauties of a *Thomson's* page.

To thee with reverence bends the raptur'd muse,
Thee to extol loud chaunts her awkward strain,
The strain tho' dissonant, sublime the theme
And copious, if she sing a *Thomson's* praise.

Nature, indulgent to a thoughtless world,
Had long display'd the wonders of her hand;
While busy man, in low pursuits involv'd,
Or in the crowded city breathing smoke,
Or else reclining on the silken couch
Of luxury, foe to nature's simple charms,
With eye averted scarcely deign'd to view
The scenes enchanting, which her pencil form'd.

The indignant goddess call'd her favourite son,
To him her pencil, and her landscape gave,
And bade him paint anew the sylvan scene.
The bard obey'd; with softened tints retouch'd,
Great Nature's work, and, when the goddess view'd,
She deeply blush'd, and own'd herself outdone.

The grateful *seasons*, in their annual round,
With ardour emulous gifts conferr'd on thee.
First, blooming *Spring* crop'd from the verdant mead
A Chaplet gay, thy temples to entwine,

And ardent *Summer*, at meridian hour,
When Phebus rag'd, and Zephyr ceas'd to breathe,
Yielded the oak umbrageous where reclin'd,
You held high converse with the sylvan gods.
Mild *Autumn*, sedulous, rang'd Pomona's grove,
And pluck'd the ripest fruits to deck thy board.
Winter came last, high pil'd the blazing hearth,
Restrain'd his winds, and gave the studious hour.

At early dawn, the evanescent forms
Of pensive Dryads breathe in fancy's ear
This plausive strain, in memory of *their* bard,
'While artful anglers lure their finny prey,
'While fervent youths bathe in the lucid stream,
'While jocund shepherds whet their sounding shears,
'Around the shepherd's cot while Boreas howls,
'And brumal snows oppress the leafless bough
'So long shall *Thomson's* wood notes charm the ear,
'So long his moral page improve the heart.'

ACADEMICUS.

Appendix D

THE FARRAGO ESSAYS

First Appearances, and Reprints in the Port Folio.

		Morning Ray 1792	*Port Folio* 1801
I	Periodical Essays	14 Feb.	———
II	Character of Meander	21 Feb.	24 Jan.
III	Meander's Journal	6 Mar.	24 Jan.
IV	———	20 Mar.	———
		The Eagle or Dart-mouthCen-tinel 1793	*Port Folio* 1801
VIII[1]	Letter from Brown, Brick-maker	17 Aug.	———
IX	Strenuous Idleness	26 Aug.	14 Mar.
X	"He Cuts a Dash"	9 Sept.	———
XI	Care-free-ness	16 Sept.	28 Feb.
XII	Taciturnity	21 Oct.	25 July
XIII	"Now I Have Got a Ewe and a Lamb"	28 Oct.	———
		1794	
XIV	Character of Charles Cameleon	27 Jan.	27 June
XV	Pleasures of Winter	10 Feb.	———
XVI	My Aunt Peg	3 Mar.	29 Aug.
XVII	Happiness of Dupes	10 Mar.	7 Mar.
XVIII	Sickness	14 July	———
XIX	"How Shall I Compass the Cash?"	21 July	———
XX	Conrad Caustic on the Sex	28 July	30 May
			1802
XXI	Worldly Prudence	4 Aug.	14 Aug.
XXII	Much Study is a Weariness of the Flesh	18 Aug.	———

1. No trace of Essays V, VI, and VII has been found. See page 94. Nos. XII, XIV, XVI, XIX, and XXI reappeared in the *Farmer's Museum*; and II, III, IX, XIV, XVI, and XVII in the *Tablet*.

		The Tablet 1795	*Port Folio* 1802
XXIII	Introductory	19 May	———
XXIV	Inconsistent Censure	9 June	31 July
			1801
XXV	Detraction of Mathematics	16 June	4 April
XXVI	Two Cheats Make an Even Bargain	23 June	10 Oct.
XXVII	Praise of Dulness	21 July	4 July
XXVIII	"Royal"	4 Aug.	3 Oct.
			1802
XXIX	A Morning in the Country	———	24 July

APPENDIX E

THE LAY PREACHER

First Appearances, and Reprints in the Port Folio.

		Farmer's Museum	*Port Folio*
		1795	1803
1.	Wine and New Wine Take Away the Heart	13 Oct.	———
2.	There Is a Lion in the Streets	20 Oct.	17 Dec.
3.	Favor Is Deceitful	27 Oct.	———
4.	Issachar Is a Strong Ass	3 Nov.	———
5.	A Man of Understanding	10 Nov.	19 Nov.
6.	Two Are Better than One	17 Nov.	12 Nov.
7.	Thanksgiving	24 Nov.	24 Dec.
8.	Against Democrats	1 Dec.	———
9.	The End Is Better than the Beginning	8 Dec.	1 Oct.
10.	By This Craft We Have Our Wealth	15 Dec.	———
11.	Idleness—Dick Dronish	22 Dec.	8 Oct.
12.	Superstition	29 Dec.	———
		1796	1804
13.	New Year's Day	5 Jan.	7 Jan.
14.	Satan in Pleasing Shapes	12 Jan.	14 Jan.
			1806
15.	"My Head, My Head!"	19 Jan.	18 Jan.
			1803
16.	The Heart of the Foolish Is Like a Cart Wheel	26 Jan.	24 Sept.
17.	Quench not the Spirit	2 Feb.	5 Nov.
			1805
18.	Cheerfulness	9 Feb.	7 Sept.
19.	A Wild Young Man	16 Feb.	———
20.	Idols	23 Feb.	22 Mar.
			1804
21.	Slothfulness	1 Mar.	14 Apr.

22.	Drink Water out of Thine Own Cistern	1796 8 Mar.	1804 ———
23.	Hate not Laborious Work, neither Husbandry	15 Mar.	21 Apr.
			1803
24.	One Thing is Needful	29 Mar.	10 Dec.
25.	A Good Wife[1]	———	———
26.	Victory after Defeat	5 Apr.	17 Sept.
			1805
27.	Practice as You Preach	12 Apr.	13 July
			1803
28.	Changeableness—in Dress	19 Apr.	27 Aug.
29.	Changeableness—in Politics, Religion etc.	26 Apr.	3 Sept.
30.	Great Is Diana of the Ephesians—Harvard	3 May	———
31.	For Lo, the Winter is Past	10 May	29 Oct.
			1806
32.	Remove Sorrow from Thee	17 May	18 Feb.
33.	What Aileth Thee?	23 May	2 Aug.
			1803
34.	Ingratitude to Humble Heroes	7 June	22 Oct.
35.	Go Forth into the Country	14 June	———
36.	The Story of Rebecca	28 June	10 Sept.
37.	Watchman, What of the Night?	5 July	20 Aug.
			1805
38.	Divisions among You	12 July	10 Aug.
			1801
39.	Fretfulness	19 July	8 Aug.
40.	Forgetfulness of Promises	26 July	26 Dec.
			1805
41.	Do Thyself no Harm	2 Aug.	20 July
42.	Honor Thy Parents	9 Aug.	———
43.	Idle Curiosity	16 Aug.	———
44.	Folly of Passion	23 Aug.	28 Apr.
			1803
45.	The Prosperity of America	30 Aug.	13 Aug.

1. Appeared in the *Eagle; or Dartmouth Centinel*, 4 April, 1796.

		1796	1801
46.	Mind Your Own Business	6 Sept.	24 Oct.
			1803
47.	Frailties of Preachers	13 Sept.	15 Oct.
			1805
48.	Sedition and Revolution	25 Oct.	27 July
49.	Choose Rulers Wisely	15 Nov.	———
50.	Melancholy of Autumn	29 Nov.	———
			1801
51.	The Story of Ruth	13 Dec.	26 Sept.
		1797	
52.	For the Workman Is Worthy of His Meat	17 Jan.	29 Aug.
53.	Desire for Novelty	24 Jan.	———
			1805
54.	Unnatural Passions—Absalom	7 Feb.	26 Oct.
			1804
55.	Loyalty in Adversity	28 Feb.	12 May
			1801
56.	Modern "Philosophers"	7 Mar.	31 Oct.
57.	It Is Foul Weather	4 Apr.	———
58.	Childishness of This Generation	11 Apr.	7 Nov.
59.	Hospitality	18 Apr.	18 July
60.	Restlessness for Gold	9 May	14 Nov.
61.	The Story of Samson	16 May	4 July
62.	Haste—Jehu	23 May	17 Oct.
63.	Love of Nature	5 June	1 Aug.
64.	Disappointment	12 June	22 Aug.
			1805
65.	Let Us Get Up Early	26 June	29 June
			1801
66.	Keeping the Sabbath	3 July	3 Oct.
67.	Newsmongers	24 July	19 Dec.
		1798	1804
68.	Here Am I, for Thou Didst Call Me	19 June	7 Apr.
69.	In Praise of Reading	26 June	———
			1806
70.	Rebellion	3 July	19 July
71.	The Power of Music—David and Saul	10 July	———

		1798	1806
72.	Modern Philosophers	17 July	16 Aug.
			1801
73.	Let Thy Garments Be Always White	24 July	12 Sept.
74.	A Dutiful Subject	31 July	———
75.	Requisites of a Good Ruler	6 Aug.	———
			1805
76.	The Story of Hagar	13 Aug.	———
77.	Moses and the Daughters of Midian	20 Aug.	6 July
78.	Criticism of the Gothic Romance	27 Aug.	9 July
			1803
79.	Criticism of Mrs. Radcliffe	3 Sept.	16 July
80.	Criticism of Mrs. Radcliffe	10 Sept.	23 July
81.	Criticism of Mrs. Radcliffe	1 Oct.	30 July
82.	Criticism of Mrs. Radcliffe	10 Dec.	6 Aug.
		1799	
83.	April Fool Customs	1 Apr.	———
			1804
84.	Truly the Light is Sweet	15 Apr.	5 May
			1801
85.	Jacob and Leah	17 June	19 Sept.
			1805
86.	Meditation	24 June	22 June
			1801
87.	Gratitude	1 July	10 Oct.
			1804
88.	Second Sight	15 July	19 May
89.	Prophecies	29 July	1 Sept.
			1801
90.	Versatility—St. Paul	19 Aug.	27 June
91.	Versatility—St. Paul	26 Aug.	27 June

		Gazette of the U. S.[1]
92.	Their Widows Are Increased	8 Nov., 1799
93.	These Be the Days of Vengeance	16 Nov.
94.	Harlotry	23 Nov.
95.	Simplicity and Sincerity	30 Nov.

1. The essays in the *Gazette* were entitled the *Lay Preacher of Pennsylvania.*

96.	Marry Thy Daughter	7 Dec., 1799
97.	Fatherhood	14 Dec.
98.	National Mourning for Washington	21 Dec.
99.	The Youth of David	28 Dec.
100.	Motherhood	30 Dec.
101.	Hardships of Genius	11 Jan., 1800
102.	Meekness More Befits a Woman than Adornment	25 Jan.
103.	The Prodigal's Return	1 Feb.
104.	Many Waters Cannot Quench Love	1 Mar.
105.	Immodesty in Dress and Ornament	15 Mar.
		Port Folio
106.	Go about the Streets	17 Jan., 1801
107.	The Story of Samuel	12 Dec., 1807
108.	Paul's Voyage	19 Dec.
109.	Christmas Gaiety	26 Dec.
110.	New Year's—Walk Circumspectly	2 Jan., 1808
111.	The Story of Esther	9 Jan.
112.	Paul's Departure from Ephesus	16 Jan.
113.	Blessed Is He Who Readeth	23 Jan.
114.	Commune with Your Own Heart	30 Jan.
115.	The Story of Job	6 Feb.
116.	The Demagogue—Adonijah	13 Feb.
117.	David and Michal[1]	28 Feb., 1818
		New England Galaxy
118.	Parental Interference in Love Affairs	10 July, 1818

1. Printed in pamphlet form.

Appendix F

Inscription on the Monument to Dennie in the Burying Ground of St. Peter's Church, Philadelphia.

JOSEPH DENNIE

Born at Lexington, in Massachusetts,
August 30th, 1768,
Died at Philadelphia, January 7th, 1812.
Endowed with talents, and qualified
By Education
To adorn the Senate, and the Bar,
But following the impulse of a Genius,
Formed for Converse with the Muses,
He devoted his life to the Literature of his Country.

As author of the Lay Preacher,
And as first editor of the Port Folio,
He contributed to chasten the morals, and to refine
the taste of the nation.
To an imagination, lively, not licentious,
A wit sportive, not wanton,
And a heart without guile,
He united a deep sensibility, which
Endeared him to his
Friends, and an ardent piety, which we humbly trust
Recommended him to his God;
Those friends have erected this tribute
To his Memory.
To the Mercies of that God is their resort
For themselves, and for Him.
MDCCCXIX.

INDEX.

Abbreviations: *F. W. M.*=*Farmer's Weekly Museum;* *L. P.*=*Lay Preacher;* *P. F.*=*Port Folio.*